BATTLE of the BANKS
How ad men, barristers and bankers ended Ben Chifley's boldest plan

Bob Crawshaw's deeply researched *Battle of the Banks* provides a unique insight into one of the foundational moments of modern Australian politics. Not only did the Chifley Government's inability to nationalise the banks reveal the limits of the possible for a federal Labor government committed to an ambitious postwar reconstruction, that failure also disclosed the powerful dominion exercised by public relations and advertising – backed by vast capital – over public opinion and political life. It is a story which retains its resonance and offers us lessons in our own era of media disinformation and propaganda masquerading as news.

Frank Bongiorno AM, Professor of History, The Australian National University

The battle over the Chifley government's bid to nationalise Australian banks was waged on the political hustings, in the boardroom, and in the courts. The failed Labor plan helped to inspire one of the most expensive and elaborate public relations campaigns in Australian political and communications history, helmed by R. G. Menzies and the fledgling Liberal Party. Bob Crawshaw has produced an impeccably researched and compelling study set against the background of the Cold War.

Bridget Griffen-Foley, Director of Research and Innovation, Department of Media, Communications, Creative Arts, Language and Literature, Macquarie University

Bob Crawshaw has written an absorbing and revealing tale of post-war political intrigue, shedding new light on the campaign against the Chifley government's plan to nationalise the banks. It's a great read and deserves a wide audience.

David Day, Award-winning Author of *Chifley*

About the Author

Bob Crawshaw began his career during the Vietnam era, serving in the Australian Army for over 30 years as a commander, trainer, long-range planner and diplomat.

As the first Director of Army Public Affairs, he gained unique insights into how governments try to shape public opinion and how communities push back to influence those in power.

After leaving the Army, Bob established a public relations agency, using his experience to help governments and community organisations effectively promote their ideas. His work received Australian and international recognition.

In recent times, Bob has focused on uncovering the stories behind the advertising and public relations campaigns that shaped Australia. Inspired by the passion and larger-than-life personalities involved in the bank nationalisation episode, he authored *Battle of the Banks*, a compelling exploration of how bold communications can either defeat big plans or make them a reality.

BATTLE of the BANKS
How ad men, barristers and bankers ended Ben Chifley's boldest plan

BOB CRAWSHAW

AUSTRALIAN SCHOLARLY PUBLISHING

© Bob Crawshaw 2025

First published 2025 by
Australian Scholarly Publishing
7 Lt Lothian St North
North Melbourne, Vic 3051
tel: 61 3 93296963
www.scholarly.com

ISBN 978-1-923267-27-5

ALL RIGHTS RESERVED

Cover Design: Amelia Walker

To Barbara

Contents

Preface	ix
Introduction	1
1 Autocrat or Visionary	9
2 Leading the Charge	18
3 Routine and Respectable	26
4 The Anti-Bank Brigade	33
5 Mobilising the Resistance	44
6 Fighting on the Front Page	56
7 Masters of the Public Mood	68
8 Battle in Canberra	76
9 One-Bank Town	86
10 Banks Raise the Stakes	98
11 Allies and Opportunities	107
12 Fantasy Fighters	117
13 Wigs at War	125
14 Collingwood versus Canberra	139
15 Menzies Roadshow and a Coal Strike	147
16 Election Blueprints	160
17 Launches and Vicious Slander	168
18 Bankers' Last Push	175
19 Shirt-Sleeve Days End	185
20 A Sickening Loss	198
21 An Erosion of Trust	202
Acknowledgments	204
Bibliography	207
Index	222

Preface

On 15 August 1945, Australian Labor Prime Minister Ben Chifley declared the end of the Second World War. Whistles blew, church bells clanged and crowds danced in the streets. Two years later, Chifley made another historic announcement. This time the public reaction was confused and sullen.

On a winter Saturday in 1947, Chifley issued a terse, forty-two-word press statement declaring the Government's intention to nationalise the banking system and eliminate Australia's wealthy private banks. The declaration landed abruptly and with no explanation. Australians were baffled. They had lived through the massive changes of the war but they had never seen a plan so radical that it could transform the entire economy for generations. The Chifley Government had emerged from the Second World War with cabinets full of audacious blueprints to reshape Australia. Arguably the bank grab was the boldest of its plans.

Shortly after the announcement, the leaders of Australia's eight largest private banks met in Melbourne to plan a response. They devised a blueprint to resist the government and whip up community outrage. They would bankroll media campaigns, legal challenges and support grassroots protests to thwart Chifley's intentions and ultimately remove the Labor Party from office. Breaking with tradition, they encouraged their normally reserved clerks and tellers to become political activists and chose for their generalissimo, Leslie McConnan from the National Bank of Australasia.

Former Prime Minister Robert Menzies and his new Liberal Party had lost the federal election twelve months before. Now Leader of the Opposition in Canberra, Menzies immediately saw the possibilities in Chifley's strange announcement. He would orchestrate a nationwide fight to save the banks and, along the way, reclaim the prime ministership. Over the next two years, Menzies blasted bank nationalisation and took every opportunity to make it an election issue. In 1949 Australians rejected Chifley and his bank plan and elected Menzies. The Liberal Party took office and remained in power for twenty-three years while the Labor Party wandered in a political wilderness.

The battle for the banks unfolded in the early days of the Cold War, a time when many believed Communism threatened the Australian way of life. Ben Chifley was strongly anti-Communist but convinced the government had to control important industries like banking to move Australia from a wartime to a successful peacetime economy. His opponents, however, saw his nationalisation plans as a blueprint for socialism.

This story is not an economics essay or a political polemic; rather it is about those who fought the last and possibly the greatest battle for the banks. The cast included politicians of the day, men who later occupied Australia's highest offices, media barons, ad men, Communists, community campaigners and thousands of bank officers who campaigned to save their banks.

This is the first detailed account of this highly contentious episode in fifty years. It draws on oral histories, political biographies, online archives and recently digitised records that show how the Labor Government planned to make Australia a "one-bank town".

This post-war crisis shows how governments can overestimate the openness Australians have for grand ideas, how bold plans need big efforts to communicate them, and that wealthy and threatened institutions always find ways to rally for survival.

Ode to Bank Nationalisation

We will not grab the hot dog stands
Nor on the pie carts lay on our hands
They're safe to ply their trade
The peanut man has nought to fear
With him we will not interfere
Nor with the fun arcade
For these things we do not need
We do not deal in chicken feed

Although we're socialists at heart
We covet not the ice-cream cart
Nor yet the oyster bar
The fish shop is as free as air
The wine saloons need have no care
We'll leave them as they are
For none of them are quite our dish
We've set our minds on bigger fish

Let no one fear we'll socialise
Cream puffs, ham rolls and apple pies
King prawns, soft drinks or lollies
Our thoughts are free of such designs
We've made our plans on other lines
And stoop to no such follies
The things for which we'd give our thanks
Are airways, shipping lines and BANKS[1]

---

1 *Uralla Times* (Uralla), 20 October 1949, p. 4.

Introduction

> "Chifley's press statement left an uneasy feeling, a foreboding,
> a grim presentiment [that] all was not well."[1]

Australia's most destructive press statement left Canberra on 16 August 1947. It was fed into a clunky teleprinter in the Press Gallery located on the upper floor of Parliament House, and moments later rattled out in the nation's newsrooms. It was Saturday and duty reporters were expecting to receive football scores, race results and other routine traffic. They were astounded when they read the press statement which said:

> Cabinet today authorised the Attorney General (Dr Evatt) and myself to prepare legislation for submission to the Federal Parliamentary Labor Party for the nationalisation of banking, other than State banks, with proper protection for shareholders, depositors, borrowers, and staff of private banks.[2]

Without warning Australia's longest-serving Labor Government had just announced it was upending the system of banking which had served Australians for over a hundred years. Labor Prime Minister Ben Chifley, barely a high school graduate, had personally written these terse forty-two words and sent them careening into an otherwise unremarkable Saturday.

No one expected the press statement. There was no financial meltdown in the country nor were depositors queueing anxiously outside the country's banks to reclaim their savings. Banking was barely mentioned in the federal election the year before. Yet the Government had now declared its intention to take over an industry with 20,000 workers that was worth almost a billion pounds. There were thousands of bank branches across the country, with one and a half million customers. If nationalisation went ahead customers would be forced to take their accounts to the federally-owned Commonwealth Bank or one of the much smaller state banks. The *Sydney Morning Herald* said Chifley was trying to create the biggest banking monopoly in the world.[3]

The timing of the press statement was no coincidence. Three days earlier, the High Court of Australia had invalidated legislation to extend

---
1 Records of the Liberal Party of Australia, Federal Secretariat, circa 1945-1990, NLA MS 5000/Nationalization of Banking, 1946-1947 (2) (File) Box 1251. Speech by Kevin Ellis on 11 September 1949.
2 *Geraldton Guardian and Express* (Geraldton), 16 August 1947, p. 3.
3 Sydney Morning Herald (Sydney), 18 August 1947, p. 1.

the Government's wartime authority over the nation's finances. Its 1945 Banking Act was meant to help the Government in the herculean task it faced in transitioning the economy from war to a peacetime footing.

Buried in the dryly worded language of the legislation was Section 48 which required state and local governments to seek approval from the Commonwealth Treasurer on where they could bank. The Labor Government wanted all governments to bank with the Commonwealth Bank which then would monitor the flow of money in the economy and regulate credit on its behalf. The country's private banks challenged this controversial provision and the High Court ruled it invalid. The High Court decision concerned the Prime Minister. He feared the private banks would now be emboldened to challenge other parts of the legislation and this could disrupt future economic planning.

Within twenty-four hours Chifley held a secret meeting in his office to review the High Court decision.[1] Present were Herbert ("Doc") Evatt, the Attorney General and Minister for External Affairs and Senator Nicholas ("Nick") McKenna, the Minister for Health and Social Services who deputised for Evatt when he travelled overseas.[2] The Commonwealth Solicitor-General, the Governor and the Secretary of the Commonwealth Bank and two Treasury officials were also there.

Evatt and McKenna were close and trusted confidants of the Prime Minister. Evatt, a former MP in the New South Wales Parliament, held a law doctorate from Sydney University and served as a Justice of the High Court from 1930 to 1940. He left the bench to become a member of parliament and in 1947 was also the Deputy Leader of the Federal Parliamentary Labor Party in addition to his portfolios.

The "Doc" was widely respected for his expertise in constitutional law but Evatt the man was less acclaimed. He had a complicated personality. He was ingratiating and curried favour with those who might help him, but was often intolerant of his peers and dismissive of his subordinates.[3] Evatt had poor listening skills and "none could speak to him on equal terms in the subjects of which he was master".[4] While Chifley and other Labor MPs respected Evatt they recognised he was a virtuoso rather

---

1 *Age* (Melbourne), 18 August 1947, p. 1.
2 G. C. Bolton, "Evatt, Herbert Vere (Bert) (1894–1965)", *Australian Dictionary of Biography*, National Centre of Biography, Australian National University, https://adb.anu.edu.au/biography/evatt-herbert-vere-bert-10131/text17885, accessed online 4 April 2022.
3 Howard Beale interviewed by Mel Pratt, 20-21 October 1976, NLA ORAL TRC 121/82.
4 *Canberra Times* (ACT), 3 November 1965, p. 2.

than a team player.¹ When Evatt visited overseas missions as External Affairs Minister, Australian diplomats could be heard in after-hours bars bemoaning the day Evatt left the High Court and became their minister. On the other hand, Tasmanian Nick McKenna was smooth, efficient and well-liked. Trained in law and accountancy, McKenna understood the Constitution and Chifley trusted him to gauge the mood in the Party.²

The men in the Prime Minister's office had been called to discuss how the Government should respond to the High Court judgment. One obvious option was to accept the ruling and amend the banking legislation so it could withstand further legal challenges. The most extreme choice was for the Government to bring the private banks under state control, effectively silencing all dissent from the banking industry. This would be an unprecedented move in Australia, and apart from the Soviet Union, there were few examples where any government had successfully taken over an entire banking system.

The Australian Labor Party (ALP) had long wanted to control Australia's banks. In 1902 the Party platform included provisions for "the nationalisation of monopolies" and nine years later the Commonwealth Bank was established as a people's bank by the Labor Government of Andrew Fisher. In 1919 an election pamphlet issued by a Labor candidate stated the banks were profiting from the hard work of farmers and the best way to get fair treatment for country people was to establish a government bank.

In 1921 the Party's national conference passed a resolution calling for "the socialisation of industry, production, distribution and exchange" to be achieved through industrial machinery and the Parliament.³ This raised concerns among moderates at the Conference who feared such a resolution could divide the Party. A compromise was proposed by Victorian delegate and lawyer Maurice Blackburn. It suggested private ownership could operate if it did so in a socially useful manner, but collective ownership of industries was acceptable to prevent the exploitation of workers. It remained unclear, perhaps deliberately, who should define what was "socially useful", "collective ownership" or "exploitation of workers". Blackburn's verbal gymnastics allowed the ALP to claim its concern was not with private ownership but about the exploitation of the working class.

After the 1921 Conference the Party had few chances to put any nationalisation plan into action. In the early 1930s, James Scullin led

---
1   *People* (Sydney), 28 March 1951, p. 10.
2   Commonwealth, *Parliamentary Debates*, Senate, 10 July 1974, 28 (Lionel Murphy, Attorney General).
3   *Sydney Morning Herald* (Sydney), 13 October 1921, p. 9.

a one-term Labor Government that was consumed with managing the Depression. A decade later, Labor Prime Minister John Curtin ruled out nationalisation while Australia was at war. Yet the feeling lingered that governments needed to regulate banking because it was a crucial national service. Labor supporters believed banks put profits before community interests and saw Australia's bankers as part of a "money power cabal" that controlled the economy through "old boy networks". The banks were considered potential obstacles for Labor's post-war plans for improved living standards, social welfare and national development.

These prevailing attitudes explained why the abolition of private banking arose so readily during the meeting in the Prime Minister's office. Evatt expressed confidence that the Constitution would allow the Government to take over the banks and said he would personally defend such an action in the courts if needed.[1] The Attorney General apparently spoke from his own knowledge and experience as there is no formal record of any advice on this matter from his Department. McKenna supported Evatt and added that the broader Labor movement would support a blow against the banks. The Governor of the Commonwealth Bank added the Government had £100 million to compensate the banks in the event of a take-over.

The meeting ended around 7 pm. Later in the evening the Prime Minister summoned an extraordinary meeting of Cabinet for the next morning to consider bank nationalisation. Government ministers were in Canberra even though Parliament was on a break. The news of the special meeting surprised everyone.

It was a cold and wet Saturday in Canberra. Since it was the weekend, Parliament House and government offices were empty. Public servants and their families shopped in Canberra's small retail centre and the local newspaper was predicting a record turnout for the rugby match between Canberra and Queanbeyan that afternoon. Some tourists were stuck in the snow on Mt Franklin, in the ranges west of the capital.

At nine o'clock that morning the eighteen ministers who made up the Labor Cabinet assembled in the otherwise deserted Parliament House. Arthur Calwell and Eddie Ward were absent in London and John Dedman was on his way to Geneva and Washington. These three were ministers and influential figures in the Parliamentary Labor Party. They supported nationalisation in principle and were vocal critics of Australian banks. That they were not told of the Cabinet meeting indicated Chifley

---

1 Evatt to Chifley, 15 September 1947, Department of the Treasury, A57 Nationalisation of Trading Banks Legislation – Banking Bill 1947, NAA 1947/2679/134304.

was confident he had the numbers to get the decision he wanted.

The Prime Minister began the meeting by reviewing the High Court decision and expressed concern the banks might challenge more provisions of the 1945 Banking Act. Evatt presented the arguments for and against bank nationalisation and concluded the Government had the legal authority to take over the banks. Then, McKenna warned the meeting that the High Court ruling could jeopardise the Government's future plans. Ministers sat in stunned silence as Evatt and McKenna briefed them.[1]

Chifley went around the table and asked each man his opinion. There was little discussion though someone mentioned the proposal might frighten people. No one mentioned that the High Court had previously blocked an attempt to nationalize the aviation industry or considered the impact of this precedent on the bank plan.[2] Chifley carefully listened but remained silent. When pressed for his opinion he said, "Something has to be done about this, boys, and I think nationalisation is our only alternative." He predicted a hostile reaction from the country's newspapers to a bank takeover and added, "I only hope you are all prepared to stick together and face the grim opposition."[3]

The Cabinet meeting ended with ministers agreeing the Government would introduce legislation to end private banking in Australia when Parliament resumed in Canberra in four weeks. The specifics of nationalisation would be sorted out before MPs returned, and would need to address fundamental issues including whether nationalisation would involve a swift decapitation of the banks or take place incrementally over several years. Would the Government acquire the private banks by compulsion? Or would the Commonwealth Bank buy a controlling interest in their shares, or use taxpayers' money to compete and force them out of business?

At this stage there were no answers to such important questions, nevertheless Cabinet ministers were confident of two things. Firstly, Australia's bankers would never meekly hand over the keys to their vaults to a Labor Government. They would fight fiercely to preserve their independence. Secondly, the ministers believed time was on their side. Ben Chifley was a popular prime minister and had won a historic election victory the year before. Labor had majorities in both Houses of

---

1 *Truth* (Sydney), 24 August 1947, p. 42.
2 *Australian National Airways Pty Ltd v Commonwealth* (No 1), 14 December 1945, 71 CLR 29.
3 Gil Duthie, *I Had 50,000 Bosses: Memoirs of a Labor Backbencher 1946–1975*, Sydney, Angus & Robertson, 1984, p. 43.

Parliament and another three years in office.

The Government was in the first year of the parliamentary term and the next election was not until 1949. That was enough time, or so they calculated, to pass legislation, overcome the opposition that was bound to follow and beat back any legal challenges the banks would mount. By 1949 banking would be an old story, voters would have seen the benefits of nationalisation and the ALP would be rewarded at the polls for its courageous decision. Ministers felt a sense of destiny as they left the Cabinet room. Bank nationalisation had been in the Party platform for decades and now the "nationalisation gun" had been taken from its dusty rack, loaded, and was primed to fire.[1]

By the time the Cabinet meeting ended, two newsmen had arrived in the deserted corridors of Parliament House. Harold Cox and Alan "Red Fox" Reid were experienced members of the Canberra Press Gallery and observers of federal politics. Cox reported for the *Herald* and worked for Sir Keith Murdoch, the Melbourne press baron. Reid reported for the *Sydney Sun*. The pair may have been tipped off that Cabinet was considering the High Court's recent ruling, or their news sense told them there must be a story in an unscheduled Cabinet meeting on a Saturday morning.

As Chifley passed the reporters he said, "Well, I have one or two things of interest for you today." He then disappeared into his office. He reappeared a short time later and handed a piece of paper to his press secretary Don Rodgers. With a look of pleasure Chifley commanded, "Get that out, Don."[2] Cox and Reid were astonished when they read what the Prime Minister had written. By one account Cox was so amazed he bit clean through the stem of his pipe. Another version said Cox's mouth dropped wide open and his pipe smashed to the floor. The press secretary was as astonished as the journalists.

Rodgers was a respected former reporter and member of the Press Gallery. He was Prime Minister John Curtin's press secretary during the war and remained in that role when Chifley became prime minister. He was adept at weaving together information, communicating government decisions with clarity, mediating between the ministry and the press corps, advising his chief about the mood in the Press Gallery or how reporters might approach a story. He had managed the Government's momentous wartime announcements and before he died claimed he wrote John

---

1 *Sydney Morning Herald* (Sydney), 2 December 1949, p. 2.
2 Donald Kilgour Rodgers interviewed by Mel Pratt, 29 April 1971, NLA, ORAL TRC 121/14.

Curtin's landmark declaration in 1941 which stated Australia looked beyond Great Britain to the United States for support.[1] Rodgers was smartly dressed, competent, perspicacious and loyal. Journalists, party officials, public servants, military officers and business leaders trusted him and knew that when Rodgers said something he had the full backing of the Prime Minister. Rodgers served Curtin then Chifley admirably and became a model for the generations of press secretaries who followed.

It was highly unusual that Chifley did not consult Rodgers before he drafted the press statement on the banks. Had he done so, Rodgers would have quickly sensed the announcement would land like a spark in summer-dry bushland. The press secretary was taken by surprise with no chance to advise the Prime Minister or suggest more consideration for such a ground-breaking idea before it became public. Instead there was no turning back once Rodgers handed the press statement to Cox and Reid who immediately catapulted it into that unsuspecting Saturday.

Chifley's press statement immediately caused alarm and people began asking questions. What did bank nationalisation mean, how and when would it be carried out? What would be the effect on personal savings, house mortgages or the overdrafts farmers needed to carry them between seasons? How would it affect exporters who needed credit or manufacturers with loans for plant and machinery? What would happen to the people who worked in the private banks, and would nationalisation harm Australia's standing with international investors? And if his Government had its way, would a future government be able to unscramble Chifley's bank omelette? Was bank nationalisation be a one-off event or the beginning of a larger plot to make Australia a socialist state?

The Commonwealth Government remained tight-lipped for eight weeks after the initial press statement. This gave the banks and other opponents a massive start to organise a nationwide resistance movement. By the time the Prime Minister stood before a packed Parliament to introduce the bill to nationalise private banking, "an uneasy feeling, a foreboding, a grim presentiment [that] all was not well" had settled over the continent.[2] Concerns were also coming from overseas. In London, *The Economist* reported Chifley had set Australia on a regrettable and foolish course.[3] The *Montreal Star* said the measure was unwise and "an imprudent experiment which bodes no good for Australia".[4] Wall Street

---
1 *Canberra Times* (ACT) 13 May 1978, p. 16.
2 Records of the Liberal Party of Australia, speech by Kevin Ellis, 11 September 1949.
3 *Sydney Morning Herald* (Sydney), 29 August 1947, p. 6.
4 *Dalby Herald* (Dalby), 10 October 1947, p. 4.

thought it reeked of Communism.[1]

The job of a press statement is both to inform and to attract attention. Chifley's was short on information but attracted massive attention. From August 1947 to the federal election in 1949 it generated thousands of newspaper stories, editorials, opinion pieces, columns, cartoons, letters, photos and ads. Radio carried a bitter debate into suburban living rooms and bush camps, and the issue was endlessly discussed in town halls and on street corners. The nation's presses rolled out bulletins, brochures, circulars, fliers, leaflets, pamphlets, petitions and posters by the millions, and the printing industry flourished.

Australians had seen political controversies before but had never witnessed the enormous energy and vast sums poured into a single issue. Chifley and his Government came under sustained attack and the Prime Minister's image as a popular leader began to crack.

---

1 *Advertiser* (Adelaide), 20 August 1947, p. 1.

1 Autocrat or Visionary

"I liked the man for his honest and forthright common sense."[1]

Joseph Benedict Chifley was an unlikely man to lead Australia. The sixteenth Prime Minister looked more like a heavyweight boxer than a prime minister and before entering politics drove trains across the central western plains of New South Wales. Photos of the time show a big-boned, grey, grizzled individual with a broad face and wide smile. Women found Chifley ruggedly attractive and Australia's first female MP, Enid Lyons, praised his sturdy good looks, immense personal dignity and friendly but reserved bearing.[2]

Not everyone found Chifley appealing. The renowned portrait photographer Max Dupain had a rare instinct for capturing the essence of his subjects. His photograph of Ben Chifley, among the few deliberate studies of the man, differed from the usual genial images and instead showed a cold, determined individual with flaring nostrils and steely eyes.[3] Like most other pictures it featured his inseparable pipe.

Chifley's pipe was the unmissable element in any photograph, cartoon or illustration of the Prime Minister. It was as much a part of his public persona as Winston Churchill's cigar or the battered grey fedora worn by Franklin Roosevelt. Cigarettes were popular after the war but Chifley remained a pipe smoker. No doubt he found the pipe pleasurable but it did no harm that a pipe could convey an air of thoughtfulness and authority. The opening of the tobacco tin, the pressing of tobacco in the wooden bowl, the striking of the match, the long draw on the stem, and afterwards the scraping of blackened ashes from the bowl, was a ritual that conveyed method and purpose and gave the smoker time to ponder the issue before him. On Chifley's desk was a small oil jar with a burning wick which he used throughout the day to light his pipe. Anyone coming into a room after Chifley knew he had been there. When the blind American author Helen Keller met Chifley on a visit to Australia, she cradled his pipe and declared, "I felt his pipe and he was very gracious."[4]

1 *National Advocate* (Bathurst), 16 July 1951, p. 1.
2 Dame Enid Lyons, *Among the Carrion Crows*, Adelaide, Rigby, 1972, p. 7.
3 Ben Chifley n.d. Max Dupain OBE, gelatin silver photograph on paper (sheet: 39.0cm x 31.5cm, image: 38.5cm x 31.5cm) © Max Dupain/Copyright Agency, 2021, National Portrait Gallery of Australia, 2017.25.
4 *Worker* (Brisbane), 3 May 1948, p. 4.

Chifley's voice, which sounded like pebbles rattling in a tin can, was another distinguishing feature. This coarseness was a result of years of speaking in all weathers on street corners, pub balconies, union halls and over the noisy clanking of steam trains. The *Australian Women's Weekly* reported, "there is a harsh, rasping quality in his voice which is partly natural, partly caused by a throat condition. Yet it is a voice that seems to bring to his listeners some intangible reminder of the bush."[1] Chifley was aware of his voice and the limitations of his oratory. He often mispronounced words, ran sentences together and spoke in flat monotones. There was no flourish or excitement in his speeches, yet Australians listened not for his eloquence but for the ordinary, genuine way he expressed his convictions.

Chifley was born in 1885 to a working-class Irish Catholic family in Bathurst, New South Wales. At the age of five his parents sent him to his grandfather's hardscrabble farm near the village of Limekilns about twenty miles away. Working alongside his gruff Irish grandfather he learned about stoicism, persistence and hard labour. He was a part-time pupil at a nearby bush school and when he returned to Bathurst at the age of fourteen he attended St Patrick's Boys' School. Chifley left school with a love of reading but an otherwise meagre education. No one including himself had any expectation he would be remarkable in any way.

Chifley's first taste of politics was in the parlours and kitchens of Limekilns listening to his grandfather's neighbours talk about the issues of the day. These left an impression because when one neighbour asked young Chifley what he wanted to be, the boy replied, "a Member of Parliament".[2] Chifley first came into contact with banking around the same time. He was in primary school when the colonial banking system in Australia collapsed in the 1890s after years of speculation and risky lending. Twenty-three major banks failed and there were hundreds of defaults among land syndicates, "fringe banks" and building societies.

Surviving institutions struggled to pay out depositors and even well-managed banks took years to reimburse their customers. Many working people lost their savings and credit evaporated for farmers, factory managers and shopkeepers. The collapse hit the elder Chifley, and his grandson witnessed his despair and anger and the distress of neighbouring families. He later recalled, "When I was a small child I can remember in the Depression of the nineties, the farmers near where I lived were lonely

---
1 *Australian Women's Weekly* (Sydney), 21 July 1945, p. 17.
2 L. F. Crisp, *Ben Chifley*, Melbourne, Longmans, 1961, p. 5.

and grief-stricken at the closing of the banks. They had no guarantee of ever being repaid and in some instances they were never repaid."[1]

Chifley's first jobs after finishing school were in a store and a tannery before he joined the New South Wales Government Railway Service in 1903. The railways were the vital links that connected major cities, provincial centres and bush towns. A job with the railways was respectable, predictable and reasonably well-paid. At night small boys dreamed of driving a locomotive as they listened to trains whistling past their bedroom windows. Small girls had no such dreams because working on the rails was a man's job. The few women who were employed served refreshments in station tea rooms and occasionally the widow of a railwayman was paid to operate the gates at a crossing close to her house.[2] In places like Bathurst the railway service was not only a major employer but also served as a community hub. Towns competed to have garden-perfect stations, and the red brick institutes where railwaymen trained, served as after-hours dance halls, public libraries and social clubs.

Chifley started by doing the dirtiest jobs in the Bathurst rail yards and through diligence and classes at night worked his way up through the ranks: yard boy, engine cleaner, fire lighter and fireman. Eventually he became the youngest first-class engine driver in the state. Piloting a 139,000-pound, D50-class locomotive around central New South Wales was a demanding job that required an expert knowledge of timetables, stations, bogies, carriages, gradients and loads. Chifley joined the Federated Engine Drivers' and Firemen's Association and ultimately became a union organiser and delegate. His deep knowledge of railway trades made him a sought-after witness in arbitration cases involving industrial issues like pay.

In 1914 Chifley married Elizabeth ("Lizzie") McKenzie, the daughter of a Scottish co-worker. Lizzie was a Presbyterian and Chifley was a Catholic and the couple had to marry in Sydney because the Catholic Church did not approve of "mixed marriages". Though the marriage separated Chifley from the Catholic Church he still attended mass in Bathurst and Canberra but sat in the back pews. He read the Bible several times from cover to cover and maintained a deep personal faith throughout his life. The Catholic Church, the ALP and the union movement had a shared Irish heritage but Chifley was less susceptible to church influence than other Labor men since the circumstances of his marriage had limited his

---
1 Crisp, p. 4.
2 Rail Trades Exhibition, New South Wales Rail Museum, Thirlmere, 2018. The first woman train driver in New South Wales was appointed in 1985.

involvement with the Church.

When they married, Lizzie's parents gave the couple a five-room cottage as a wedding present. The house in Busby Street was close to the centre of Bathurst and a short walk to the railyards. It was their first and only home and was simply furnished and unpretentious. Lizzie was a capable and frugal homemaker and apart from work and night-time study, Chifley enjoyed reading and caring for his backyard vegetable plot. In his younger married days Chifley was also active in local sports clubs and an accomplished footballer.

The couple had no children, probably because of Lizzie's poor health, and were described as devoted and close. There was speculation Chifley had long-running relationships with Phyllis Donnelly and her sister Nell. Both women were from Bathurst and Phyllis worked for years as Chifley's secretary and general factotum. Any relationship with the two sisters however was closely guarded and Chifley's biographer David Day notes, "Whatever journalists might have known or suspected about the complications in Chifley's private life they kept a discreet silence. It was the public man and his public responsibilities that interested them."[1]

Chifley might have continued along unremarkably – a respectable married man in Bathurst with a solid railway career – but for the events of 1917. In July the New South Wales Railways introduced a time-and-motion system to improve worker efficiency but failed to consult the unions about the changes. Rail and tram workers walked off the job in Sydney and the strike soon spread across New South Wales. Eventually, eighty thousand workers, numerous trades and mines, steelworks and ports nationwide were involved in what became known as "The Great Strike". Some railway workers did remain on the job but the State Government dismissed strikers including Ben Chifley and recruited "scab" labour to help run essential services.

The public mood soured on the strikers because the country was at war. After six bitter weeks, isolated and exhausted, the unionists returned to work. Striking railwaymen had to reapply for their jobs and Chifley, who had been an engine driver, was reinstated at the lower rank as a fireman on reduced pay. His rating as an engine driver slumped to number 1,186 out of about 1,300 drivers in the state and he was now subordinate to men he had trained and supervised. "The Great Strike" scarred Chifley, who remembered the "legacy of bitterness and a trail of hate" it caused between those who walked off the job and those who stayed.[2] Chifley's

---
1 David Day, *Chifley*, Sydney, Harper Collins, 2001, p. 441.
2 Crisp, p. 22.

commitment to his union was unwavering but the personal legacy from that strike was to convince him that political rather than industrial action was a better way to safeguard the interests of working people.

Chifley turned to politics and was an unsuccessful ALP candidate in state and Commonwealth elections between 1922 and 1925. In 1928 he was elected as the Federal Member for Macquarie, representing an area from Bathurst to the Blue Mountains. The novice MP was a diligent and hard-working member of the Scullin Labor Government and briefly the Minister for Defence and the Minister Assisting the Treasurer. In Canberra he forged a lasting friendship with fellow freshman John Curtin from Western Australia.

Lizzie Chifley supported her husband but had little interest in politics or the role of a politician's wife. She remained in Bathurst and made only occasional trips to Canberra even when her husband became prime minister. On one occasion she advised the wife of a nephew who was thinking about a career in politics, "Don't let him do it. You'll lose him."[1]

The Scullin Government wrestled with the economic turbulence of the Depression and voters came to believe it was ineffectual in managing the crisis. Scullin was defeated in the 1931 election by Joseph Lyons who had been the Labor Treasurer but defected from the Party over serious policy differences. Chifley lost his seat and returned to Bathurst. Fortunately Lizzie had received an inheritance from her father so the couple were financially independent. He was able to occupy his time volunteering with community organisations in Bathurst. He was on the board of the District Hospital and became a director of the *National Advocate*, one of Bathurst's two newspapers.

In 1933 Chifley was elected as a councillor of the Abercrombie Shire Council which covered the rural district encircling Bathurst. He went on to serve fourteen years in local government including a term as Shire President. Though Chifley kept busy in Bathurst, his volunteering days were a significant change from his former status as a Commonwealth minister. Lizzie shared the indignity and some local women "chose not to recognise her when they met her about the shops and streets".[2]

Jack Lang was the Labor Premier of New South Wales when Chifley was back in Bathurst. Lang was a big, bellicose and intimidating figure whose bully-boy style and unorthodox economic policies split the Labor Party in the state. Chifley, by this time a respected figure in the ALP,

---

1 "Mrs Prime Minister: Public Image, Private Lives", Museum of Australian Democracy, https://mrspm.moadoph.gov.au/private-lives.html, accessed online 4 April 2022.
2 Crisp, p. 65.

worked towards unifying the fragments of a now dispirited organisation and became state president of what remained of the Party in New South Wales. In the 1935 New South Wales election he contested Jack Lang's seat of Auburn but lost by 2,400 votes. It was an ugly and bruising campaign but Chifley's dogged performance resurrected some of his Party's fortunes. The clash between the two men turned Lang into a lifelong critic of Chifley.

Five months after Chifley's loss in Auburn, Prime Minister Joseph Lyons appointed him to the Royal Commission on Monetary and Banking Systems. The Commission was established due to the widespread dissatisfaction with Australia's banks during the Depression and pressure from the Country Party. Commission members came from legal, finance and economics and pastoral backgrounds. Lyons thought Chifley's union and ALP credentials would add balance to the Commission and help win public confidence. Chifley received a sitting fee of £5 a day (nearly $600 today) plus travel expenses, which was a large sum given hundreds of thousands were out of work.

Commissioner Chifley listened intently and contributed freely. His formal education had stopped after two years at St Patrick's College, so he eagerly took the chance to learn about economics, finance and public policy from the witnesses who appeared before the Commission. Chief Commissioner Justice John Napier from South Australia regarded Chifley as his most valuable member.

The Commission's final report concluded private banking was still the most suitable system for Australia although it recommended the Commonwealth Bank should have wider powers in order to give governments greater control over the economy. Chifley, wary of banks since the days on his grandfather's farm, submitted a minority report that challenged this view. After hearing hours of testimony and reading millions of words, he concluded, "There is no possibility of ... well-ordered progress being made in the community, under a system in which there are privately-owned trading banks which have been established for the purposes of making profit ... the best service to the community can be given only by a banking system entirely under national control."[1] Though Chifley's opinions on banking never wavered, at the time they did not overly concern Australia's bankers who assumed he would go back to the political wilderness of Bathurst. The Lyons Government shelved the

---

1 D. B. Waterson, "Chifley, Joseph Benedict (Ben) (1885–1951)", *Australian Dictionary of Biography*, National Centre of Biography, Australian National University, https://adb.anu.edu.au/biography/chifley-joseph-benedict-ben-9738/text17199, accessed online 4 April 2022.

Royal Commission's recommendations because of the impending war.

At the onset of the Second World War the Menzies Government appointed Chifley as the Federal Director of Labour Supply and Regulation in the Ministry of Munitions. He resigned from that position to contest the 1940 federal election and successfully regained his old seat of Macquarie. A year later he became Treasurer after John Curtin formed the first Labor Government in ten years.

Chifley's time on the Royal Commission proved invaluable preparation for the new role. He quickly gained a reputation as a first-class financial mind, knowledgeable administrator and canny politician. Even Opposition Robert Menzies acknowledged his grasp of finances and policy. Treasurer Chifley bankrolled the expansion of the armed forces to almost a million servicemen and women and massive industrial developments. He supervised the biggest loans in Australian history and overhauled the tax system to pay for the war effort. John Curtin also entrusted Chifley with the leadership of the Department for Post-war Reconstruction, a small yet influential agency tasked with shaping Australia's future after the war. These dual roles made Chifley simultaneously responsible for funding the war and planning the peace.

Chifley and Curtin had a warm personal and professional relationship and Chifley was happy being Treasurer. When Curtin died six weeks before the war ended, the Federal Labor Party elected Chifley as its new leader. As Prime Minister he continued as Treasurer, giving him unique authority in the Government, Cabinet and Caucus and influence in the remotest federal outpost. Chifley continued to draw on the support of the talented university graduates the Government had recruited during the war. Herbert "Nugget" Coombs, Douglas Copeland and other forward-thinking minds provided him with economic advice and progressive opinions and soon "Chifley men" were on every significant Commonwealth committee.

Public servants liked the Prime Minister because he was a strong and straightforward leader with clear principles and precise objectives. He meticulously collected facts, considered different views and then logically built an argument. Yet once he made up his mind there was little prospect of change or compromise. The journalist Alan Reid said when Chifley decided something it was like closing a book and pushing it away.[1] Labor MP Fred Daly, who was elected in 1943, said Chifley was "probably was too rigorous in regard to some things".[2] This unwillingness to compromise

1   Alan Reid interviewed by Mel Pratt, 28 February 1973, NLA ORAL TRC 121/40.
2   Fred Daly interviewed by Mel Pratt, 26 August–25 November 1976, NLA ORAL TRC 121/96.

was to become increasingly apparent as the bank nationalisation drama played out and eventually cost the Prime Minister and his Party dearly.

Chifley's work ethic was legendary and the lights in the Prime Minister's office were the last to burn in Parliament House. Days started early and ended around midnight and were filled with appearances in the House of Representatives, in Cabinet and Caucus and as many as fifteen appointments a day. His door was always open for colleagues including Opposition Leader Robert Menzies who could just drop by. He used the Prime Minister's office for appointments and the Treasurer's office to work on his ministerial papers. He took few breaks during the day apart from regular catnaps, a routine he had developed during his train-driving days, and always seemed alert and in command.[1]

Chifley enjoyed the occasional dinner or drink with co-workers but meals mostly consisted of copious cups of tea and dry toast, produced from a kettle and pressed-tin toaster he kept in his office.[2] Chifley had little time for things beyond work. He had been a handy footballer and cricketer in his younger days but rarely attended sporting matches because they robbed him of time.[3] He occasionally bet on horse races, liked listening to brass bands and attending live theatre and swapped crime and cowboy novels with Robert Menzies and other bibliophiles in Parliament House.[4]

Lizzie Chifley cared for her nonagenarian mother in Bathurst and rarely came to Canberra. Chifley chose not to live at the Prime Minister's official residence but stayed at the Hotel Kurrajong near Parliament House. From here he walked to work rather than being chauffeured in his official limousine. On weekends he met informally with other MPs and used any free time to reflect and refine his ideas. On Sunday mornings he walked to St Christopher's Cathedral in nearby Manuka for mass, and in the afternoons lay in bed snoozing, reading a thriller or studying official papers. On designated weekends his chauffeur Ray Tracey drove him back to Bathurst but even then Chifley worked. He toured his electorate, attended meetings of the Abercrombie Shire Council where he was still a councillor, and caught up with old mates from railway days. Back home in Busby Street he read the paper, listened to the radio, chatted with neighbours and pottered about his garden.

---

1 Alan Reid interviewed by Mel Pratt.
2 Don Rodgers interviewed by Mel Pratt, 29 April 1971, NLA ORAL TRC 121/14.
3 *Australian Women's Weekly* (Sydney), 28 July 1945, p. 20.
4 Hazel Craig interviewed by Ken Begg, 25 March 1996, Museum of Australian Democracy, OPH-OH13, accessed online 4 April 2022.

An effective prime minister must be an effective politician and Chifley was very good at both. He mixed easily with people and though he came across as amiable and open, journalist Edgar Holt noted that he never really gave a great deal of himself to others.[1] Someone arriving at his office upset or flustered, left soothed after he made them a cup of tea from his kettle and listened patiently to their worries. He accepted criticism without anger, bitterness or the volcanic eruptions of lesser men, and though he respected all viewpoints he often used the dry humour of the bush to end an argument. Typically in a heated debate he would sum up by saying the topic was of such great principle, it demanded action. Or he would say the situation demanded a cautious approach because a great principle was at stake. He had a wealth of experience in economics, finance and public administration and deftly used it to shape or limit a discussion with peers in Cabinet and Caucus. He was happy to recognise their good ideas but would leave them unactioned if it suited his purpose. He joked that the ideal committee would be two in number with one away ill.[2]

For a man making crucial decisions in war and its aftermath, Ben Chifley made no personal enemies.[3] He showed no trace of self-importance nor sought special treatment and would abhor today's environment where prime ministers are cocooned behind minders, media advisers and security officers. In 1945, when Chifley succeeded Curtin, Menzies lamented, "Why did they choose him … how can we fight him?"[4] Before bank nationalisation Chifley was popular and Australians liked his genial, robust style. Admirers saw a nobility in his politics perhaps best summed up by Chifley himself in a 1949 speech, "We have a great objective – the light on the hill – which we aim to reach by working for the betterment of mankind not only here but anywhere we may give a helping hand."[5]

---

1 Edgar Holt interviewed by Mel Pratt, 2–3 May 1978, NLA ORAL TRC 121/93.
2 Leslie Haylen, *Twenty Years' Hard Labor*, South Melbourne, Macmillan, 1969, p. 35.
3 *Armidale Express and New England Advertiser* (Armidale), 15 June 1951, 8.
4 *Australian Women's Weekly* (Sydney), 27 June 1951, p. 21.
5 "The Light on the Hill: Celebrating 75 Years", Chifley Centre, 10 July 2020, https://www.chifley.org.au/publications/the-light-on-the-hill-celebrating-75-years/, accessed online 4 April 2022.

2 Leading the Charge

"Have they now assumed the role of defenders of the freedom of the common people of Australia?"[1]

In 1947 Robert Gordon Menzies was the Opposition Leader in the House of Representatives. His reacted with disbelief when he heard about Chifley's bank announcement and called it "a staggering statement".[2] The next day he went further: "The Government's decision was the most spectacular move toward complete socialisation ever made in an English-speaking country. For any parallel, we must go to Soviet Russia."[3] Chifley and Menzies were friends but their political relationship though respectful, could be lively and combative. From the moment he learned about bank nationalisation Menzies believed it was his duty to warn Australians that Ben Chifley was leading them down a dangerous path.

Robert Gordon Menzies was born in 1894 in Jeparit in the Wimmera region of north-west Victoria. The town was surrounded by farms and was a hub for telegraph, rail and postal services. Jeparit had only 250 people so everyone knew James Menzies and his general store. James and his wife Kate had five children and impressed on them the need to do well at school. Robert applied for and won scholarships to prestigious private schools and colleges in Victoria.

In 1916 Menzies graduated in law from the University of Melbourne with a "galaxy of prizes". He began his legal career under Owen Dixon who was later to play a pivotal role in the bank nationalisation case and become Chief Justice of the High Court. By the 1920s Menzies had earned a reputation as an accomplished constitutional lawyer and was appointed a King's Counsel by the end of the decade.

Menzies was drawn to politics possibly because his father and two uncles served in the Victorian Parliament and his maternal grandfather was a senator. In 1920 Menzies married Pattie Maie Leckie, the daughter of a Victorian senator who was later a minister in Menzies' first government. Unlike Mrs Chifley, Pattie Menzies actively supported her husband's political career and went on to be the role model for modern prime ministerial partners.

---

1 *Barrier Daily Truth* (Broken Hill), 30 October 1947, p. 2.
2 *Herald* (Melbourne), 16 August 1947, p. 1.
3 *Argus* (Melbourne), 18 August 1947, p. 1.

Menzies was elected to the Victorian Parliament in 1928 and served in both the Legislative Council and Legislative Assembly. He rose through the conservative ranks to become Deputy Premier, Attorney General and Minister for Railways. His star was rising and he was encouraged to enter national politics on the understanding that he would eventually replace Joseph Lyons as Prime Minister in the United Australia Party (UAP) Government. In 1934 Menzies won the Melbourne suburban seat of Kooyong and weeks later Lyons made him Attorney General and Minister for Industry.

A tall, handsome man with slightly curly hair Menzies had refined features and a commanding presence. He dressed impeccably and looked a prime minister in waiting. What really set Menzies apart however was his ability to speak in public, his photographic memory and a remarkable ability to absorb detail. A secretary remembered that Menzies "probably would do in a quarter of an hour what it would take another man an hour and a half to do".[1] Unlike Chifley who was an uninspiring speaker, a Menzies address was powerful and lyrical. He had a pleasing tonality, a strong sense of humour and could use the lofty language of the law.[2] The Melbourne *Herald* called him "the easiest politician to listen to in Australia".[3]

Menzies' razor-sharp wit could both energise and alienate and some critics said he could not relate to ordinary people. Before the war his battles with the Waterside Workers' Federation earned him one of the most unattractive and enduring nicknames in Australian politics. Then Attorney General, Menzies battled workers on the docks when they refused to load crude iron for shipping to Japan. The wharfies called him "Pig Iron Bob" and it would take a concerted public relations effort a decade later to try to shake off that unflattering title.

In April 1939 Menzies became the UAP's second Prime Minister when Joseph Lyons died. This was despite a vicious personal attack launched by the Leader of the Country Party, Sir Earle Page. Using parliamentary privilege Page savaged Menzies and questioned his lack of military service in the First World War, highlighted his character flaws and questioned Menzies' fitness to lead the government.[4] Even some Labor MPs came to Menzies' defence and years later many still remembered Page's verbal lashing.

---

1 Hazel Craig interviewed by Ken Begg, 25 March 1996, MOAD Oral History.
2 Heather Henderson (daughter of Sir Robert Menzies) in discussion with author, 6 July 2021.
3 *Herald* (Melbourne), 24 July 1934, p. 8.
4 *Sydney Morning Herald* (Sydney), 21 April 1939, p. 12.

Five months later Germany invaded Poland and Menzies went on nationwide radio to declare Australia was at war. He was now responsible for mobilising the country for a global war. Despite criticisms of his efforts in the first two years of the war, Menzies always maintained his Government laid the foundations for those who followed to effectively prosecute the war. One of his initiatives was to create the Department of Information and task it with providing Australians with news of the war, preparing them for the hardships ahead and winning public support for the regulations and restrictions to come. While one part of the Department moulded public opinion, another part censored information, sometimes in a heavy-handed way.

In 1941 Menzies visited the Middle East and the United Kingdom. While he was away his support within his Party waned because a number of his colleagues were offended by his management style and concerned about serious shortcomings in how the war was managed. After he came home Menzies tried but failed to establish a national, all-party government to oversee the war effort. He resigned and was replaced by the Leader of the Country Party, Arthur Fadden, who headed a government that lasted thirty-nine days. Fadden was succeeded by the Labor Party's John Curtin and Menzies became an ordinary backbencher in a bruised and diminished party.

In opposition Menzies mostly supported Curtin's handling of the war but also set out to rebuild conservative politics and revive the spirit of liberalism in Australia. He believed Australians accepted government interference with the country at war but would reject regimentation when the fighting finished. He presented his philosophy of government in weekly and nationwide radio talks that broadcast between 1942 to 1944. The *Age* lauded them for their unequalled merit, quiet distinction and firm reasoning. Transcripts from these weekly programs became a book.

The best remembered of these talks was "The Forgotten People" broadcast in 1942 when Menzies spoke of the middle-class Australians who were squeezed between wealthy elites and the unionised working class. He championed their ambitions and values. They were the strivers and planners and their approach to family and work contrasted sharply with those of the spineless and effortless who relied on the state to "dole out bread and ideas with neatly regulated accuracy".[1]

In October 1944 the UAP was in serious decline and a handful of MPs and fourteen conservative organisations met to talk about forming a new

---

1   Robert Menzies, "The Forgotten People", http://www.liberals.net/theforgottenpeople.htm, accessed online 4 April 2022.

conservative party. Menzies was chosen as leader of the newly formed Liberal Party whose aim was to champion "all that is sane, responsible, enterprising and generous in the Australian spirit".[1] At its core the new Party wanted individuals to be responsible for their futures and for private enterprise to flourish. It implacably opposed socialism and Communism. This ideology appealed to young people, veterans and women wanting change after years of being told what to do. Soon the new Party had nearly 40,000 members.[2]

Menzies and his new Party unsuccessfully contested the 1946 federal election. Australians rewarded the Labor Party for its wartime performance and returned it to government. The *Sydney Morning Herald* reported, "Mr Menzies proved unable to overcome the handicaps of personal unpopularity (leading) a reorganised party which has not yet established itself in public favour."[3] The election loss cast doubts about Menzies' future and he briefly considered quitting politics. However, he was re-elected as Liberal leader despite dark whispers that "you can't win with Menzies".

In August 1947 the Liberal and Country Parties were struggling to gain traction against the Government. Prime Minister Chifley was popular and the Labor Government in a historic third term was very much in control. Chifley's bank nationalisation statement shifted the dynamics of Australian politics almost overnight. For the Opposition Leader it was like rain after a summer drought. Menzies had been saying for five years that Labor governments were predisposed to state control and socialism and Chifley's bank press statement now provided irrefutable proof he was right.

Chifley had gifted Menzies the chance to rally his "forgotten people", oppose the Government and make a political comeback. He immediately marched his Party to the head of a national protest movement, and took every opportunity for the next two years to condemn the Government and its bank plan. Australian newspapers cheered on Menzies and the banks were delighted to have someone of his calibre to defend their interests. Soon Menzies broadened the issue. His fight with the Government was not just about banking but about who had the best vision for the future of Australia as it headed into the next half century.

Ben Chifley and Robert Menzies were from humble backgrounds but Richard Gavin Gardiner Casey had a privileged upbringing. His father was involved in pastoral and gold mining interests and his mother's

1 *Advertiser* (Adelaide), 12 May 1945, p. 7.
2 Edgar Holt, *Politics is People: The Men of the Menzies Era*, Sydney, Angus and Robertson, 1969, p. 42.
3 *Sydney Morning Herald* (Sydney), 30 September 1946, p. 2.

family included three Queensland parliamentarians, one of whom served as Premier of Queensland. Casey attended the Melbourne Church of England Grammar School and then the University of Melbourne. He graduated with honours in mechanical science tripos from Cambridge University. Casey enlisted in the Australian Imperial Force during the First World War and served at Gallipoli and in France. He was Mentioned in Dispatches and was awarded the Military Cross and the Distinguished Service Order. While Casey held important staff appointments he never commanded troops, a trend that continued throughout his life. Richard Casey was always near the top but never the top leader.

Casey stayed in London after the war and worked as a political liaison officer between the Australian and British Governments. In this quasi-diplomatic role he developed a lifelong affection for British institutions and often referred to Australians as "we British". The *Bulletin* magazine said Casey's time in the United Kingdom gave him a Whitehall manner which Australian politics never managed to scrape off.[1]

Casey had a warm relationship with Australian Prime Minister Stanley Bruce. When the Scullin Labor Government replaced the Bruce Government in 1929, Casey and his wife Maie decided to return to Australia. They settled in Melbourne where Maie's family connections made them part of the Melbourne establishment. In 1931 Casey successfully stood as the UAP candidate for the seat of Corio in Victoria. As a politician he kept aloof from the grubby squabbles of Canberra but was recognised for his energy and organisational abilities.

Casey's ambition made him an early aspirant for Cabinet rank and in 1935 he became Treasurer in the Lyons Government. He was in the running for the UAP leadership when Joseph Lyons died, but lost to Menzies. His Party probably felt the very English Casey was too stiff and formal for Australian voters. He served as Minister of Supply in Menzies' first government.

In 1940 Casey quit politics to take up the newly created role of Australian Minister in the United States, which was equivalent to the modern position of Australian Ambassador in Washington. America had yet to enter the war and Australia was looking for support from the Roosevelt Administration. Casey was well-liked in Washington because of his polished presentation and unflagging work ethic. He made close connections in the White House and with the politicians and pressmen of Washington. He became fascinated with the emerging profession of

---

1 *Bulletin* (Sydney), 27 January 1940, p. 10.

public relations and how political parties and big business used it to promote their agendas.

The British Prime Minister Winston Churchill knew Richard Casey and offered him the position of British Minister of State in the Middle East. Casey left Washington for Cairo and later accepted Churchill's offer to become the Governor of Bengal in India. Casey spent the war years outside of Australia and his decision to work for the British Government led some in the Labor Party to doubt this loyalty. The Australian press called him "the Bengal Tiger".

Casey returned to Australia after the war with an impressive resume. He had served in the Great War with distinction, been a competent Treasurer in the Lyons Government and succeeded in his diplomatic postings. Some whispered he might replace Menzies as the leader of the Liberal Party but Casey returned home too late to either find or be offered a winnable seat in the 1946 election. The following year Casey was elected Federal President of the Liberal Party, which ruled out any immediate leadership challenge from him. The Party Leader and the new President were not especially close but Menzies recognised that Casey's energy, organisational skills and ambition could help him restore the Liberal Party's fortunes after the election defeat.

Casey and Maie were wealthy, well-connected and part of Melbourne's elite. They dressed impeccably, belonged to the right clubs and divided their time between a country property and a fashionable townhouse in East Melbourne. They could have easily and comfortably retired and basked in the glow of past achievements. Instead, in his new job as Federal President Casey propelled himself into the national spotlight with the full support of his wife. Casey was never anti-worker or even anti-Labor but he now vigorously opposed the Chifley Government. He set out to use his remarkable ability to organise, to rescue the banks, drive his Party to victory at the next election and preserve the Australia that had so generously blessed him.

Bankers could recall the moment they heard about Chifley's announcement. The General Manager of the English, Scottish and Australian Bank (the ES&A Bank) saw a newspaper poster at a railway station and promptly alerted his board in London. Harry Jago, an officer with the Bank of New South Wales, was gardening at home in Sydney. Young Army veteran and bank officer Bob White heard the news from a Melbourne paperboy in Swanston Street.[1] Leslie McConnan was the

---

1   White had a very successful banking career, finishing as Chief Executive of Westpac.

General Manager of the National Bank of Australasia (National Bank) and was on the golf course when word reached him. McConnan calmly finished his game as pressmen gathered to hear his reaction.

Leslie James McConnan was born in 1887 in Benalla in north-east Victoria to a father who was a Presbyterian minister and a mother from South Australia. The McConnans were originally from Scotland and were proud of their Celtic ancestry. Their family home had an atmosphere of "plain living and high thinking".[1] McConnan matriculated from a private school in Benalla and instead of going to university joined the National Bank. His early career was spent as a junior bank officer in branches around Victoria and as a travelling country accountant. His diligence and hard work led to management roles in Sydney and Adelaide and to a prestigious appointment in the Bank's office in London. In 1935 at the age of forty-eight he became head of the National Bank and tried to humanise banking by being more reasonable than rigid.[2] The rise of the "Boy from Benalla" to the peak of the banking industry had been quick and stuffy insiders said he was too young for such role.

The renowned Australian artist William Dargie painted McConnan before the banker retired. The painting, which won the 1950 Archibald Prize, shows an intelligent and thoughtful man with determined eyes. At first glance he looked approachable but on closer inspection his manner suggested he could be abrupt with those who wasted his time. McConnan was charming, well-regarded and respected. He set high standards for himself and others, inspired loyalty and coaxed rather than commanded his people. He stood out from other bank chiefs of the day because he was unafraid to go public with his views. McConnan and Chifley first met when the banker gave compelling testimony before the Royal Commission on Banking. National Bank historian Geoffrey Blainey said McConnan showed "an absorbing interest in politics and public affairs, unusual in a chief officer of an Australian bank".[3]

McConnan led his bank through some of its most difficult moments: the Depression, the Second World War and the post-war attempt to abolish the banks. In 1947 McConnan was the Chairman of the Associated Banks, the committee of bank chiefs that met a couple of times a year to coordinate an industry response to topical issues. The role of chairman rotated annually among the general managers and mostly involved

---

1 *Benalla Ensign* (Benalla), 23 December 1954, p. 1.
2 *Canberra Times* (ACT), 23 December 1954, p. 9.
3 Geoffrey Blainey, *Gold and Paper: A History of the National Bank of Australasia Limited*, Melbourne, Georgian House, 1958, p. 358.

arranging meetings and hosting lunch.

As chairman during the war, McConnan had bristled at the Curtin Government's wartime controls on banking. He was especially exasperated in 1942 when the Minister for War Organisation of Industry, John Dedman, declared banking to be a non-essential service. Dedman tried to close and amalgamate bank branches and dispatch surplus staff off to "real" wartime jobs. The Minister was an abrasive figure and the banks had little option other than to comply with his demands because the country was at war. The Minister's measures ultimately produced few savings but had the effect of making the banks suspicious that Dedman's rationalisation could lead to post-war nationalisation.

In 1945 McConnan was the most vocal critic of the Government's banking legislation which extended wartime controls over banking. He warned of the threat it posed in radio broadcasts, press interviews and letters to his customers. The other banks mounted a listless and eventually ineffective protest, and finally the general managers said that while they would comply with the legislation they reserved the right to challenge it in future. That moment came in early 1947 when Chifley instructed government bodies they needed his permission to bank with any institution other than the Commonwealth Bank. The private banks supported the successful challenge by the Melbourne City Council against that ruling. McConnan, sensing trouble ahead, quietly reinstated the Bank's public relations office, which had disappeared amid wartime staff cuts.

McConnan finished his game of golf after hearing the news about Chifley's statement on bank nationalisation, then told waiting journalists, "If I understand today's announcement correctly, the objective is that every citizen's financial affairs will be subject to Government inspection and control."[1]

In the normal course of events, McConnan should have stepped down from the chairmanship of the Associated Banks at the end of 1947. However, supported by the other banks, he continued in the role for two more years and led a devastating campaign that saw the defeat of nationalisation and the Labor Government. McConnan was the *generalissimo* behind the bank victory and was recognised as the man who saved Australia's banks.

---

1 *Mail* (Adelaide), 16 August 1947, p.1.

3 Routine and Respectable

"Fear of losing high profits has added to the volume of the bankers' squeal."[1]

Private banking had been integral to Australian life for over a century and over that time many banks had failed many customers. Despite its imperfections, banking was widely recognised as one of those industries that had helped build the nation. Now, the Chifley Government aimed to replace this industry with a state-run banking system.

Australian banking began with the Bank of New South Wales in Sydney in 1817. Starting with capital of £11,000, the bank went on to play a significant role in developing colonial agriculture and manufacturing. By 1947 "The Wales", as it was generally known, had 800 branches and 6,000 staff nationwide. It saw itself as the premier bank and when a switchboard operator answered calls at head office, she simply said, "The Bank". Further identification was unnecessary.

The Head Office of the Bank of New South Wales was in Martin Place in Sydney and next door was the Commercial Banking Company of Sydney which was the second-oldest bank in the country. It operated mainly in Victoria and New South Wales. Between them the two banks managed some of the country's largest and most profitable accounts. Australia's other major banks were headquartered in Melbourne on leafy Collins Street. The National Bank was the largest of these, and further up Collins Street were the head offices of the mid-sized Commercial Bank of Australia and the three "English banks". The Bank of Australasia, the Union Bank and the English, Scottish and Australian Bank (ES&A) were incorporated in the United Kingdom and controlled from London. At the start of the year the Bank of Australasia and the Union Bank had announced plans to merge.

The much smaller Bank of Adelaide and the Queensland National Bank were state-based operations, while the Bank of Ballarat and the Brisbane Permanent Building and Banking Company were hometown concerns. There were three banks owned by the New Zealand, French and Chinese governments but their focus was on serving the occasional traveller and facilitating trade with Australia.[2]

---

1 *Tribune* (Sydney), 26 August 1947, p. 1.
2 RBAA: Research Department; C3.22.3.2, Research Department – Legislation – Banking Act 1947 – Memoranda and Correspondence – June–September 1947, p. 146.

After Chifley's press statement, there was speculation that the Bank of Adelaide might be the first candidate for the executioner's block. It was the smallest of the eight private banks and could be a useful laboratory for the nationalisation process. On the other hand, the Bank of New South Wales would likely be the last to go since it was the most established and the largest. Insiders said international investors would be scared off if the Government was too heavy-handed. Dismantling the "English banks" would require deft management and careful diplomacy, as would the small banks owned by the New Zealand, French and Chinese governments. One thing was certain. Even the simplest path to nationalisation would be complex.

To pass by the headquarters of the large private banks was to sense their power and respectability. Their head offices occupied classically designed, steel and stone buildings on the best streets of the busiest cities. Inside were high-ceilinged and spacious banking chambers finished in copper, marble and rich timbers. On the upper floors bank executives worked in comfortable offices and lunched in private dining rooms. Massive, undrillable steel vaults full of bullion, cash, records and valuables sat below the public spaces.

This architectural splendour went beyond the cities. The Berry branch of the ES&A Bank in New South Wales resembled a Scottish baronial hall with a crenelated tower and gothic entrance. It was designed by the same architect who built St Patrick's Cathedral in Melbourne. The Union Bank in Boorowa in New South Wales had an arched entrance and large palladium windows. The Bank of New South Wales branch on Karangahape Road in Auckland was a three-storey building with an imposing Georgian doorway and an oversized flagpole. The National Bank branch in Jeparit was far humbler, built of wood and galvanised iron, it was still among the most substantial buildings in the district.

The private banks provided services through a network of 2,500 branches across the country. A decent-sized town or suburb had two or more banks. Though they claimed to be competitive, rivalry rarely extended beyond poaching marginal customers and offering ancillary services. Branches displayed different signs but inside interest rates and loan arrangements were remarkably similar. In small villages and outback areas, the private banks operated through licensed agencies in chemist shops, grocery stores and news agencies. These back-corner kiosks provided basic services, but made up a quarter of the banking outlets in the country. Together, city offices, branches and licensed agencies managed more than ninety percent of the country's bank accounts, worth £650 million.

Banking however was more than buildings and branches. Almost 100,000 people were involved in the industry and whatever Chifley planned would affect all of them. First there were around 70,000 bank shareholders, two-thirds of whom lived in Australia. Their average shareholding was about £600. Although these investments earned a predictable but modest annual dividend, it was no match for an investment in the far more lucrative mining, agriculture and manufacturing sectors.[1] After the shareholders came the 20,000 people employed in banking. Their careers were defined by hierarchy, seniority, loyalty and duty and it was common for them to work for the same bank for their entire working life.

Starting in a bank required passing an exam and impressing at an interview. It helped if the local bank manager knew the applicant's parents. Juniors started on mundane tasks supervised by three or four seniors. Their next step was to become a teller. Working behind a polished counter in a local branch or from an ornate brass cage in head office, the teller was the link between the bank and the customer. Ambitious junior officers studied accountancy or economics part-time and aspired to go beyond the teller's cage into the prestigious research and economics departments run by their banks.

Next came the branch manager. He supervised the operations of his branch with the precision and poise of a surgeon in an operating theatre. Banks selected managers for their competence, character, cultural adaptability and ability to work in a local community. A manager enjoyed a social status similar to a clergyman, doctor, leading grazier or prominent merchant. Town and district newspapers reported their appointments and promotions and the social pages noted their attendance at gatherings and events.

Many people who started in a bank went on to have illustrious careers. Arthur Tange worked for the Bank of New South Wales and after joining the Commonwealth Public Service eventually became the High Commissioner to India and the Secretary of the Department of External Affairs and the Department of Defence. Robert Askin started as "a boy in short pants" with the Rural Bank and ended up as Premier of New South Wales.[2]

At the pinnacle of each bank was the board of directors who approved

---
[1] National Bank Information Circular no. 8, September 1947, Records of the Liberal Party of Australia, Federal Secretariat, circa 1945–1990, NLA MS 5000/ Banking, 1946–1960 (8) (File), Box 1232.
[2] Robert Askin interviewed by Mel Pratt, 7--11 October 1976, NLA ORAL TRC 121/83.

major investments and loans, ratified significant policies and had the final say on promotions and terms of employment. Shareholders elected directors for their commercial experience and their business and social connections. Typically a director served on a board until retirement or resignation because of poor health. Bank boards were bound by class and club. Directors attended the same schools, dined at the same clubs, waltzed at the same balls and golfed the same greens. The boards of the English banks included major generals, right honourables, dukes and knights of the realm.

Bank directors generally had ties to other industries. Bank of Adelaide directors also sat on the boards of insurance, construction and brewing companies. The Chairman of the Union Bank chaired the country's leading pastoral company. Bank of New South Wales directors sat on the boards of the Australian Mutual Provident Society and the *Sydney Morning Herald*. The owners of the same paper sat on the Bank of New South Wales board. The Chairman of the National Bank was the Vice Chairman of the *Herald and Weekly Times* and the Deputy Chairman of the Bank was a prominent politician.

Board members were well paid. National Bank directors got £4000 a year (around $250,000 today) and those of the Bank of Australasia received four times as much. The Bank of New South Wales probably paid the same but never publicly disclosed its fees.[1] Given their social affiliations, commercial connections and handsome entitlements, it was easy for critics to claim bank directors had little in common with factory workers and farmers. Or that they belonged to the "money power", those privileged few who controlled the economy and put the interests of their banks ahead of those of ordinary people.

There was a not a single female bank director in the country because post-war banking offered few opportunities for women beyond traditional roles. They were employed as secretaries, typists or on the head office switchboard, and should a woman work at a higher level, she was not as well paid and had less status than the men she worked with. It was another fifteen years before a woman became a bank teller and forty years later the first woman was appointed to the board of a major bank.[2]

For a short time it had seemed the prospects for women in banking would change. Eight thousand bank men had enlisted in the services during the Second World War, all with the full encouragement of their

---
1 *Herald* (Melbourne), 28 April 1947, p. 11.
2 Kim Eberhard, "The Super Legacy of Bank's First Females", *Westpac Wire*, 8 March 2018, accessed online 15 September 2021.

employers. Indeed, some banks supplemented the military pay of those who signed up, and kept their jobs open until they returned. This exodus of male officers forced the banks to hire more women and for different roles. Even so, women were prohibited from duties deemed as "masculine" such as carrying a pistol or escorting a payroll. Many older bank officers resented the presence of women. They bemoaned the "girls" treated their bank like a marriage bureau and quit as soon as they found a husband.[1] After the war, as veterans returned to banking, women reverted to their old roles or left the industry.

Men or women, board members and branch juniors, everyone "in the banks" were expected to follow a strict code of behaviour. Officers of the Bank of New South Wales were bound by rules which forbade them to enter hotels, gambling houses and betting shops, and young officers needed permission to marry.[2] Even in the 1960s, bank officers were instructed not to be bad-mannered, speak rudely or be "men of untidy clothes and unkempt hair".[3] Banks expected their people to be loyal, and in most cases bank officers were intensely loyal. In 1945 an armed man confronted Eric Hine, the manager of the Liverpool Street branch of the Bank of New South Wales. Hine stared down the robber and when a judge later asked why he risked his life, Hine said he would willingly die for his bank.[4]

This degree of loyalty was noteworthy, since most bank officers could have earned considerably more elsewhere. In 1946 *Banker* magazine reported some officers had trouble maintaining the lifestyle expected of them and struggled to pay for food, rent and clothing.[5] This was the case for Keith Morris, a junior bank officer who supported his family on a weekly wage of £3/10/- (around $200 today). The Morris family lived comfortably but carefully, in a rented, modestly furnished home. Mrs Morris won a *Women's Weekly* cooking competition in 1948 for the best budget meal and was dubbed "Mrs Careful" because she made her children's clothes and prudently planned each shopping trip.[6]

Spouses like Mrs Morris and board members, female employees, older officers and younger veterans all felt part of a bigger "bank family". Banking provided income, lifestyle and status, and when their chief executives asked them to oppose bank nationalisation, this hierarchical

---

1 *Daily News* (Perth), 20 May 1950, p. 4.
2 Bob White and Cecelia Clarke, *Cheques and Balances: Memoirs of a Banker*, Ringwood, Viking Press, 1995, p. 25.
3 *Banker* (Sydney), November 1967, p. 22.
4 *Sydney Morning Herald* (Sydney), 2 November 1945, p. 6.
5 *Banker* (Sydney), December 1946, p. 5.
6 *Australian Women's Weekly* (Sydney), 13 November 1948, p. 17.

but tightly knit community turned out in force.

Chifley's nationalisation plan expressly omitted one important slice of Australian banking: the Commonwealth Bank and the banks owned by the state governments.

If nationalisation went ahead, the Commonwealth Bank would be the biggest winner. In 1912 the Labor Government of Andrew Fisher established the Commonwealth Bank with the vision of it becoming "the people's bank". This was despite strong resistance from the private banks. The Bank had a sluggish start and during the First World War was preoccupied with financing the country's war effort. In 1924 the pro-business government of Prime Minister Stanley Bruce forbade the Commonwealth Bank from directly competing with the commercial banks and installed influential businessmen on its board to make sure it stuck to a fairly narrow trajectory. Even though the bank was owned by the Federal Government, for the next decade and a half, it exercised very few powers of a central bank. At the start of the Second World War it operated within a largely unregulated banking system which the pressures of war would soon change.

The governments of Robert Menzies and John Curtin faced an unprecedented effort to finance Australia's part in a global war. Menzies preferred to work with the banks but Curtin and Treasurer Chifley were far more interventionist. They gave the Commonwealth Bank the responsibility to set policies on credit, foreign exchange and interest rates and forced the private banks to lodge any "surplus investible funds" with the Commonwealth Bank.[1] By the war's end the Commonwealth Bank was uniquely placed in the Western world, having the powers of a central bank yet providing services to the public.[2]

By 1947 the Commonwealth Bank employed 9,000 people in 320 branches coast to coast, in the Pacific and in the United Kingdom. Its footprint was such it operated its own C47 aircraft, piloted by a stylishly dressed crew who ferried executives around their empire. The bank provided customer services, managed government accounts and supported new industries, cooperative societies and trade boards. One section ran a financial literacy program for 4,500 schools across the country. Each week teachers collected pennies from their pupils and stamped their Commonwealth Bank passbooks. It was an uncontroversial service even though it brought in £1 million a year (almost $70 million

---
1 *Bulletin* (Sydney), 17 September 1947, p. 26.
2 "Information Booklet", Bank Employees Protest Committee, June 1949, National Bank, National Australia Bank Archives/Bank Nationalisation.

today) and was the undeclared gateway for young Australians to become lifetime Commonwealth Bank customers.[1]

State-owned banks completed the banking landscape although they managed only ten percent of the nation's loans, mortgages and overdrafts. The Rural Bank in New South Wales was the biggest state bank and worth £43 million. Its fifty-seven branches served communities throughout the state, and every year issued thousands of small personal, home and business loans and sponsored scholarships, radio shows, farm visits, open days and agricultural research. The Western Australian Government owned the Rural and Industries Bank. Victoria had a state savings bank and Tasmania operated a state agricultural bank. The South Australian Government ran a savings bank for individuals and a second bank financed government projects, housing estates and land releases.[2]

State Premiers were protective of their small banks, and the constitutional challenge to fold them into the nationalisation plan was too formidable even for a determined Prime Minister.[3]

---

1 *Courier Mail* (Brisbane), 18 August 1947, p. 1.
2 *South Eastern Times* (Millicent), 21 June 1949, p. 2.
3 *West Australian* (Perth), 4 November 1947, p. 21.

4 The Anti-Bank Brigade

"As an instrument for controlling all industries from the largest to the smallest ... it will be the most powerful (bank) ever created."[1]

The banks were prepared to wage a war to save themselves from nationalisation, yet there was no guarantee they would succeed. They were up against a respected Prime Minister, a government adept at pushing through policies and sections of the community who believed the "banking system is the product of greed, ignorance, and superstition".[2] Many people felt the banking industry had deserted them during the Great Depression, and older Australians like Ben Chifley remembered the bank collapses before Federation. In some quarters bankers were viewed with mistrust, cynicism even hostility.

The Depression affected Australia like few events before or since. It began in 1929 when prices for Australian exports like wheat and wool fell, and foreign investment slowed to a dribble. Stanley Melbourne Bruce's conservative Nationalist Government responded with spending cuts, new taxes and measures to temper industrial unrest. Bruce lost the 1929 election and James Scullin led Labor into office. The new Prime Minister's timing was unfortunate. Wall Street crashed a few weeks after Scullin took over and his newly minted ministry faced the worst economic downturn in Australia since Federation.[3]

Australia was far from the New York Stock Exchange but was not immune to the chaos. In August 1930 Scullin invited Sir Otto Niemeyer of the Bank of England to visit Australia and advise the Government on what should be done. Niemeyer's prescription was harsh: he recommended lower production costs, a balanced budget, deep spending cuts, more taxation and foreign debts to be repaid.

The Government accepted Niemeyer's harsh recipe, leading to a split in the ALP. New South Wales Premier Jack Lang, who wanted to default on loan obligations, led his supporters into "Lang Labor". Joseph Lyons, a senior minister, quit the Scullin Government and left the ALP. With a small group of dissatisfied Labor MPs and support from the Opposition

---

1 *Daily News* (Perth), 18 August 1947, p. 1.
2 *Burra Record* (South Australia), 13 May 1931, p. 4.
3 James Scullin led the ALP to victory on 12 October 1929 and Wall Street crashed on 29 October 1929.

he formed the United Australia Party. Scullin lost the 1931 election and Prime Minister Joseph Lyons was left to oversee an agonisingly slow economic recovery.

During the Depression industrial production fell, construction stalled and migration declined. Unemployment hit over thirty per cent and lines of unemployed men snaked outside factories looking for work or waited for a chance to wield a pick and shovel on a relief project. Dole queues, evictions and hunger were bleak realities for hundreds of thousands. Unemployed men went "on the track", travelling the country looking for work, handouts and rations. Less visible but equally miserable were unemployed and unmarried women whom everyone seemed to forget.[1] A Queensland observer wrote about the plight of women forced into homelessness: "If [she was] a criminal she would get care and attention in the prison infirmary, but because her only crime is poverty she is worse off than a stray dog."[2]

Those with jobs found life precarious. Bank clerks, school teachers and other professionals had their pay reduced. Domestic workers, maids and cooks often worked just for food and lodging. Women with clerical, retail and factory jobs became family breadwinners, and parents pressured daughters to postpone their weddings because households depended on their wages. Property values around the country collapsed but interest rates stayed the same. Couples who had purchased a home in more prosperous times risked financial ruin if they lost their jobs or their wages were cut.

Commonwealth and state governments provided some relief but it was generally uncoordinated and poorly administered. The unemployed quickly learned not to upset a bureaucrat in case they jeopardised their benefits. Benevolent societies, churches and charities were stretched to exhaustion helping the unemployed and homeless. One religious writer noted "the distress is widespread and the misery appalling".[3]

Many Australians looked for someone to blame for this wretchedness. They criticised governments, political parties, businesses and the banks who they thought conspired to drive them into poverty. The *Australian Worker* described bankers as "financial vultures [who] are ever at their best when their greedy claws are searching out to grab blood money".[4]

The Depression deepened antagonisms between workers and

---

1 *Westralian Worker* (Perth), 29 April 1932, p. 6.
2 *Telegraph* (Brisbane), 31 August 1935, p. 10.
3 *Age* (Melbourne), 28 September 1935, p. 20.
4 *Australian Worker* (Sydney), 4 February 1931, p. 11.

managers, labour and capital, and the ALP and the banks. Labor folklore was replete with stories about "the bastard banks", how they caused the Depression and then refused to help the Scullin Government. Queensland Labor MP Harry Bruce told State Parliament about a sugar cane farmer who could always get loans before the Depression. Then his local bank manager suddenly refused his request for an overdraft. "The man lost the whole of his property at that time, and the last time I saw him he was working for the council, whereas he should have been on one of the best sugar farms on the Burdekin."[1]

Lieutenant Gordon Wilkins, who lost a leg in the First World War, ran a garage west of the Blue Mountains. When sales slumped Wilkins' bank demanded he repay his loans. The ex-digger valiantly tried to clear his debts, even signing over his disability pension. The bank still pressed for payment and eventually the disabled veteran was forced out of business. Wilkins, who went on to be a New South Wales MP, later recounted how he was "handed over to the banks bound hand and foot so they could put the boot into me".[2]

Federal Labor MP Fred Daly, who entered Parliament in 1943, said the banks "took in the umbrella" when they refused credit and almost forced his family into poverty.[3] Many on the land felt they tilled their soil for the banks, sowed seed for the banks and reaped their harvests for the banks.

The banks rejected this criticism and showered Australia with statistics that showed even as deposits flatlined and investment returns fell, they increased lending. Some bankers imperiously argued that instead of restraining lending they were too liberal with their loans. They opposed any change and as historian Boris Schedvin wrote, saw it as their right "to determine their own policies and to guide the economy as they thought fit".[4]

The banks knew they had to win approval and looked for support from the Lyons Government, friendly state governments, the non-Labor parties, media owners, chambers of commerce and business groups. The "Wales" supported pro-bank bodies such as the Sound Finance League, the New Democratic Committee and other groups. Other banks published literature and encouraged local personalities to write letters and

---

1 Queensland, *Parliamentary Debates*, Legislative Assembly, 16 October 1947, p. 809 (Harry Bruce, Member for The Tablelands).
2 *Tribune* (Sydney), 27 September 1947, p. 6.
3 Fred Daly interviewed by Vivienne Rae-Ellis, 2 August–19 September 1983, NLA ORAL TRC 4900/63.
4 Boris Schedvin, *Australia and the Great Depression: A Study of Economic Development and Policy in the 1920s and 1930s*, Sydney University Press, Sydney, 1970, p. 78.

newspaper articles arguing things would be far worse but for the banks.

The Melbourne and Sydney banks decided to help Joseph Lyons at the 1934 federal election, since James Scullin and the ALP had made it clear there would be an inquiry into banking if Labor won. The banks ran a £38,000 ($3.8 million today) campaign to support the Government, masking their involvement in case Labor won the election.[1] They trained staff to talk about banking, sent out agents to branches to counter anti-bank feelings, and encouraged pro-bank letters in hometown papers. They offered speaking notes to non-Labor candidates and gave money to sympathetic groups to help with advertising, radio time and printing. Lyons won the election but widespread discontentment and pressure from the County Party led him to call a royal commission into banking and appoint Chifley as a commissioner.

If people were dissatisfied with the banking system they were not about to tear down capitalism or Australia's system of government. They wanted a political and economic system that worked for them and someone to fix the country's economic malaise. Many middle-class Australians felt "the party system of government was morally bankrupt [and] led politicians to put the petty, parochial interests of their party and supporters above the interests of the nation".[2] Exasperated, they formed groups that stood for "sane and honourable" management of the nation's finances, smaller government and fewer MPs.

These organisations were pro-capitalism, pro-British and anti-Communist. A handful like the paramilitary New Guard said they were ready to fight against socialism and defend Australia.[3] However, most of these groups soon ran out of steam.

The Douglas Credit Movement was such a group. It started in Canada after the First World War and spread to Australia. It believed nations had abundant resources but failed to organise their economies for the benefit of their citizens. It advocated utopian ideas like the "Age of Plenty", the "Time of Leisure" and a universal wage, and said there was a banking conspiracy against the people. By the mid-1930s there were 6,000 members in Australia including some from the ALP. The "Movement" fielded candidates in state and federal elections, but only one was successful. By 1939 the Douglas Credit Movement had lost energy and influence mainly because it could

---

1 Warwick Eather & Drew Cottle, *Fighting From the Shadows: the Private Trading Banks, Political Campaigns and Bank Nationalisation 1930-1949*, China: Australian Centre for Labour and Capital Studies, 2012, pp. 23-30.
2 Matthew Cunningham, *Mobilising the Masses*, Canberra, ANU Press, 2022, p. 6.
3 *Argus* (Melbourne), 20 February 1931, p. 8.

never explain how it could achieve its lofty ambitions.

The Australian Communist Party (ACP) was one of the rare organisations to endure beyond the Depression and was the most fervent supporter of bank nationalisation. In 1920 twenty-six men and women met in a drab Liverpool Street storefront to establish the ACP. They wanted to improve conditions for working people, dismantle capitalism and turn the country into a Marxist-Leninist state. They promised better jobs, education, culture, gender equality and Indigenous rights and longed to nationalise banks, insurance companies, railways and big department stores.

The Communists made inroads in the trade union movement during the next two decades and came to dominate important unions like the Miners' Federation, the Seamen's Union and the Waterside Workers' Federation. Communist officials did win genuine improvements in industrial conditions in some areas but many Australians were alienated by their confrontational tactics. In the post-war period Communist-controlled unions were responsible for 84 per cent of time lost in industrial action. The US Central Intelligence Agency (CIA) reported the Australian Communists could, if they wanted, temporarily cripple the national economy.[1]

The Labor Party as an organisation opposed the Communists' belligerent approach to industrial affairs and regarded them as rivals for the loyalty of union members. The ALP rejected several overtures from the Communists to affiliate and work together. Communist candidates contested every election in the 1930s but Australian voters were wary of them. Their best result was in 1934 when the Communists won 50,000 votes of the 3.5 million votes cast, but they failed to win a single federal seat in that and other elections. By 1937 the Communist vote had dropped by nearly two-thirds although their presence in key unions remained strong. With the Communists fully behind Chifley's bank nationalisation ambitions, it was easy for opponents to claim the Communist Party and the ALP had similar goals. This forced the Government to distance itself publicly from the Communists.

After the Depression peaked in 1932–33, the economy painfully but slowly improved. The opprobrium around the banks subsided, although there was a lingering antipathy between the banks and the ALP and disenchanted Australians challenged the whole concept of private banking. McConnan and his more savvy peers knew the Depression had dented

---

1 Crisp, p. 355.

the image of banking and understood the need to restore its reputation. Yet by 1939 the banks were as profitable as ever, and the *Sydney Morning Herald* reported, "the financial strength of the great banking institutions of Australia certainly inspires confidence".[1]

From 1939 to 1945 the Commonwealth Government spent unprecedented sums to mobilise the nation for war, and introduced regulations, rationing and controls of all kinds to direct the nation's resources to this massive effort. Money poured into agriculture, industry, communications and transport, and to recruit and keep nearly a million service men and women in the field. The economy was awash with money and there was the danger the banks could make massive profits from the war if left unchecked.

The Menzies Government managed the banks with a light touch but the new Labor Government, facing an ever worsening situation, soon introduced more prescriptive measures. These included unprecedented national security regulations to curb excessive profits, control lending, set interest rates and force the private banks to deposit surplus funds into special Commonwealth Bank accounts. These restraints, though new for Australia, were similar to how allies were treating their banks.

In 1942, John Dedman, a senior government minister, declared banking to be a non-essential service and set out to close or amalgamate bank branches and dispatch surplus bank officers to wartime roles. Dedman's plan unnerved the nation's bankers who figured the longer such wartime measures were in place, the harder they would be to unravel when peace finally arrived.

The banker's ideal future would be a return to the comfortable days of pre-war banking, which historian Geoffrey Blainey described as "the responsible position that they [the banks] had held since the early days of the Australian economy".[2] But the Chifley Government believed the wartime financial controls had to continue because they were critical for funding reconstruction and checking inflation. And, with most of Europe and Asia in ruins, tighter controls would brace Australia against international shocks or another depression. The economy was beginning to improve but Chifley told Parliament, "No responsible government could afford to move forward into the post-war period without adequate means to cope with inflationary and deflationary movements in the monetary and banking system."[3] In 1945 Parliament passed the Commonwealth

---

1 *Sydney Morning Herald* (Sydney), 30 August 1939, p. 10.
2 Geoffrey Blainey, p. 362.
3 Commonwealth, *Parliamentary Debates*, House of Representatives, 9 March 1945, 533 (Ben

Bank Act and a separate Banking Act, both of which dismayed the banking fraternity.

The 1945 Commonwealth Bank Act embedded the central banking powers handed to the Commonwealth Bank during the war. It maintained a role for the bank in setting credit policy and interest rates, and providing favourable loans to farms, factories and other sectors sometimes overlooked by the private banks. The Act abolished the Commonwealth Bank Board and dismissed its directors because Labor claimed they had too much influence on bank policy. The Governor was made solely responsible for the bank and would work within broad guidelines from the Treasurer. The legislation turned the Commonwealth Bank into both a central bank and a rival with access to unlimited taxpayer funds.

The 1945 Banking Act also raised concerns, in particular for two controversial sections. First, despite the end of the war, the private banks wre forced to continue to deposit their excess funds into the special accounts supervised by the Commonwealth Bank. They had already deposited £250 million in these accounts and were unlikely to see this money any time soon. Now future profits were also to be locked away at the dismal interest rate of one percent per annum.

Section 48 was equally contentious. It mandated that state and local governments needed the Treasurer's approval for their choice of bank. Journalist Harold Cox wrote, "It was a very strong point of principle with the Labor Party that the Commonwealth Bank should have all government and municipal banking business."[1] Without Chifley's express permission, the largest state government agency through to the poorest borough would be forced to bank with the Commonwealth Bank. This would cut off the private banks from managing public money and their most lucrative customers, and give the Treasurer a peephole into the finances of every level of government.

As sweeping as these 1945 Acts were, John Dedman and other hard-liners wanted an outright takeover of the banks. Chifley disagreed and feared the timing was not right. It would "give rise to much criticism in Parliament and also in the press and every opportunity will be taken to frighten depositors".[2]

The wartime anxieties of the private banks were realised and they

Chifley, Prime Minister).
1   Harold Cox to Sir Keith Murdoch, 18 August 1947, *Typescript Reports of Erle Harold Cox*, 1944–1964, National Library of Australia (NLA), MS 4554 Folder 3. Sometimes, Chifley and Evatt shared confidences with Cox who reported them to Sir Keith Murdoch.
2   David Stephens, "Three Labor Veterans Look Back", *Australian Quarterly* 46, no. 3 (1974), pp. 84–89.

responded with a public relations campaign that framed the debate as the people's banks versus a politically controlled bank. In 1946 the banks discreetly supported those who opposed the new legislation. The Bank of New South Wales gave a five-figure sum to the Liberal and Country parties in New South Wales and smaller amounts in Queensland, South Australia and Western Australia.[1] The involvement of the banks went largely unnoticed, and banking was scarcely mentioned during the election. The Labor victory voided any challenge the banks might make to the Government's plans and they would need to bide their time before they could agitate for a return to their pre-war independence.

The opportunity came in 1947 when Treasurer Chifley set Section 48 in motion and instructed 200 municipalities and local governments to seek his approval for their banking arrangements. Before this the Commonwealth Bank was not ready to take on new state and municipal business. The Governor of the Commonwealth Bank, knowing the private banks would not unwillingly surrender a single government account, hinted he might compensate for their losses by releasing money from their special accounts.[2] The banks were not impressed with the prospect of being compensated with their own money and were adamant they would not abandon a single customer.

The private banks stood to lose millions of pounds in annual revenue, and state agencies faced the prospect of public servants in the Commonwealth Bank handling their affairs. Mayors and shire presidents were angry at being forced to switch from local branches which had stood by them for years. A councillor in western New South Wales said the Government was trying to socialise finance and "in a few years we will not have a soul to call our own".[3] The Bridgetown Roads Board in Western Australia reluctantly voted to change to the Commonwealth Bank but the Melbourne City Council refused to quit the National Bank.

Melbourne was among the wealthiest and most conservative municipalities in the country and was not about to take orders from Canberra. The Shire of Coreen was a pocket-sized concern in southern New South Wales and its Shire Clerk claimed being forced to switch to the Commonwealth Bank would cost an additional £2000 per year.[4] Blessed by the private banks, mighty Melbourne joined tiny Coreen to

---

1 Eather & Cottle, *Fighting From the Shadows*, p.54
2 Reserve Bank of Australia Archives (RBAA): Research Department; C.3.6.19.2, Banking Section – Conferences with Private Banks – October 1946–November 1951, p. 217.
3 *Sydney Morning Herald* (Sydney), 6 June 1947, p. 3.
4 *Corowa Free Press* (Corowa), 15 August 1947, p. 5.

challenge Section 48 in the High Court. By any account it was an odd pairing, and most likely fabricated to show that neither big city interests nor battlers in the bush would tolerate government interference in their affairs. The South Australian and Western Australian governments were also unhappy with the Commonwealth intrusion into their affairs and joined the litigation.

The *Melbourne Corporation* case was eventually decided on 13 August 1947 when the High Court ruled the Commonwealth Government could not instruct state and local governments how to bank.[1] The reaction was immediate. The Lord Mayor of Melbourne was pleased but unsurprised. The Secretary of the Victorian Municipal Association blurted out "Whacko!" when he heard the news. The Australian Associated Chambers of Commerce said the High Court had saved the community from Canberra.[2] Most observers thought that was the end of the matter and no evidence ever emerged that the banks wanted to challenge other parts of the 1945 Act.[3] Chifley, however, did not believe the banks would stop and so he set out to nationalise them.[4]

Attorney General Evatt flew to Sydney straight after the Prime Minister issued his banking statement. There, a team of economists, lawyers, parliamentary draftsmen and officials from the Commonwealth Bank was tasked to turn Chifley's skimpy announcement into draft legislation. Evatt told journalists it would be some time before they could expect an official statement from the Commonwealth.[5]

The Prime Minister needed something to present to the Labor Caucus. When Parliament resumed Chifley needed the support of his MPs, though Caucus was expected to endorse whatever he presented. A bill could then go before Parliament. The Prime Minister insisted the draft legislation had to be watertight. Poor drafting could lead to legal challenges from the banks or amendments being thrown together as the bill passed through Parliament. The bill also had to be simple enough for people to understand and to get the nationalisation process quickly underway.

Evatt was to fly to New York for a meeting of the United Nations General Assembly and then go on to London to represent Australia at the wedding of Princess Elizabeth and Prince Philip. That left a week for the Attorney General to supervise the preparation of a bill the scale of

---

1 *Melbourne Corporation v Commonwealth* (Melbourne Corporation case) 1947, 74 CLR 31.
2 *Sydney Morning Herald* (Sydney), 14 August 1947, p. 1.
3 *Herald* (Melbourne), 18 March 1950, p. 6.
4 Lloyd Maxwell Ross interviewed by Suzanne Walker, 16 August–17 October 1973, NLA TRC 236.
5 *Border Mail* (Albury), 21 August 1947, p. 3.

which no Australian parliament had ever passed. With Evatt overseas, the team worked quickly and navigated a complex stew of options. The Commonwealth marshalled the "biggest battery of legal talent" including two King's Counsels and other legal experts to provide constitutional advice to the drafting team. Everyone working in Sydney knew lawyers of distinction and talent would contest whatever they came up with, and some of the wealthiest organisations in the country would spare no expense to defeat what they finally delivered.

The group worked in the Martin Place headquarters of the Commonwealth Bank. The Governor made typists, printers, security guards and cooks available, and the bank's aeroplane (callsign VH-CBA) was on standby at Mascot to ferry passengers between Sydney and Canberra. Drafts of the legislation sped back and forth between Canberra and Sydney and there were frequent conferences with the Prime Minister and his advisers.

The task of nationalising the banks was immense and no English-speaking country had ever attempted the wholesale takeover of a banking system. In 1931 the Government Savings Bank of New South Wales was forced to amalgamate with the Commonwealth Bank but that was hardly of the magnitude Chifley proposed. In 1945 the New Zealand Government nationalised the Bank of New Zealand but Kiwis still had private banks including branches of the Australian banks.

After the war the British Labour Government of Clement Attlee nationalised the Bank of England but the bank was already an instrument of government policy so there was minimal structural and management change. The Attlee Government also provided warnings of what not to do. Its efforts to nationalise British coal mines, power plants, steel mills and railways had been marred by difficulties.[1] In some cases the owners of the newly nationalised industries were poorly compensated, a lack of investment led to falls in productivity, and inexperienced civil servants bungled the nationalisation process. There had been limited attempts at nationalisation in Europe. The Dutch Government brought the Bank of Netherlands under state ownership and Belgium nationalised the Bank of Belgium. The French Government nationalised the Bank of France and some private banks and that went reasonably smoothly.

Vladimir Lenin and the Communists calculated bank nationalisation was the fastest way to turn Czarist Russia into a socialist state, and private

---

[1] In addition to the Bank of England Act 1946, other UK legislation included the Gas Act 1948, Electricity Act 1947, Transport Act 1947, Cable and Wireless Act 1946, Civil Aviation Act 1946, and the Coal Industries Nationalisation (Collieries) Act 1946.

banking had long since disappeared in the Soviet Union. Communist regimes in post-war Eastern Europe were following the same pattern. Argentinian President Colonel Juan Peron had nationalised his country's Central Bank, stacked its board and prohibited private banks from withdrawing their funds. Australian newspapers called Peron's measures dictatorial. Though Evatt's team in Martin Place reviewed the Leninist and Argentine approaches they were hardly models an Australian Prime Minister could use.[1]

---

1 RBAA: Secretary's Department; S-d-125, Secretary's Department – Banking Legislation – Banking Act 1947 – Section 26 – Nationalisation of Banks in Germany, Italy & Russia, 1947, p. 2.

5 Mobilising the Resistance

*"I went abroad to fight for freedom, but I think we should
get together again in our own country to fight Chifleyism."*[1]

Forty-eight hours after Chifley's press statement, eight grim-faced men sat around a polished oval wooden table in the boardroom of the National Bank in Melbourne. Leslie McConnan, the Chairman of the Associated Banks, had called them together. Dressed in dark serge suits and stiff collars, the general managers of Australia's private banks were in their late fifties and early sixties and had been with their banks their whole working lives. The bankers had been aware the Prime Minister had been thinking about nationalising their banks for a very long time and they understood the grave risk his statement posed to their institutions.

Ten years earlier Ben Chifley had advocated state control of banking in a minority report he prepared for the Royal Commission on Banking. As Treasurer he had introduced onerous wartime regulations on banking and introduced the two bank acts into Parliament in 1945 that continued to curtail their independence. He had lost the High Court case which had challenged his powers and now he had suddenly announced a takeover. The Prime Minister's reputation told the bankers that he had little appetite for compromise or negotiation when he had vested interests and old-boy networks in his sights.

The general managers faced two choices. If they did not act, the Government would liquidate their banks. If they resisted, they might be able to block state control but resistance would set them on the most consequential journey of their working lives. By the time the Melbourne meeting ended, the bankers had chosen their path. They would fight Chifley in the nation's courts and the court of public opinion. They intended to create a campaign of nationwide protest that would force the Government to abort its plan or call a referendum or so damage the Labor Party it would lose the next election.

On paper the legal battle seemed straightforward. The banks would mount a High Court challenge to whatever legislation the Government created. If they lost, they would appeal to the Privy Council in London, Australia's highest court of appeal. Their immediate response was to retain

---

1 *Smith's Weekly* (Sydney), 4 October 1947, p. 19.

some the country's most accomplished barristers and enlist support from the Australian Law Council and the Victorian Bar. The general managers agreed to use the media and advertising to press their case and recruit community activists as well as their bank staff, shareholders and customers to oppose nationalisation. They would become corporate activists for the next two years or however long it took.

They divided Australia into operational zones. The Bank of New South Wales and the Commercial Bank of Sydney would focus on New South Wales and Queensland. The Bank of Adelaide was responsible for the fight in South Australia. The Melbourne banks would take care of the other states. It was evident from the start that the Sydney and Melbourne banks had different cultures.

The Bank of New South Wales and the Commercial Bank would mount the high moral ground. They would talk about totalitarianism and how nationalisation would damage the Constitution. They would prefer to remain in the background and work through others as they had done years before when they supported Joseph Lyons. The Melbourne bankers intended to be visible and make a personal case. They would claim nationalisation affected every family, factory owner, farm labourer and pie cart vendor. Richard Casey described the difference: "The New South Wales banks want to do impersonal, long-range stuff and the Victorian banks rather shorter range and more direct stuff in their own names."[1]

Leslie McConnan as the Chairman of the Associated Banks would be the industry spokesperson, although this did not stop other general managers from speaking publicly. A committee would coordinate the activities of the Melbourne banks and a similar committee would mesh the efforts of the Bank of New South Wales and the Commercial Bank. A joint committee with representatives from all the banks would operate in each state and a Bank of New South Wales officer would liaise with the banks in Melbourne.

When the Melbourne meeting ended, the General Manager of the Bank of New South Wales, Thomas Heffer, issued a press statement. The other general managers were undoubtedly happy for Heffer to speak because he managed the largest and most prominent bank. Heffer was usually "a retiring personality, persuasive in a quiet way, with the power of intense concentration and a gift for a sudden transition from serious thought to smiling geniality".[2] This time Heffer thundered. Nationalisation threatened

---

1 *Papers of the Casey Family, 1820-1978* (Manuscript), National Library of Australia, MS 6150, R.G. Casey diary entry: 5 December 1947.
2 *Smith's Weekly* (Sydney), 22 May 1948, p. 11.

the prosperity and liberty of the community and was an attempt to regiment every Australian. The Government had all the banking powers it needed and there was no mandate for the Commonwealth Bank to become a monopoly. "The nationalisation proposal must be a fight by the people and the banks would play their full part."[1]

The Liberal Party mounted an Australia-wide campaign to oppose the Government's bank plan. The first major event was on 26 August 1947 when Menzies spoke at the Sydney Town Hall in front of 3,000 people. Nearly as many again clustered around mobile loudspeakers outside on George Street.[2] This was the first significant anti-nationalisation rally and there was a visible police presence because no one knew what to expect. Constables diverted traffic around the Town Hall, others guarded doorways and plainclothes officers mingled with the crowd on the lookout for trouble. A radio hook-up relayed Menzies' speech to homes, offices, factories and shops throughout New South Wales.

The crowd cheered as the former Prime Minister ascended the stage and fell silent as he began to speak. Menzies' attack on the Government came in savage salvos. He said if the bank plot succeeded it would as if Hitler captured London and hoisted a swastika over Westminster. He declared war on the Australian fascists behind the bank plot. The applause was loud and sustained.

Menzies said similar things in Melbourne three days later when he addressed a lunchtime audience at the Princess Theatre a few blocks from the Victorian Parliament. Again, the venue was packed. An overflow crowd listened to amplifiers outside and thousands heard him on radio.[3] The audience shouted encouragement as Menzies said nationalisation was about dictatorship and told the audience that people "politically dead for years" were now aroused.

Newspapers positively reported on the size and enthusiasm of the Sydney and Melbourne crowds as Menzies left on a speaking tour of Victoria. The Liberal Party anti-nationalisation campaign had started well. Labor supporters countered by saying there were no working class people at Menzies' meetings and he spoke to exclusive audiences.

Liberal Party President Richard Casey went on the road when Menzies returned to Canberra for the spring session of Parliament. It was the first time the ex-Bengal Viceroy and gentleman farmer had returned to the national spotlight and his comeback began at a packed Sydney Town Hall

1 *Argus* (Melbourne), 23 August 1947 p. 1.
2 *Dubbo Liberal and Macquarie Advocate* (Dubbo), 23 August 1947, p. 1.
3 *Herald* (Melbourne), 28 August 1947, p. 3.

and with an eighty-eight-station live radio broadcast.[1] The Town Hall crowd cheered as Casey spoke to them as one Australian to another and said bank nationalisation was "the gravest issue, political or otherwise, that had ever come to the people of Australia".[2]

Then Casey flew to Brisbane to blast the "Chifley's bombshell" before 2,500 people at the Town Hall. They clapped for a minute when he said, "The pipe-smoking J. B. Chifley is Australian enemy number one." In other Queensland centres he urged locals to get into the fight and then flew to Adelaide and Perth to deliver the same message.[3]

Casey's most notable performance was in September 1947 during the ABC's *Forum of the Air*, a weekly radio broadcast. The program was a debate on issues of the day and on this occasion the topic was bank nationalisation. Casey and another conservative argued against Dr Lloyd Ross and a top union official. Ross was a committed Labor man and worked for the Department of Post War Reconstruction. It was strange that a senior public servant was participating in a political debate and his participation angered the Opposition. Stranger still was the absence of a Labor politician to defend bank nationalisation before a national audience.

The debate was broadcast live before a studio audience who soon expressed their feelings. The crowd cheered Casey and his colleague and booed Ross and his offsider. The heckling was continuous and the chairman frequently had to call the audience to order. The next day angry callers complained to the ABC switchboard about the bitter tone of the debate and the disgraceful behaviour of the audience. Ross later claimed the audience was stacked with bank officers and "nothing was more intolerant or irrational than the attack of bank clerks on anyone who was supporting bank nationalisation".[4] Casey was pleased with the outcome.

In the weeks that followed there were over 1,000 meetings around Australia and 500 in New South Wales alone.[5] The *Sydney Morning Herald* reported the mere mention of a protest was enough to draw a crowd.[6] Speakers said Chifley's bank plan would reduce competitiveness, jeopardise privacy and debauch democracy. The Prime Minister was acting in a socialist, communist or fascist manner. Meetings usually closed with a motion demanding a referendum on bank nationalisation so people had a say on the future of their banks. Chifley's press statement

---

1 A.L. May, *Battle for the Banks*, Sydney, Sydney University Press, 1968, p. 29.
2 *Sydney Morning Herald* (Sydney), 17 September 1947, p. 4.
3 *Daily Mercury* (Mackay), 23 September 1947, p. 5.
4 Lloyd Maxwell Ross interviewed by Suzanne Walker, 16 August–17 October 1973, NLA TRC 236.
5 May, p. 23.
6 *Sydney Morning Herald* (Sydney), 22 September 1947, p. 4.

had surprised everyone including those on his own side, so there were few pro-nationalisation meetings in those early weeks and even these were mostly small.

Parliament was not in session so Labor MPs were in their home districts or abroad when they heard the news. Arthur Calwell and Eddie Ward were in London. When reporters told them about Chifley's press statement Calwell blurted out, "You must be kidding."[1] John Dedman was in Geneva and could only say he supported the proposal a hundred percent.[2] Labor MP Fred Daly recalled "The forty-three word statement rocked the political world for the next three years".[3]

Back in Tasmania Labor MP Gil Duthie remembered how "The Opposition and their backers declared war and went into action. No army could have been recruited, trained and sent to war more quickly."[4] Labor state premiers were as surprised as everyone else. Queensland's Ned Hanlon said bank nationalisation was inevitable. Tasmanian Premier Robert Cosgrove welcomed the move but "Big" Jim McGirr, the New South Wales Premier, was less forthcoming. He thought the Commonwealth Government already had too much power.

ALP branches passed motions of support, although no one really knew what nationalisation entailed at that stage. Some Party members saw it as the chance to finally put the nation's finances in the hands of Parliament and the people. For others nationalisation was the first phase in replacing capitalism with socialism. The trade union movement was strongly pro-Labor so most unions and union newspapers supported nationalisation. The *Brisbane Worker* said bank nationalisation was a triumph. The *Maritime Worker* said working people welcomed it and called for demonstrations to counter bank propaganda. The *Australian Worker* blasted anti-Labor propagandists, the press and the banks.

The Australian Communist Party applauded Chifley's press statement. State control of banking had been instrumental in turning Czarist Russia into a socialist economy and they wanted the same outcome for Australia. Chifley's announcement was an historic chance to snap the vice-like grip bankers, industrialists and media barons had on money and information. Communist speakers addressed factory meetings and the Party circulated half a million leaflets supporting the Government.[5] The Communist

---

1 Fred Daly interviewed by Mel Pratt.
2 *Advertiser* (Adelaide), 27 August 1947, p. 3.
3 Fred Daly, *From Curtin to Kerr*, Melbourne, Sun Books, 1977, p. 58.
4 Duthie, p. 40.
5 May, p. 51.

Workers' Star ran editorials and stories and a cartoon which showed a pompous Menzies asking a farmer, "My dear friend, are you going to stand by and let Mr Chifley's nationalisation rob you of your debts?"[1] The ACP congratulated the Prime Minister and urged him to also take over industries such as brewing, tobacco, sugar and steel.[2] However, the ACP grew impatient with the Government's reluctance to expand state control. Support began to wane and cartoons in Communist newspapers switched from mocking Menzies to taunting Chifley.

The early Communist endorsement did Chifley no favours. Some people wondered about the difference between Labor and the Communists since both wanted to abolish banks. Critics used bank nationalisation to associate the Government with Communism. Arthur Fadden of the Country Party declared, "The Government's decision brought into the open the complete similarity and unity of plan of the Labor and Communist Parties."[3]

The banking issue was more than just a stoush between politicians and bankers. Because banking was such an important part of Australian life, people in cities, country towns and bush blocks began to voice their opinions. The feeling in rural Australia was mixed. Many farmers still blamed the banks for the Depression, but as many were suspicious of anything that could upset the relationships they had built up with their bank managers over many years. Dairy farmers, orchardists, cattlemen, wheat farmers, wool growers and market gardeners relied on their local bank manager to carry them between seasons and lend money for fuel, stock, seeds and machinery after bushfires and floods. *Queensland Country Life*, the *Pastoral Review and Graziers' Record* and other country publications damned the Government and hinted Communists in Canberra were grabbing power. The Graziers' Association of Victoria predicted a bank takeover would regiment farming and called on the Victorian Government to hold a referendum on banking even though nationalisation was a federal matter.

Graziers in Central Queensland said they would have switched to the Commonwealth Bank years ago if it was competitive. They also wanted a referendum. Wool merchants said the private banks understood the wool industry and worried nationalisation would mean bureaucracy and delays that would threaten their export markets. The Tasmanian Farmers' Federation passed protest motions, and the Oatlands Branch in

---
1 *Workers Star* (Perth), 12 September 1947, p. 3.
2 *Tribune* (Sydney), 3 September 1947, p. 6.
3 *Argus* (Melbourne), 25 August 1947, p. 3.

the centre of the State endorsed a petition calling for Tasmania to quit the Commonwealth.¹ A few Tasmanian farmers said they would refuse to send their produce to market until they realised a boycott would hurt them more than the Government.

Employer groups were universally against any nationalisation. The Associated Chamber of Manufacturers said nationalisation would wipe out free enterprise and worried that a person's political sympathies would influence who got credit from a government-run bank.² Retailers protested too. The David Jones department store said the private banks had provided it with satisfactory service for 109 years and doubted if government bankers could do better.³ Shopkeepers placed anti-nationalisation petitions on their counters and shut their businesses to join customers at protest meetings. The trade journal *Radio Electrical Weekly* warned that electrical appliance shops and radio stations might well be future Labor targets, and builders thought nationalisation would be a bureaucratic nightmare for their industry. An ironmonger compared the Chifley Government to mobsters. "Al Capone and Ned Kelly were guardian angels compared to this mob."⁴

Chifley's press statement shook the property market and the Government's silence compounded concerns. People rushed to buy or sell property while there was still a choice of banks. Real estate slumped in Victoria and a Brisbane agent reported that thirty cashed-up buyers called him each day but he had little to offer. Vendors were nervous about selling their homes in case money from their sale ended up in a strange bank. Estate agents speculated that the Commonwealth Bank might eventually hold the mortgage of every home, farm and factory in the country.⁵

Many wanted to know if the Christian churches would use their considerable influence to sway opinion on bank nationalisation one way or the other. The Church of England was the country's largest denomination with three million followers. The Baptist, Methodist and Presbyterian churches had significant flocks. Protestant congregations outnumbered Catholics three to one. Jews, Muslims, atheists and agnostics were a tiny fraction of the population.

Catholic thinking was important because the Catholic Church in Australia shared a common Irish and working-class heritage with

---

1 *Mercury* (Hobart), 27 September 1947, p. 2.
2 *North West Champion* (Moree), 8 December 1947, p. 5.
3 *Sydney Morning Herald* (Sydney), 24 October 1947, p. 10.
4 *Sydney Morning Herald* (Sydney), 28 August 1947, p. 5.
5 *Construction* (Sydney), 22 October 1947, p. 1.

the ALP, and the Prime Minister and half the Labor MPs in Canberra were Catholic. Pundits and parishioners waited to hear the views of the Catholic hierarchy. Newspapers speculated that if Catholic clergy were against nationalisation, working-class support for the ALP might peel away, and Catholic Labor MPs might be forced to choose between faith and party.

Norman "Bluey" Gilroy was Australia's most senior Catholic, a man who "combined prayer and action ... and [moved] from one to the other with no pause between". Gilroy came from a modest Irish family.[1] In 1946 Pope Pius XII delighted Australia when he appointed Gilroy the first Australian-born cardinal. Sixty thousand well-wishers lined the streets of Sydney to cheer Gilroy when he returned after his installation in Rome.

Gilroy was overseas when Chifley announced nationalisation so the Catholic laity, politicians and pressmen eagerly awaited his return. Gilroy flew back to Sydney in early October and said he needed more information before he could advise Catholics whether nationalisation was a moral or a political issue.[2] Matthew Beovich, the Archbishop of Adelaide, said nationalisation was not necessarily wrong if it produced a common good. If it was just about politics, then citizens needed to make up their minds. Beovich encouraged Chifley to include protections for the Church's finances in any nationalisation legislation.[3] Eighty-three-year-old Archbishop Daniel Mannix of Melbourne said he supported neither side and that the Government should make its case in Parliament. He wryly noted his dealings with the banks had always been happy and any banking monopoly would delight the Communists.[4]

After a trip abroad, the Archbishop of Brisbane reported he met no one overseas who supported bank nationalisation and it was "too revolutionary to be made law without a mandate from the people".[5] Initially Catholic newspapers were ambivalent. Melbourne's *Advocate* reached no conclusion on bank nationalisation and the *Catholic Weekly* in Sydney urged the Prime Minister to provide more information. The *Weekly* also withheld judgment but later ran an editorial stating papal teachings opposed socialism but supported nationalisation in some cases. It concluded Catholics could not vote for the ALP and Catholic MPs

---

1 T. P. Boland, "Gilroy, Sir Norman Thomas (1896–1977)", Australian Dictionary of Biography, National Centre of Biography, Australian National University, https://adb.anu.edu.au/biography/gilroy-sir-norman-thomas-10308/text18241, accessed online 4 April 2022.
2 *Central Queensland Herald* (Rockhampton), 2 October 1947, p. 15.
3 *Argus* (Melbourne), 15 September 1947, p. 3.
4 *Southern Cross* (Adelaide), 10 October 1947, p. 7.
5 *Daily Telegraph* (Sydney), 21 September 1947, p. 30.

should resign if the Government had a socialist agenda. A pamphlet the following year asserted the Church's right to speak on issues of morality, justice and equality but distinguished between government control of everything and government control of industries that were vital for the common good. The pamphlet concluded by telling the faithful to make up their own minds.[1]

Monsignor Thomas J. O'Donnell in Tasmania wanted no part of this delicate ecclesiastical juggling. The stocky prelate railed against nationalisation from the pulpit.[2] O'Donnell was already a controversial figure. During the First World War he was a battalion chaplain in France. In 1919, while he was on leave in Dublin, British authorities arrested him for supporting the Irish struggle for independence. He was jailed in the Tower of London for a short time and court-martialled in a widely reported trial. He was acquitted, awarded £3,000 in compensation, and promptly shipped back to Tasmania. The Catholic leadership posted him to a remote corner of the state, although by 1947 O'Donnell was sufficiently rehabilitated to have a parish in Hobart.

Two weeks after the nationalisation announcement, the Monsignor ascended the pulpit in St Mary's Cathedral in the Tasmanian capital. The Sunday Gospel was Luke 14:1. Instead of speaking about the exalted being humbled and the humble being exalted, O'Donnell attacked the bank plan. "The Federal Labor Party, unconsciously bent on the destruction of Australian liberty, is forging chains for the limbs of our people ... to seize the banks is to seize the property and the rights of hundreds of small shareholders ... it would be the first step towards making Australia a totalitarian State and its people slaves."[3]

Was it planned or by coincidence that reporters were present at that mass? Soon O'Donnell's stinging comments were national news. Later O'Donnell addressed a public meeting in Hobart, debated the Labor Premier through the pages of the state's largest paper, and addressed the nation in a radio broadcast to which the Melbourne-based banks contributed a substantial sum.[4] O'Donnell gained national attention when he called for Catholic MPs in the Labor Caucus to refuse to vote for nationalisation and if expelled from the ALP, they should establish a new

---

1 *Advocate* (Melbourne), 2 September 1948, p. 6.
2 L. L. Robson, "O'Donnell, Thomas Joseph (1876–1949)", *Australian Dictionary of Biography*, National Centre of Biography, Australian National University, https://adb.anu.edu.au/biography/odonnell-thomas-joseph-7880/text13699, accessed online 4 April 2022.
3 *Examiner* (Launceston), 1 September 1947, p. 2.
4 Summary of Activities of The Banks' Central Committee, 10–27 September 1947, National Bank of Australasia (NABA)/Bank Nationalisation, p. 5.

Christian democratic party.[1]

Liberal President Richard Casey met O'Donnell when he visited Hobart. He found a "portly comfortable-looking old priest who broadcast lately on the banking issue and likes his drink".[2] The Monsignor told Casey the nationalisation issue might end up in Rome and hinted "a satisfactory answer would be forthcoming".

O'Donnell died in 1949 but his involvement raised curious questions. Why had the cautious Catholic hierarchy not shut down the fiery priest? Or was O'Donnell let loose to express what the Church's leadership thought about nationalisation?

Several Protestant clerics attacked nationalisation but none matched O'Donnell's national profile. The Presbyterian Moderator of New South Wales said "the Federal Government was making a systematic attack on the personal liberty of the individual".[3] A Presbyterian minister in Bundaberg published *Advance Australia Where*, a pamphlet that declared "the banking proposals mark the official repudiation of our blood-brought liberties and herald the demise of Australian democracy".[4]

Brisbane businessmen asked the Anglican Synod to step in to stop power-sated politicians and Communists. The Rector of St Matthew's in Manly said "the whole of the Anglican Church in Australia was strongly opposed to the dangerous proposal".[5] Someone anonymously published a pamphlet of criticisms from leading Protestants. One notable exception to the religious anger was the Anglican priest in Goulburn who believed bank nationalisation was the most progressive policy in years.[6]

The Returned Sailors, Soldiers and Airmen's Imperial League of Australia (RSL) had 400,000 members, and like the churches, could wield significant political influence when it wanted. However the 1947 National Congress refused to debate nationalisation and the RSL directed sub-branches not to pass resolutions on the bank plan. Its only request of the Government was that veteran bank officers would be protected if they were forced to work for the Commonwealth Bank.[7]

Most sub-branches accepted the direction from their national headquarters but a few were strongly opposed to nationalisation.[8]

---

1 *Kalgoorlie Miner* (Kalgoorlie), 23 September 1947, p. 4.
2 Casey diary entry: 3 October 1947.
3 *Sydney Morning Herald* (Sydney), 27 September 1947, p. 5.
4 *Inverell Times* (Inverell), 14 April 1948, p. 2.
5 *Daily Telegraph* (Sydney), 21 September 1947, p. 30.
6 *Tribune* (Sydney), 24 September 1947, p. 6.
7 *Age* (Melbourne), 31 October 1947, p. 3.
8 *Forbes Advocate* (Forbes), 12 September 1947, p. 9.

Canowindra veterans censured their own State Council for not fighting the proposal and Armidale ex-servicemen said the Government was attempting to suspend individual freedom and make Australia a totalitarian state.[1] Veterans in Queensland demanded a referendum on the issue and veterans employed by the Bank of New South Wales said nationalisation would open the door to a Nazi-type state which was the very thing they had fought against.

Individual veterans expressed their opposition. Some addressed protest meetings while others sent letters to the newspapers signing off as "Ex-Digger" or with their service number. Veteran Bob White was a junior officer with the Bank of New South Wales. He recalled, "As a young man I found the anti-nationalisation propaganda totally convincing. I was still at school when the war started and spent five years in the Army. In that time away from 'civvy street' I was bitter about the impact of the war on my life. I disliked the constraints of Army life and longed for the freedom and security of life back at the bank. Now that my job security was threatened by nationalisation, I like many young people had no problem with the argument that it was a socialist plot."[2]

Lieutenant General Gordon Bennett was the highest-ranking veteran protester. Bennett had served at Gallipoli and commanded the Australian 8th Division in Malaya during the war. He fled to Australia when the Japanese captured Singapore leaving his soldiers to march into years of captivity as prisoners of war. He arrived home amid controversy that he had abandoned his command, though supporters claimed he came back to pass on valuable intelligence about Japanese tactics. A Royal Commission in 1945 vindicated Bennett's decision to leave Singapore and the returning POWs remained loyal to him. The dour, moustachioed general toured New South Wales and Queensland lashing the Government and declaring the bank move would lead to Soviet-style oppression. He said Australia needed volunteers to fight an enemy who was intent on introducing alien ways into Australia.[3]

Amid growing community anger the Prime Minister was seemingly content to puff his pipe and not say much. Usually Chifley was accessible to reporters but now he refused to explain or further elaborate on his press statement. He said he would give more information and answer his critics when Parliament came back in the spring. A few ministers who ventured a public opinion blundered badly.

---

1 *Armidale Express and New England Advertiser* (Armidale), 12 September 1947, p. 8.
2 White and Clarke, p. 37.
3 *Tribune* (Sydney), 6 December 1947, p. 1.

Claude Barnard, the Minister for Repatriation, told Tasmanian bank managers the insurance industry might also be nationalised. The Postmaster General Senator Don Cameron said bank buildings would make excellent telephone exchanges. "If I could get hold of a couple of banks it would suit me fine."[1] John Dedman speculated that nationalisation could save 5,000 jobs and hinted bank officers who were made redundant might be deployed elsewhere. Chifley quickly silenced his ministers.

It is hard to understand Chifley's decision not to promote his revolutionary banking policy. He was a respected and canny politician and as Treasurer oversaw major wartime loan drives which had succeeded because of innovative advertising, marketing and public relations. Was he waiting for Labor MPs to return to Canberra so he could brief and prepare them for the fight ahead? Was he reluctant to go public while Evatt's team was in Sydney thrashing through the takeover details? Or was Chifley less interested in selling his historic idea than he was in making it work.[2] Whatever his motives, his silence gifted the Opposition and the bankers time to prepare nationwide protests and allowed the country's newspapers to ignite a firestorm.

---

[1] *Daily Telegraph* (Sydney), 29 August 1947, p. 9.
[2] Crisp, p. 244.

6 Fighting on the Front Page

"Mr Chifley has given them (the newspapers) a genuinely startling shock."[1]

Newspapers dominated the post-war media landscape and shaped public opinion. They were the lens through which the vast majority of Australians viewed issues and the press lens on nationalisation was decidedly dark. The country's newspapers relentlessly attacked Labor's bank ambitions from the moment Chifley's press statement landed in their newsrooms through to the election in December 1949.

In 1947 there was no national newspaper but each capital city had its major mastheads. Sydney had four big dailies and as many on Sunday. Melbourne had similar numbers but no Sunday paper. The *Brisbane Telegraph* and the *Courier Mail* competed in Queensland and the *Advertiser* in Adelaide was "the paper" in South Australia. People in Perth read the *West Australian* and *Daily News*, while the *Mercury* on Macquarie Street in Hobart published Tasmania's most serious paper.

Provincial centres like Newcastle, Townsville and Launceston had daily papers and even small towns like Gundagai and Gympie had publications. The most influential papers syndicated their stories, dispatches, comic strips and political columns. Because of this, Australians across the continent could count on learning about critical developments at roughly the same time.

The *Sydney Morning Herald*, the *Herald* in Melbourne and other major newspapers had teams of editors, sub-editors, roundsmen, columnists, cartoonists, illustrators, freelancers and social diarists who supplied an astonishing amount of information. A newspaper could keep the average person busy for an hour or more each day if they chose to read overseas, national and state news, political round-ups, editorials, gossip columns, finance reports, movie and book reviews, church notices, garden jottings, real estate bulletins, cinema schedules, radio timetables, racing results and football scores. There were special weekly supplements for women, racegoers, children, gardeners, book lovers and other groups and most days newspaper cartoonists pilloried politicians, pricked powerful egos and cast an ironic eye over post-war life.

The largest newspapers had several daily editions while bush papers

---
1 *Smith's Weekly* (Sydney), 30 August 1947, p. 16.

like the *Koorda Record* in Western Australia were published weekly or fortnightly. Communities depended on their local paper, and while city newspapers had departments full of people, the one or two people on a country paper attended events, filed stories, sold advertising, laid out and printed the paper and then trucked their newspaper to the farm gates of district subscribers.

Australian newspapers were as affordable as any in the world and they prided themselves on providing news and entertainment to readers at a low price. Sydney's *Daily Telegraph* sold for two pennies (about sixty cents today) as did *The Advocate* in Burnie and *The Guardian Express* in Geraldton. The primary revenue for a paper was, however, from advertising. Each edition carried page after page of classified ads for jobs, real estate and cars and announcements of births, deaths and marriages. Governments used newspapers to communicate essential notices and job vacancies, and political parties advertised during election campaigns. Display advertising combined text with illustrations or photographs and promoted the products of major brands and rural shopkeepers.

Ownership of the nation's newspapers was tightly held by a select group of wealthy men, always willing to use their barrels of ink and rolls of newsprint to vent their feelings. Among this exclusive group were Frank Packer, the Fairfax family and the highly visible Sir Keith Murdoch. Murdoch controlled the *Herald* and *Sun News-Pictorial* in Melbourne, the *Advertiser* in Adelaide, Perth's *Daily News*, and the *Courier Mail* in Brisbane. He also held substantial investments in commercial radio stations. He established the Australian Associated Press news service and pioneered the domestic newsprint industry and public opinion polling in Australia.

Murdoch started in newspapers as a suburban roundsman and became an unofficial war correspondent during the First World War. His most famous reporting was a scathing assessment of the performance of British commanders at Gallipoli. Later he dispatched opinionated reports from the battlefields in France. In wartime London Murdoch saw how Fleet Street press barons used their newspapers to influence the British Government. Back in Melbourne, he became the energetic and passionate editor of the *Herald* and sailed the paper from one political storm to the next. He was never afraid to take on an issue especially if it involved a Labor government.

At the start of the Second World War he was appointed the Commonwealth Director General of Information but quit after a short time. For the rest of the war Murdoch used his papers to offer spirited reviews on the competence of Australian and Allied governments. Harold Cox, the *Herald's* political reporter in Canberra, provided Murdoch with regular, confidential political reports for years, and his assessments proved remarkably accurate.

The *Canberra Times* described Frank Packer as an "unreconstructed nineteenth-century capitalist, robber baron and press baron rolled into one".[1] Packer was the son of a small newspaper proprietor and worked briefly as a journalist. He acquired his newspapers through financial shrewdness and pugnacious deal-making. His holdings included Sydney's *Daily Telegraph* and the *Sunday Telegraph* which together had the largest newspaper circulation in New South Wales. Like Murdoch, Packer was ever ready to bludgeon a Labor government.

Packer also owned the *Australian Women's Weekly* which had the largest circulation of any Australian publication. Each week 700,000 copies provided entertainment and advice to Australian women on fashion, cooking, raising children and keeping a husband happy. The *Weekly* was the most democratic of all the most important publications and was read by the wives of bank managers, women at home, shop girls and union women on the factory floor. That separated it from the major papers where readership was determined by occupation and class. Melbourne hoi polloi like crane drivers, labourers and cleaners read the *Herald* and *Sun News-Pictorial*. Sydney's blue-collar workers bought the *Daily Telegraph* and the *Sun*. Doctors, accountants, university professors and bank managers preferred the *Sydney Morning Herald* and the *Argus* in Melbourne.[2]

The *Sydney Morning Herald*, owned by the Fairfax family, was the country's oldest paper. Irascible Ezra Norton owned the *Daily Mirror* in Sydney and the *Truth* newspapers whose motto could have been "'vice is news and virtue isn't". Hugh Syme, a retired decorated naval officer, was General Manager of the *Age* and ex-Brigadier E. G. Knox and a group "known as the colonels" managed the *Argus*. Chifley thought the *Sydney Morning Herald*, the *Age* and the *Argus* were the most even-handed of the major dailies.

The press proprietors became quickly combative if an issue threatened their interests. Bank nationalisation was such an issue although it served to magnify the distaste owners already felt for the ALP. In 1939 the Menzies

1 *Canberra Times* (ACT), 2 May 1974, p. 2.
2 Newspaper and Magazine Survey circa 1940, *Collection 1: Ashby Research Service Records*, ca. 1937–ca. 1972, State Library of New South Wales, MLMSS 8907/Box 06/Item (6).

Government had introduced press censorship to block any reporting that could help Australia's enemies. The Curtin Government continued and tightened these arrangements despite the objections of newspaper owners and editors who reckoned their judgment was sufficient to decide what to publish. The owners petulantly accepted censorship in much the same way the banks accepted restrictions on wartime banking.

Tensions peaked in 1944 when the Curtin Government suspended major Sydney papers over an alleged censorship breach. The tipping point came when a Commonwealth policeman drew his pistol to stop a newspaper lorry delivering copies of the *Sunday Telegraph*. The incident descended into farce as newsboys dodged police and journalists threw newspapers from their office windows to cheering crowds in the streets below.[1] The proprietors challenged the suspension in the High Court but eventually compromised with the Government.

The wartime shortage of newsprint also exasperated the owners. Before the war Australian newspapers sourced newsprint from Canada and Scandinavia but newsprint was rationed because of a lack of wartime shipping. Sir Keith Murdoch established a paper pulp mill in Tasmania but it was unable to fully supply industry demands. The proprietors argued for more inbound cargo space because they regarded newsprint as an essential product. Paper shortages continued after the war because the Government regarded newsprint as a low priority import. At one point the proprietors hired an advertising agency to run a campaign against newsprint rationing. When that failed the pressmen were forced to go cap in hand to the Government to appeal for increased allocations. The shortage of newsprint forced newspapers and magazines to reduce the size of their editions, which meant fewer stories, fewer ads and less revenue. The editions of the *Newcastle Morning Herald* halved in size in 1948 and the *Australian Women's Weekly* dropped its page with letters from readers and a popular beauty column.[2]

The Labor Government had its own vexations with the newspaper proprietors. The Minister for Information Arthur Calwell was a fierce newspaper critic and described the Australian press as "owned by financial crooks and edited for the most part by mental harlots".[3] Chifley colourfully characterised the media as "paid stooges with pen and tongue and radio voice [who] are prepared to sell the cause of truth and their

---

1 *Daily Telegraph* (Sydney), 18 April 1944, p. 3.
2 *Newcastle Morning Herald and Miners' Advocate* (Newcastle), 30 December 1947, p. 2.
3 Commonwealth, *Parliamentary Debates*, House of Representatives, 13 November 1941, 430 (Arthur Calwell, Minister for Information).

own souls at a lesser price than that for which Judas sold his master, that is when one takes into consideration the increased cost of living since biblical times".[1]

In 1944 Calwell, frustrated with the press coverage of the Government, presented Cabinet with a plan to curtail press privileges, redeploy journalists to wartime work, tax advertising revenue, cut the price of newspapers and limit supplies of newsprint. He also wanted newspaper owners to surrender their investments in radio stations and guarantee Australians had a right of reply if newspapers misrepresented them.[2] Cooler heads in the Cabinet knew these measures would ignite an all-out war with the media. Calwell's plan was not adopted but it did illustrate the deep distrust many in Labor had for the press.

In 1947 Calwell criticised the patriotism of Australian newspapers and said they used stunts to increase circulation and were unconcerned with telling the truth.[3] Twelve years later he was still complaining, when as Leader of the Federal Parliamentary Labor Party, he claimed the Australian press had opposed every Labor Government since Federation. Newspapers had slanted the news, ignored or misrepresented Labor's programs, favoured the Opposition and encouraged columnists and editorialists to savage the ALP.[4]

The Fabian Society of New South Wales, though modest in size, was an influential organisation with close ties to the ALP. Amid the nationalisation uproar, it published a pamphlet that was highly critical of the media. It noted newspapers had generally reported responsibly on wartime events but attacked the Labor Government once the war was over. The Fabians claimed major papers routinely misreported Labor achievements and often manipulated information, used deceptive headlines, buried stories, misquoted spokespeople and suppressed opinion polls favourable to the Government. It was little wonder Australians could not learn the facts when editors and reporters mirrored the prejudices of their bosses.[5]

The ALP talked about having its own national daily to counter the pro-capitalist, anti-Labor media. Little progress was made because Labor

---

1 *Examiner* (Launceston), 3 September 1948, p.1.
2 National Archives of Australia (NAA) Department of the Treasury, CP184/8 Bundle 1, Copies of Cabinet Agenda Papers, Cabinet Agenda No 673: Urgent and Necessary Measures for the Reform of the Daily Press, 8 June 1944.
3 *News* (Adelaide), 25 July 1947, p. 3.
4 Arthur Calwell, *The Australian Labor Party and the Press: Twenty-Second Arthur Norman Smith Memorial Lecture in Journalism delivered at the University of Melbourne, 30 July 1959*, Carlton, University of Melbourne Press, 1959.
5 The Fabian Society of New South Wales was established in 1947 to contribute to progressive thinking and popular culture and had close ties to the ALP.

papers struggled to attract advertising revenue and Party officials never could agree on how such a paper would operate. Most importantly the Party never had the funds to maintain a credible national publication. Some suggested the Government could run a paper just like it ran a national radio network through the Australian Broadcasting Commission (ABC). Even advocates of a government-operated newspaper had to admit it would be too dull to succeed.

There were ALP and union newspapers like the *Westralian Worker*, *Labor Call* and the *Maritime Worker* but only party loyalists and union members read them. Likewise leftist regional papers like the *National Advocate* in Bathurst and the *Barrier Daily Truth* in Broken Hill had pocket-sized circulations.

The press barons were immediate and visceral opponents of nationalisation. They believed it was bad for their interests, terrible for the country and reeked of socialism. They launched an all-out assault on bank nationalisation. Copy editors plastered their pages with critical headlines. The front page of Melbourne's *Herald* cried, "Dictator Risk" and Mackay's *Daily Mercury* declared, "Bank Plan is Death Knell of Freedom". The *Daily News* proclaimed the battle of the banks had begun. Reports and commentary below such lurid headlines were laced with inflammatory quotes and peppered with words like *revolution*, *dictatorship* and *communistic*.

Traditionally the editorial reflected the political voice of the newspaper and now editorial after editorial condemned bank nationalisation. The Sydney *Sun* published the most editorials, one of them entitled "The Police State and You". The *Mail* in Adelaide said bank nationalisation was a new rabbit in the hat of political tricksters and one more step toward a socialist Eden.[1] An editorial in the *Daily Telegraph* lambasted the "Caesars of Canberra".[2]

Newsrooms were awash with letters to the editor. A minority supported a bank takeover but most correspondents disapproved. Mr H. Cootes told the *Daily Telegraph* that Australians had fought fascism only to discover it alive and well in Australia and ready to stab them in the back.[3] Mr F. T. Gratwick from Mount Gambier said the Klansman's "fiery cross" should inspire people to sign a petition demanding a referendum on banking.[4] A Lismore reader said "one can no longer wonder that such

---
1 *Mail* (Adelaide),16 August 1947, p. 1.
2 *Daily Telegraph* (Sydney), 23 August 1947, p. 2.
3 *Daily Telegraph* (Sydney), 19 August 1947, p. 6.
4 *Border Watch* (Mount Gambier),13 September 1947, p. 5.

a mass of ineptitude, crass idiocy and general incompetence known as the Chifley Government exists".[1] Cartoonists reflected the growing anger. George "Mo" Molnar was the *Daily Telegraph's* cartoonist. Previously he drew Chifley as a sympathetic figure with a pipe and squiggly necktie who meant well. Now his cartoons showed an unsympathetic politician treating public opinion with contempt. A cartoon in *Smith's Weekly* showed Chifley in cricket flannels bowling to a nervous citizen with balls marked "rising prices", "high taxation" and "bank bill".

A Sydney *Sun* cartoon pictured Minister John Dedman luring bank officers deep into a dark forest with false promises. Chifley was angry when John Frith of the *Sydney Morning Herald* portrayed him as a masked burglar stealing a piggy bank. Evatt was infuriated when Frith drew the Prime Minister as Abraham Lincoln urging his Foreign Affairs Minister to have slave chains ready for the bankers.

Opinion polls reflected the restlessness in the country. American newspapers had published polls since the thirties, but polling was relatively new in Australia. In 1940 Sir Keith Murdoch encouraged one of his junior reporters, Roy Morgan, to study the polling methods of Dr George Gallup in the United States. When he returned to Melbourne, Morgan established Australian Public Opinion Polls (APOP) in the belief polling could be a valuable community service and offer insights into what Australians thought about major issues.

A poll could identify topics people were either unaware of or misunderstood. It could allow politicians to "engage their publics in debate across a range of matters beyond the electoral cycle".[2] By 1947 Morgan was paying 300 interviewers to question men and women across the country about specific issues. Surveys were mailed to Melbourne, data collated and analysed and then metropolitan newspapers with links to Murdoch published the results. Morgan never claimed polls were perfect. However, he successfully predicted the results of the 1946 federal election, the Victorian state election the following year and the outcome of a New South Wales referendum on hotel closing times.

Morgan was Melbourne-based, and Sylvia Ashby in Sydney did similar work for newspapers there. She had studied market research abroad and then started her own agency in Sydney where her client roll included banks, department stores, oil companies, advertising agencies and radio

---

1 *Northern Star* (Lismore), 25 August 1947, p. 5.
2 *Southern Argus* (Port Elliot), 23 July 1941, p. 1. R. Macreadie, "Australian Public Opinion Polls", Victorian Department of Parliamentary Services, July 2011, p. 22.

stations.¹ Sometimes Ashby did political work: in 1943 she surveyed Dr Evatt's Sydney electorate and worked on referenda and elections. Like Morgan, Ashby never claimed perfection but said her surveys were accurate within "one, two or three percent of known facts".² By 1947 Ashby employed 100 mostly middle-aged and married women because she believed women were the most conscientious researchers.³ Ashby was a leader in her industry and among Australia's best-paid women.

A Morgan poll in September 1947 showed a swing to the non-Labor parties and that Australians were against a bank takeover nearly three to one. A *Daily Telegraph* survey based on Ashby's research revealed a majority of people in every state were against the bank plan, and that Queenslanders and Tasmanians were particularly incensed.⁴ Another poll showed most Victorians did not favour bank control.⁵ These findings were consistent with a 1945 survey that found most people, including ALP supporters, believed the Government should not control banking.⁶

Interviews with people in the street were another gauge of the public mood. An *Age* journalist talked to a carpenter, chartered accountant, electrician, farrier and tile layer in Melbourne. They said the Government had no right to interfere with their money and even the Labor supporters said they were prepared to vote against the ALP over the issue.⁷

The *Sydney Morning Herald* sent two reporters to the Riverina to interview a hundred people. Business people, farmers and graziers were against bank nationalisation. A librarian in Wagga Wagga said women were particularly hostile. A car salesman said, "We might as well have Hitler or Mussolini as a government controlled by a few caucus heads." Only fifteen people said nationalisation might be good including one who thought it might help rural development.⁸

The *Sydney Morning Herald* sent another reporter into the safe state Labor seats of Bondi and Hurstville. Most small business owners and shopkeepers opposed bank nationalisation, though some supported government control despite confessing they had little idea how it might

---

1   Murray Goot, "Ashby, Sylvia Rose (1908–1978)", Australian Dictionary of Biography, National Centre of Biography, Australian National University, https://adb.anu.edu.au/biography/ashby-sylvia-rose-9390/text16499, published first in hardcopy 1993, accessed online 4 April 2022.
2   *Newspaper News* (Sydney), 1 August 1946, p. 8.
3   *Daily Telegraph* (Sydney), 19 September 1947, p. 14.
4   *Daily Telegraph* (Sydney), 19 September 1947, p. 14.
5   *Advertiser* (Adelaide), 7 November 1947, p. 1.
6   *Herald* (Melbourne), 23 May 1945, p. 5.
7   *Age* (Melbourne), 20 August 1947, p. 3.
8   *Sydney Morning Herald* (Sydney), 26 August 1947, p. 4.

work.¹ The *Border Watch* in Mount Gambier asked seventeen business owners how nationalisation would affect their business. The consensus was people resented being told where to bank and felt the Commonwealth Bank already had enough power. Most said the bank plan would create bureaucracy and lead to the nationalisation of other industries. Some interviewees provided anonymous comments, fearing government retaliation or a backlash from their customers.²

Polls and interviews in the street were not wholly reliable but did offer insights into what voters thought. Labor however was untroubled by these revelations because it had been suspicious of public opinion polling from the start.³ Chifley doubted Morgan's accuracy and said he "would like to be informed of the people responsible for the votes, of votes unrecorded and informal votes".⁴ The ALP suspected polls because Sir Keith Murdoch was backing Morgan and they were published in conservative newspapers. It suspected the media barons skewed their polls to slant public opinion. Besides Labor had won the previous election just twelve months ago and its MPs believed they knew what people were thinking because they were in regular contact with their electorates. It would be another twenty years before Labor commissioned its first professional research survey.

Bank nationalisation inflamed the simmering tensions between Labor and the newspaper proprietors although the Government generally had good relations with the Canberra Press Gallery. Prime Minister John Curtin had been a journalist and editor and adroitly managed the wartime Press Gallery. He held two daily briefings for his 'travelling circus', the term he used for the dozen or so senior journalists in Canberra. He freely shared confidences on parliamentary and military matters and the 'circus' never abused his trust.⁵ Chifley like Curtin was relaxed around reporters although he scaled back prime ministerial press conferences to twice weekly.

Journalists liked Chifley. He was a strong character, had a good sense of humour and meant what he said. The Prime Minister and his Press Secretary Rodgers rarely played games with reporters, though both could use an off-the-record conversation to test an idea or shut down premature reporting of a Government plan. Chifley rarely discriminated

---
1 *Sydney Morning Herald* (Sydney), 28 August 1947, p. 5.
2 *Border Watch* (Mount Gambier), 11 September 1947, p. 5.
3 Roy Morgan studied the survey methods of Dr George Gallup in the United States. In the early days of polling in Australia newspapers used the terms Morgan Poll, Gallup Poll and Australian Public Opinion Poll interchangeably.
4 *Herald* (Melbourne), 12 November 1941, p. 3.
5 Joseph Alexander interviewed by Mel Pratt, 2 March 1972, NLA ORAL TRC 121/10.

between reporters even though he disliked the men they worked for. He seldom took press criticism to heart or took issue with journalists who filed unfavourable stories. But the Prime Minister was combative if he believed a story about his Government was unfair or inaccurate and would robustly share his views on a call to the offending paper's general manager or senior editor.

The Canberra Press Gallery only had thirty journalists though extra staff descended on Canberra when Parliament was in session. The Gallery pumped out national and political news to major newspapers, radio stations and the still-new Australian Associated Press wire service. Some Gallery members doubled as correspondents for foreign papers and news services so a significant story could be dispatched overseas quickly.

The most respected journalists wrote syndicated columns with titles like "This Week in Politics" or "Political Roundabout" which explained issues of the day, offered pen portraits of politicians and generally traded gossip. Canberra was like a country town and people knew each other. Yet if journalists knew the peccadilloes of politicians and public servants their reporting was rarely salacious. No major paper ever mentioned Chifley's alleged long-running affair with his secretary Phyllis Donnelly. Completing the Press Gallery line-up were one or two individuals who owned subscription-based newsletters. The most reliable were *Inside Canberra* and *Canberra Survey*, both edited by Eric White, the former Liberal Party public relations officer. White's sources inside Parliament and the public service were extensive and his analysis and forecasts were uncommonly accurate.

The first radio broadcast in Australia occurred in 1919 when the national anthem was broadcast between two buildings in Ash Street in Sydney. By 1947 radio was an established source of news and entertainment and listening to the radio was more popular than reading, visiting friends or going to the cinema.[1] In 1947 the 15,000 people employed in 129 radio stations throughout Australia served up an astonishing range of news bulletins, religious broadcasts, women's features, children's shows, serials, quiz programs, soap operas, concerts and live sports broadcasts. Like most Australians Ben Chifley was an avid listener and enjoyed news bulletins, light music programs and sports broadcasts. Nearly every room in his Busby Street home had a radio set.

Commercial radio copied American broadcasting and relied for revenue on advertising, sponsorships and private money. Sir Keith

---
1 *Herald* (Melbourne), 6 September 1947, p. 13.

Murdoch controlled about twenty stations. Associated Newspapers controlled stations in Sydney, Adelaide, Canberra and Melbourne and the *Argus*, the *Age* and the *Mercury* had interests in radio. The ALP and some large unions also owned radio stations. 2KY in Sydney billed itself as the world's first labour station and the ALP and the Newcastle Trades and Labour Council jointly owned 2HD in the Hunter Valley. The Trades Hall Council in Melbourne ran 3KZ and the Australian Workers' Union operated the "Voice of the West" or 6KY in Perth.

The government-owned Australian Broadcasting Commission (ABC) was modelled on the British Broadcasting Commission and operated as a national public service. Established by Joseph Lyons in 1932, the ABC was funded through annual Commonwealth allocations and receipts from radio licences that all listeners were obliged to purchase. One in five radio stations was an ABC outlet.

The ABC operated metropolitan and regional networks and a third of commercial stations belonged to a national or state network. The Macquarie Network, the largest commercial network, operated from 2GB in Sydney where forty managers, announcers, producers, copywriters and technicians produced programs in state-of-the-art studios for partner stations. Syndication and affiliation meant radio was the great cultural connector and listeners in bush camps and mining towns heard the same popular shows and about significant news, often at the same time, as those in suburban bungalows and city barber shops.

Commercial stations sourced their news bulletins from the newsrooms of major papers as did the ABC. In 1942 the ABC became the world's first government broadcaster to run an independent news service, despite the protests of newspapers that resented taxpayer-funded competition. Radio news bulletins, whether ABC or commercial, tended to relay essential facts with little attempt to provide context, explanation or interpretation. It was said the ABC bureau in Canberra was a clearing house for government handouts.

Radio took on a political role in 1922 when Billy Hughes made the country's first prime ministerial broadcast. Joseph Lyons and James Scullin used radio in the 1931 federal election, and the New South Wales Premier and Opposition Leader broadcast their campaign launches live during the 1932 state election. During the war, radio became indispensable for front line and home front listeners. It informed Australians about major events and provided entertainment. Prime Minister Robert Menzies used radio in September 1939 to announce the country's entry into the war, and

John Curtin's broadcasts kept Australians up to date about the progress of the war. In opposition Robert Menzies was an excellent radio performer and used radio to develop and promote his political philosophy. Richard Casey, the new Party President, appreciated the intimacy of radio and its ability to connect with Australians in ways newspapers never could. Casey may not have known American broadcasting executive Frederick Willis but certainly shared his views. Willis maintained radio was most effective when it wrapped drama, entertainment and humour around politics and other serious subjects.[1] Casey would have been aware of the role that radio played in the 1944 US Presidential election when it provided Americans with more accurate campaign coverage than newspapers.[2] He was keen to embark the Liberal Party on a daring electronic adventure to defeat the Labor Government.

---

1 *Radio Pamphlet No 22*, Melbourne, Australian Army Education Service, 1945, p. 18.
2 *Inter-university Consortium for Political and Social Research* (Ann Arbor, Michigan, 1971), National Election Study 1944, p. 53.

7 Masters of the Public Mood

> *"Political press advertising ... functions as a medium of polemics, extending the debate from Parliament House to the electorate."*[1]

Australia's earliest recorded advertising is a handbill for a theatre production in Sydney in 1796. From that, a small advertising industry grew in fits and starts from colonial times to the early Federation period. After the First World War hucksters, stunt men and insiders captured the fledgling industry and threatened to permanently damage its reputation. In the 1930s the Victorian Government legislated to curb objectionable practices and protect the public from false and fraudulent advertising. The industry regained respectability and in 1939 a visiting American movie executive proclaimed Australian newspapers led the world in print advertising.[2]

Historically, governments limited their advertising to job vacancies, tenders and official announcements, but that changed during the war. From 1939 to 1945 Commonwealth and state agencies served up a "literary and vocal burgoo" designed to influence public opinion, promote patriotism and sell sacrifice.[3] For the first time government advertising dominated the airwaves, newspapers, magazines and movie screens.

The Treasury Department created a special division to coordinate Commonwealth Government advertising. Along with the newly created Department of Information it standardised procedures, managed contracts and worked with peak bodies like the Australian Advertising Council which represented the major advertising agencies. Arrangements with the Council reduced rivalry between ad agencies, newspaper chains and radio stations and shielded public servants from charges of favouritism and corruption. They also allowed bureaucrats to navigate the unfamiliar world of the advertising industry. The Government also worked with the Australian Association of National Advertisers which represented companies with the biggest advertising budgets. Early in the war the Association joined the Department of Information in an £80,000 campaign (nearly $6 million today) to encourage businesses to support newly introduced financial and industrial relations regulations.[4]

---

1 Andrew Kaldor, "Liberal and Labor Press Advertising", *The Australian Quarterly* 40, no. 2 (1964) p. 58.
2 *Sydney Morning Herald* (Sydney), 18 August 1939, p. 13.
3 *Australian Women's Weekly* (Sydney), 4 April 1942, p. 10.
4 *Canberra Times* (ACT), 3 February 1941, P.1.

The war also brought price controls, rationing, fewer consumer goods and a shortage of newsprint. In 1942 Rationing Order No. 15 severely restricted commercial advertising to the point where advertising could not induce people to buy. Clothing ads had to tell buyers how to make items last longer and some advertising asked customers if a purchase was essential.[1] Restrictions in the early war years even ensnared Santa Claus when Christmas ads discouraged non-essential shopping in stores with fewer staff and less to sell. To stay in the public mind and be ready when people could spend freely again, major brands draped their ads in khaki. Ads for Turf cigarettes encouraged customers to buy war bonds and Cadbury proudly announced it was the official chocolate supplier to the armed forces.[2] Fantales and Minties asked customers to be patient with limited stocks because getting confectionary to the troops was their top priority.[3]

The war helped advertising shake off the shady edges of previous years. By the end of the decade the advertising industry was well-respected and worth £10 million a year. Government advertising shifted to promoting resettlement, reconstruction and immigration. At the same time the private sector advertised to persuade Australians to spend on travel, cars, appliances, cigarettes, alcohol and other luxuries the war had denied them. The banks also resumed advertising. However, their ads were as stiff as a bank manager's collar. They laboriously stressed the need to save for uncertainty or were deliberately bland to avoid upsetting anyone.

Advertising in Australia has always had its fair share of colourful characters. In the post-war period Frank Goldberg stood out as creative, competent, part-buccaneer, part-pioneer.[4] As a young man Goldberg migrated from England to New Zealand where he started in department store sales. He established an advertising agency and eventually had offices in Sydney, Melbourne, Dunedin, Wellington and London. Goldberg's clients included major international brands like General Motors, Johnnie Walker and the cosmetics manufacturer Max Factor. During the war he served on the Commonwealth War Effort Publicity Board and from that experience concluded, "Advertising is part of a wide-spreading propaganda machine concerned with the all-important task of moulding public opinion ... advertising can no longer be regarded purely as a commercial entity but as a department of the much wider and essentially

1 *Commonwealth of Australia Gazette* (National), 3 November 1942, p. 2577.
2 *Sporting Globe* (Melbourne), 6 March 1943, p. 1.
3 *Newspaper News* (Sydney), 1 May 1944, p. 13.
4 Valerie Lawson, "Goldberg, Frank (1889–1958)", *Australian Dictionary of Biography*, National Centre of Biography, Australian National University, https://adb.anu.edu.au/biography/goldberg-frank-10318/text18261, published first in hardcopy 1996, accessed online 4 April 2022.

modern science of propaganda."¹

Goldberg was an aggressive competitor and chased down accounts like a Caribbean pirate running down Spanish galleons. When news reached Australia that an executive from a famous whisky brand was sailing to Australia, the largest ad agencies were keen to win his business. One agency booked a car and a chauffeur to collect the executive when his ship docked in Sydney. Another chartered a launch to meet his boat before it entered Sydney Harbour. Goldberg flew to Perth, boarded the vessel and landed the account while the ship was still at sea.²

Beyond the bluster Goldberg was an advertising pioneer. He was an early advocate for display advertising where imagery and text combine to present a message. His agency was the first to have a radio studio and he handled the radio launch of the *Australian Women's Weekly*. While visiting the United States after the war Goldberg ambitiously placed an order for a television transmitter even though it would be another decade before Australia had television.

Goldberg also relished political campaigns and delighted in turning stodgy campaign promises into compelling messages. He worked for the UAP in the 1935 and 1938 elections in New South Wales and managed the Liberal Party's advertising in the 1946 election. Still it was surprising when the private banks in Melbourne chose Frank Goldberg to run their anti-nationalisation campaign. The fifty-eight-year-old ad man was more flamboyant than the people bankers normally dealt with, but they knew he was ingenious, politically astute and a master with print advertising. Advertising agencies were often reluctant to take on contentious issues like bank nationalisation, fearing they might upset existing clients or jeopardise future business. But Goldberg was unafraid of controversy and the banks knew they had to be bolder than ever.

Richard Casey was also looking for an innovative agency. Menzies was not happy with the Party's election advertising in 1946 and Frank Goldberg was out of favour with the Liberals. Ironically, Casey chose an advertising agency that had worked with the ALP for years.

Solomon (Sim) Rubensohn ran one of the most successful agencies in the country and had worked for Labor for over a decade. Apart from being an accomplished advertising executive Rubensohn was a strategist, a lobbyist and fundraiser for Labor. He was friends with Calwell and Evatt and an admirer of Chifley. *Truth* newspaper reported he was someone

---

1 Robert Crawford, *But Wait There's More: A History of Australian Advertising 1900–2000*, Carlton, Melbourne University Publishing, 2008, p. 68.
2 Crawford, p. 41.

who "pow wows with all the big chiefs of business and politics from day to day".[1] Chifley's move on the banks had unnerved Rubensohn and his creative director Pip Cogger. The pair thought the Prime Minister had overreached and seriously misread the public mood. An agency spokesman (mostly likely Cogger) said "the bank grab was the last straw. We just couldn't put our heart and soul into trying to sell such a policy to the people."[2]

Casey first meeting with Rubensohn developed into a lifelong friendship. Rubensohn appreciated Casey's enthusiasm for modernising political communications and said it was the first time in his life that "he had heard such an intelligent and rational approach from anyone connected with any political party". For his part Casey said, "I continue to get a good and improving impression of Rubensohn."[3]

Rubensohn agreed to switch his agency in the Liberal cause but not before he flew to Canberra to tell Chifley. Rubensohn insisted there be no contract with the Liberal Party and either side need only give twenty-four hours' notice before terminating their arrangement. He would receive a 3.5 percent commission on the outlay for Liberal advertising and keep the ALP account in New South Wales.[4] Around the same time Casey recruited a new public relations officer for the Party. Allan Dawes, a Falstaffian figure, former war correspondent and experienced writer with the Melbourne *Herald*, started on an annual salary of £1500 (or over $100,000) today. His first assignment was to read Casey's views on public relations then spend a week with Rubensohn in Sydney. Casey's selection of Rubensohn and Dawes showed the value he placed on communications and his willingness to invest to ensure it was as effective as possible.

Today sharp distinctions exist between the disciplines of advertising, public relations and propaganda. Advertising deals with the paid promotion of a client's goods or services, while public relations focuses on unpaid strategies like staging events and working with influential third parties or the media to tell a story. Although now a negative term, in 1947 propaganda was a catch-all word to describe reaching out and persuading an audience. In post-war Australia a sole operator or single agency might offer clients one or more of these disciplines.

The value of public relations in Australia really began to be recognised during the war. In 1939 Prime Minister Menzies established the

---

1 *Truth* (Sydney), 24 February 1946, p. 18.
2 *Scone Advocate* (Scone), 16 March 1948, p. 3.
3 Casey diary entries, 12 and 13 November 1947.
4 Goot, "Rubensohn".

Department of Information to inform Australians at home and abroad about the war effort. The Curtin Labor Government continued with the Department and made the energetic Arthur Calwell its minister. Calwell claimed his agency was "one of the most efficient national publicity units in the world" and in 1945 it had generated £20 worth of publicity for every £1 spent.[1] The Australian Army and the Royal Australian Air Force had sophisticated public relations set-ups and the Royal Australian Navy established a branch late in the war. The Department of Labour and National Service, the Department of Munitions and other agencies had public relations staff, and ministers had press officers and public relations advisers.

The Postmaster General's Department (PMG) was perhaps the best wartime example of government public relations. The PMG managed the nation's postal, telegraph, telephone, broadcasting and radio services and had 10,000 post offices, agencies and offices around Australia. The war saw a massive expansion in PMG services and the Department's public relations officers educated the public about the changes taking place. They also had to tamp down expectations of how and when the public could access these new services.

The PMG provided information to newspapers, answered media inquiries, arranged press tours, sponsored radio broadcasts, talked to schools and business groups and commissioned short films. Yet though the PMG public relations people were good they must have marvelled at the sophisticated public relations outfit that arrived in Australia in the autumn of 1942.

On 21 March 1942 government ministers, military men and civic fathers gathered at Spencer Street railway station in Melbourne to welcome US General Douglas MacArthur. MacArthur had fled from Japanese-occupied Philippines to continue the Allied war effort from Australia. These were dark times for the country. The Japanese had just captured Singapore and 15,000 Australian soldiers had become prisoners of war. Shortly after, Darwin was bombed by the Imperial Japanese Navy. MacArthur's arrival assured Australians that the United States would stand by them.

MacArthur came with his own public relations team, tasked with ensuring Australians remained grateful for his presence. US public relations officers took pictures, massaged information, charmed the media and shielded the General from anything that might harm his image.

---

1 *Newspaper News* (Sydney), 15 December 1945, p. 10.

They performed with such mastery that the American public remained largely unaware of the sacrifices made by Australian troops in the Pacific, and Australians were only slightly better informed. A US admiral said MacArthur was more interested in taking "all the credit for the entire Pacific war" than working with the Navy.[1]

When MacArthur finally departed he left two legacies. Some of the young Australian officers who worked for him later became public relations pioneers after the war. Additionally, smart organisations inspired by MacArthur's example set up their own small, public relations offices to promote their interests.

The Liberal Party was one such organisation. It recruited Eric White, a former reporter and veteran, as its first public relations officer. Ahead of the 1946 election White along with the Party's Federal Director toured the states to review the Party's preparedness. They found a "weak and spasmodic" organisation where state divisions were like fiefdoms and only one state had a public relations capacity. One state president had never met the owners or editors of the major papers on his patch.[2]

Richard Casey as incoming Federal President believed the Party's 1946 campaign had been dull and unconvincing and appealed only to voters already predisposed to the conservative cause. He wanted to change how the Party engaged with the media, kept contact with voters between elections and recruited allies. He intrigued the Federal Executive when he presented his views on political communications and fascinated Party officeholders when he spoke at meetings and dinners on his first whistlestop tour of the country.[3] State by state Casey convinced the Party to accept centralised administration and overhaul its approach to publicity.

Casey was a rather stiff and formal individual so his enthusiasm for advertising and public relations seemed incongruous. Most likely his interest was sparked during his time in Washington DC when he saw how American politicians and corporations using public relations to further their interests. He networked with journalists and public relations professionals including Earl Newsom, known as "counsellor to the corporates" and whose clients included Standard Oil, Campbell's Soup and the Ford Motor Company. Newsom helped his clients experiment with new communications strategies and to establish their

---

[1] Felix E. Larkin interviewed by Jerry N. Hess, Harry S Truman Library and Museum, September–October 1972, trumanlibrary.gov/library/oral-histories/larkin, accessed 24 September 2021.
[2] Ian Hancock, "The Origins of the Modern Liberal Party", NLA 1994, https://www.nla.gov.au/ian-hancock/the-origins-of-the-modern-liberal-party, accessed 4 April 2022.
[3] Casey diary entry: 2 September 1947.

own communications teams. He preferred to work in the background nevertheless his rivals and supporters kept a close eye on what he was doing.

After the war Newsom was worried that Americans might lose faith in capitalism since they had embraced the New Deal and accepted wartime controls imposed by the Roosevelt Administration. They were used to the idea of central planning and big government. Newsom therefore advocated a program of "educational propaganda" to sell the public on the "restorative and invigorating qualities of free enterprise."[1] Casey and Newsom corresponded after Casey returned to Australia and the American was only too willing to offer ideas and encouragement to the new Liberal President. Some of Newsom's ideas probably made it into Casey's "sermon on the mount" speech which argued for communicating with voters not just during campaigns but between elections.

The ALP had no Casey-like evangelist urging it to re-imagine its approach to a new generation of voters. Don Rodgers was "a master of political communication" yet he had no remit from Labor to champion change.[2] Party leaders, a handful of officials and a part-time and honorary national secretary, all of whom seemed stuck in the past, were responsible for ALP communications. In 1946 a review of the ALP's Victorian branch found "traditional methods of political propaganda had been rendered largely ineffective by the increase in popular available entertainments" and the Party had not kept up with the times.[3] The review recommended changes, but little happened. Those in charge of communicating party policies either overestimated their abilities or seriously miscalculated the effort needed to persuade Australians when it came to something as contentious as bank nationalisation.

Two Labor parliamentarians had the necessary expertise and experience but were largely ignored. The MP for Parkes, Les Haylen, was a former reporter and had worked for newspapers and the *Australian Women's Weekly*. Alan Fraser, the Member for Eden Monaro, was a journalist for over twenty years. He reported for the *Times* in London and worked in the Parliamentary Press Gallery. Haylen circulated manifestos, and Fraser had good suggestions for improving party communications. Both were keen supporters of the Chifley's bank plan yet their ideas were

1 "How a Standard Oil PR Guy Shaped Post-War America", *Rigged*, 7 December 2021, https://podcastaddict.com/episode/132324745, accessed 5 April 2022.
2 C. J. Lloyd, "Rodgers, Donald Kilgour (1906–1978)", *Australian Dictionary of Biography*, National Centre of Biography, Australian National University, https://adb.anu.edu.au/biography/rodgers-donald-kilgour-11553/text20615, published first in hardcopy 2002, accessed online 4 April 2022.
3 *Age* (Melbourne), 20 April 1946, p. 3.

overlooked perhaps because they were independent thinkers and neither achieved Cabinet rank.

Ben Chifley was ultimately responsible for how his Government and his Party related to voters and would have known how effective advertising and public relations could be. As wartime Treasurer he had overseen some of the Government's most successful campaigns. Yet as his biographer L. F. Crisp noted, public relations "was not a field where he had any talent or flair, and whether in consequence of that personal deficiency or not, the subject never seemed to spark his imagination".[1]

Chifley's success as a communicator rested on his frankness, sincerity and humour. Years later the Chairman of Rolls Royce Australia, Geoffrey Remington, described Chifley as "a first-class exponent of self-activated public relations [who] won and deserved to win the respect, understanding and confidence of the Australian people".[2] People liked the Prime Minister and even when the Government introduced unpopular measures some preferred to blame Canberra rather than Chifley. Yet the Prime Minister's native talents were no match for the communications blitz his opponents were about to launch against his nationalisation scheme.

---

1 Crisp, p. 243.
2 G. C. Remington, *Public Relations: An Integral Part of Policy Making; Building of Public Confidence and Public Interest*, Sydney, Public Relations Institute of Australia, 1964, p. 7.

8 Battle in Canberra

> *"It is becoming clear that Government tactics will be to press forward with the [bank nationalisation] scheme with all possible speed."*[1]

Post-war Canberra was a country town of 17,000 people where most people either worked for the government or provided services to the government. There was an acute housing shortage in the city, as elsewhere in Australia, and new arrivals could wait thirty or more months for a house. Single public servants lived in hostels where they complained about poor meals and no hot water, and tradesmen made do in huts and tents. Lucky public servants lived with their families in modest government homes in new suburbs with English names like Ainslie and Kingston. The city had some small shopping areas and five pubs, fewer than most regional centres. The few tourists who came to Canberra were directed to the Australian War Memorial and Parliament House but otherwise there was little to see.

The Lodge had been the official prime ministerial residence since 1927. Stanley Bruce and Joseph Lyons lived there and John Curtin had been a bachelor there while his family stayed in Perth. Ben Chifley chose to live in a government-run hotel, though he occasionally occupied The Lodge when his wife visited Canberra. Few MPs rented or owned homes in Canberra. Liberal and Country Party members tended to reside at the Hotel Canberra and Labor men preferred the Hotel Kurrajong.[2]

The Kurrajong catered for parliamentarians, ministerial staffers and public servants who lived in Canberra when Parliament was in session. Chifley, like other guests, lived in a small single room, with toilets and showers down the hall. The Kurrajong's polished dining room was arranged by rank. Chifley and his group sat in the middle. On one side were their secretaries. Public servants sat in another area and those of lesser status occupied the edges. Food rationing was still in force so the Kurrajong kitchen drew coupons for each guest. Meals were good but hardly fancy. Breakfast was often a disappointment but dinner was solid with soup, meat, three vegetables and chicken once a week. Some Labor old-timers had lived at the Kurrajong for years and claimed privileged places at the bar or by the fire. The few wives who accompanied their

---
1 *Sunday Mail* (Brisbane), 7 September 1947, p. 2.
2 A notable exception was former Labor Prime Minister James Scullin, who lived in the Hotel Canberra, where his status qualified him for a private table in the dining room.

husbands set up in the small lounge room opposite the front door to watch who came and went. The Kurrajong was a short distance from Parliament House so the Prime Minister and most members saved their petrol coupons and walked to work.

Parliament House was a low, elongated white building and looked more like a wedding cake than Australia's seat of power. Inside was a warren of party rooms, small offices, long corridors and the two legislative chambers which were the nerve centres of the building. The House of Representatives was furnished in mahogany and green and the Senate was finished in dark wood and deep red, the colours copying those of the British House of Commons and House of Lords. Party leaders sat at ornate tables in the centre of both chambers and behind them were concentric circles of seats occupied by government and opposition members. Newsmen sat in a small gallery above the Speaker of the House and the President of the Senate.

Ministers and senior MPs worked from cramped offices often shared with a secretary-typist and one or two staff. Junior members worked from their wooden desks in the House or Senate and locked away their papers in small drawers under their seats. Or they gathered in their party rooms where they answered mail, made phone calls, listened to the radio and bet on the races. Kings Hall was the ample foyer between the Senate and House of Representatives. Open to the public, it was a favourite spot for newsmen intent on ambushing ministers or ambitious backbenchers.

The 18th Commonwealth Parliament sat from 1946 to 1949. There were thirty-six senators, forty-three Labor MPs and thirty-two non-Labor MPs who would decide the fate of Australian banking. Among them were only four female parliamentarians, although women made up half the voting population. Even this small number was historically high. Dame Enid Lyons, the wife of the late Prime Minister Joseph Lyons, was the first woman elected to the House of Representatives, after winning a seat in Tasmania in 1943. Independent Victorian Doris Blackburn, the other woman in the House of Representatives, contested the seat of her late husband Maurice Blackburn in 1946. Labor's Dorothy Tangney was elected to the Senate in 1943 as the first woman to be a federal parliamentarian. Liberal Senator Annabelle Rankin was elected in 1946.

An MP served a three-year term and a senator was elected for six years. A backbencher earned £1500 a year, four times the average salary, and received a pension of £8 per week when he or she retired after eight years in parliament. The Speaker of the House, the President of the

Senate, committee chairmen and ministers received considerably more. Their privileges included a private bar and dining room, subsidised accommodation, meal allowances and a gold railway pass which entitled the holder to free travel and free entry to some racecourses. These benefits might seem desirable but the lifestyle of a parliamentarian was onerous especially for those from faraway states like Western Australia.

Members only went home between parliamentary sittings and even then divided their time between family and electorate duties. Country members travelled large distances to connect with voters and could spend £200 or more a year (nearly $17,000 today) on hotel, car and travel expenses.[1] MPs paid taxes, contributed to election campaigns and were expected to donate to local charities and sporting bodies. Some ALP MPs such as Chifley and Evatt were financially independent and Liberal and Country Party members from professional backgrounds or from the land tended to be better off than most Labor men.

Parliament was in recess and MPs were in their electorates when Chifley released the press statement on bank nationalisation. There was no talk of abolishing the banks before backbenchers left Canberra so the announcement surprised them as much as anyone. Some Government MPs were frustrated with the lack of warning and not knowing what the Prime Minister was thinking. They would remain ignorant until they returned to Canberra in the spring. In the meanwhile they faced angry deputations, phone calls, telegrams, letters and petitions. Tasmanian Labor MP Gil Duthie wrote that "the enemies of Labor came out of the woodwork. The lukewarm became fanatics overnight. The fence-sitters became violent antagonists. Only dyed-in-the-wool Laborites remained unmoved and loyal."[2]

In 1947 few Australians could pick up the phone and call their MP or senator. Phones were scarce and there were tens of thousands of people on the waiting list to have a phone installed in their home or business. Even so telephone networks between big cities and major regional centres were often congested. A telegram was the fastest way for a voter to make their local MP know their feelings on an issue. A person went to their local post office, scribbled a few sentences on a blank yellow form and paid a few pennies for each word. A counter clerk arranged to dispatch their message by morse code, teleprinter or teletype to the post office closest to its final destination and from there a telegram boy couriered it by bicycle

---

1 *Sun* (Sydney), 14 November 1949, p. 12.
2 Duthie, p. 43.

to the receiver. It took just a few hours to go from sender to receiver.

Immediately after the Prime Minister's 16 August press statement, forty telegrams arrived at Parliament House. All supported nationalisation. Then a barrage of hostile telegrams began arriving and soon those opposed to the bank scheme were spending nearly £2,000 a week (over $160,000 today) on a telegraphic torrent directed at the national capital.[1] During the first week that MPs were back in session, the Canberra Post Office received more letters and telegrams than it had in twenty years.[2] Staff worked fourteen-hour days, and exhausted postal workers sent their own telegram to Chifley complaining about their workload.[3] Only one in every twenty telegrams favoured nationalisation, and their terse comments ranged from "'Communists rule the Labor Government and you are in that boat'" to the more temperate "Our federal representative is expected to oppose bank nationalisation".[4]

Letters completed this bombardment. A letter took longer than a telegram to reach an MP but allowed a voter to say much more. The volume of protest letters was so great there was a temporary shortage of envelopes and one cynic suggested the Government had deliberately cut off supplies of envelopes to stem the flow.[5] Twenty-five Victorian MPs shared rooms in Melbourne and normally an MP might get ten letters a day. Now they received five times that number and the officer in charge noted that, judging by the handwriting, many were from women.[6]

Letters arrived in all sorts of formats. Some appeared to have been hastily scrawled under a hurricane lamp in a bush shack. A few were neatly typed and with official-looking crests. Some letters were templates duplicated from mimeograph and stencil machines. The Fighting Services Political Association of Western Australia published protest coupons in newspapers and invited veterans to clip and post them to Canberra.[7]

Most writers were courteous. They rejected the Government's plan and demanded a referendum. Occasionally a correspondent threatened that if an MP did not oppose nationalisation the writer would work to unseat him at the next election. The emotions in Dorothy Tangney's mailbags were typical of what MPs were exposed to. The Senator from

---

1 *Daily Telegraph* (Sydney), 16 September 1947, p. 1.
2 *Mercury* (Hobart),16 September 1947, p. 4.
3 *Herald* (Melbourne) 16 September 1947, p. 3.
4 Commonwealth, *Parliamentary Debates*, House of Representatives, 5 November 1947, 1709 (Edgar Russell MP).
5 *Telegraph* (Brisbane), 14 October 1947, p. 2.
6 *Herald* (Melbourne), 13 September 1947, p. 3.
7 *West Australian* (Perth), 11 September 1947, p. 8.

Western Australia got protests from farmers, wool merchants, veterans, road boards, hospital committees, pastoral unions, citizens' groups, families and individuals. One woman wrote: "These past years have been trying for all, but terrible for women. I ask you to please do your utmost to stop nationalisation of banking and urge you to vote against it. Almost everyone has someone dear to them who will have their lives again disorganised should this come about." Occasionally there was encouragement. Thirty-two voters from the wheatbelt towns of Narrogin and Kulin urged Tangney to support the Government and a few unions and party loyalists congratulated the ALP for its bold banking measure.[1]

Initially Labor MPs tried to answer telegrams and letters but were overwhelmed by the volume. When they did reply their responses ranged from polite to contemptuous. Nelson Lemmon, the MP for Katanning in Western Australia, received a telegram from the Katanning Freedom League inviting him to attend a public meeting to explain the Government case. Lemmon stiffly replied that he would give a full account of the Government's intentions at the next election. When pressed he dismissively said the League should listen to the debate coming up in Parliament.[2] The Minister for Commerce, Reg Pollard, replied to one bank officer: "Your assurance that you will do your utmost in the Ballarat electorate to remove me as the Ballarat representative means nothing to me … in any case I owe nothing to you as far as my previous elections are concerned as no doubt you always voted anti-Labor." The bank officer promptly handed Pollard's letter to Menzies who read it at a protest meeting in Ballarat.[3]

By mid-September trolleys piled with telegrams and letters trundled through the corridors of Parliament House and ministerial offices reported that "the pressure of protests is extremely heavy".[4] Then the petitions arrived.

At Federation the Commonwealth Parliament established the petition as a way for citizens to request a course of action or ask Parliament to redress a grievance. For the first three decades the House of Representatives received a smattering of petitions each year and fewer still in the Senate. In 1947 the House received ninety-two anti-nationalisation petitions.[5] The largest had hundreds of thousands of signatures and the smallest bore sixteen names. In one way or another each declared there was no mandate

---

1 Papers of Dame Dorothy Margaret Tangney, 1938-1986 (Manuscript) NLA MS 7564, Box 24.
2 *West Australian* (Perth), 27 September 1947, p. 16.
3 *Argus* (Melbourne), 12 September 1947, p. 1.
4 Letter: Cox to Murdoch, 11 September 1947.
5 May, p. 23.

for a bank takeover and each demanded a referendum. A petition from the Prime Minister's own electorate demanded the banks not be touched until the issue was decided at an election.[1] Only four petitions were tabled in the Senate because there the ALP had an overwhelming majority. Unsurprisingly all supported bank nationalisation and were from ALP branches or unions.

On the day Parliament resumed, the Opposition tabled five protest petitions in the House of Representatives. Each was solemnly received and duly recorded. Soon there were so many petitions they hardly attracted attention and one minister quipped, "Give us this day our daily petition."[2] Some Opposition MPs seemed to attract petitions. Archie Cameron of the Liberal Party and the Country Party's Larry Anthony tabled a third of all petitions. None were from Queensland, presumably because protesters in that state were too busy sending 12,000 letters to Canberra.[3] Petitions needed to be correctly formatted before they could be tabled in Parliament so the Opposition arranged for poorly designed petitions to be handed to the Prime Minister. Chifley made no commitment to read any of them, even one that completely covered his desk.

The banks quickly realised petitions were a convenient way for people to record their disapproval of Labor's announcement. Bank officers placed petitions on the counters of branches around the country and in some areas set up tables on the street or visited workplaces and shops to collect signatures. The United Bank Officers' Association in New South Wales (UBOA (NSW)), the union representing bank officers in the state, organised a petition with half a million signatures.[4]

Victorian and Tasmanian bank officers organised a "monster" petition and invited people to drop into their local bank branch to add their names to one of thousands of printed petition forms. In some areas 2,000 people a day signed these forms and eventually the petition had hundreds of thousands of names. The *Argus* said it could be the largest petition ever prepared in the Commonwealth and there was even talk of sending it to King George VI, though it was unclear what the Sovereign was expected to do with such a document.[5]

The reaction of Government MPs to this immense flood of letters, telegrams and petitions was to discount what landed in their in-trays. MPs

---

1 *Canberra Times* (ACT), 15 September 1947, p. 1.
2 *News* (Adelaide), 26 September 1947, p. 3.
3 Liberal Party Press Statement, 2 October 1947, NLA MS 5000/ Banking, 1946-1960 (8) (File), Box 1232.
4 *Sydney Morning Herald* (Sydney), 3 October 1947, p. 1.
5 *Argus* (Melbourne), 9 September 1947, p. 17.

said they knew their electorates and these protests did not reflect local feelings. They treated with suspicion any letter with similar handwriting or in matching envelopes or sent from the same town. There were claims that bank managers bullied customers into signing petitions or forced staff to chase signatures. Some said petitions were circulated in school yards and the same people signed the same petition multiple times. Perhaps the haughtiest dismissal was that people did not understand what they were signing. When a petition from the Northern Territory was tabled, Arthur Calwell called out, "How many Aborigines signed it?" referring to the fact that Indigenous people had no right to vote.[1] The Minister responsible for the Australian Capital Territory refused to accept petitions from Canberra residents.[2]

Labor MPs and Senators returned to Canberra before Parliament was due to sit. As they approached Parliament House they were confronted by demonstrators and cars festooned with signs such as "Hands off the people's money" and "Stop the bank grab". Three sedans had ferried a bank officer's petition to Canberra the previous day. Twenty volunteers divided the document into electorates so they could give MPs a tailored version with familiar names. As Labor members arrived, bank officers ambushed them with these customised petitions. One banker even entered Labor's meeting room and handed out protest letters and petitions. The Clerk of the House of Representatives politely evicted him but promised to deliver his offerings to any MP he had missed.

The meeting of the Labor Caucus before Parliament sat was the largest gathering of ALP parliamentarians in Canberra. Rarely had a party meeting attracted so much interest. Though the Caucus rarely meddled in the government's daily affairs it was no rubber stamp. Caucus approval was needed before a proposal became government policy. It could revise or block whatever a minister presented but when a decision was made everyone had to support it. That day's Caucus agenda was busy and bank nationalisation was the last item of the day. For the seventy members attending this was their first opportunity to ask questions, debate the issue and then decide for themselves if what the Prime Minister wanted was worth the backlash they faced.

Around 8 p.m. Caucus began to discuss Chifley's bank proposal. Evatt was abroad so Senator Nick McKenna, the acting Attorney General, outlined the banking legislation the Prime Minister intended to present

---

1 *Northern Star* (Lismore), 4 October 1947, p. 1.
2 *Press* (New Zealand), 17 September 1947, p. 7.

to Parliament. Members heard him in silence and then Chifley spoke. He said the takeover would be a complex undertaking and would be done in stages. The first stage would take one or two years during which the private banks would become agents of the Commonwealth Bank. Managers and staff would remain with their banks and Treasury officials would be placed on the boards of the private banks to ensure they complied with instructions. The Prime Minister said compensating the private banks would cost around £100 million. This would come from the special deposits held by the Commonwealth Bank and into which the private banks had to lodge funds. The banks would effectively fund their demise. Chifley assured members the Constitution allowed for the bank takeover and finished by inviting MPS to express their views. Greying Melbourne MP Frank Brennan was the sole objector. A former Attorney General, Brennan told his colleagues "the Australian Labor Party has foundered on the rock of experimental financial policy before" and warned nationalisation could cost Labor the next election.[1]

Around 10 p.m. cheers broke out when Caucus unanimously endorsed bank nationalisation. It was a safe decision for Chifley, Evatt and other Labor MPs with "sandbagged" seats and large majorities. It was far riskier for men like Les Haylen who held the seat of Parkes by just 164 votes and former timber cutter Jim Hadley who won Lilley by not much more in 1946. Yet even MPs in such marginal seats applauded the decision. Haylen excitedly declared that Chifley had taken "the holy ikon of socialism off the walls of Caucus and marched with it into the House".[2]

In hindsight it seems astonishing Caucus took this monumental step after little more than two hours of discussion. Yet it was understandable given the collective life experiences of Labor members, the internal discipline that bound them together and Chifley's prominence in Caucus. Older members, like Brennan, Evatt and Chifley, had lived through the depression before Federation, the First World War, the Great Depression and more recently the Second World War. Younger members like Dorothy Tangney and Fred Daly had sad memories of the Depression and the war.

Two generations of Australians had been robbed of opportunities and the nation had been deprived of the full use of their talents. Now this was a chance to launch Australia into its greatest era and build a future worthy of past sacrifices. Chifley said as much during the 1946 election when he described Australia as on the threshold of a "wondrous commercial and

---

1 *Economist* (UK), 10 January 1948, p. 65.
2 Haylen, p. 31.

industrial age". He went to that election with a vision of unprecedented and improved social, health and education services and a resettlement scheme for veterans superior to what the original Anzacs had received.[1] He presented a bold vision which demanded Government intervention in the economy.

Apparently Caucus did not go into detail on how to present the idea of bank nationalisation to the public or to consider how the country's bankers might react to being driven out of business. It accepted what had been briefed and did not ask for a blueprint or timetable of the bank takeover. It was four weeks since Chifley's momentous announcement but the public and the Party had seen little detail. Still the Parliamentary Labor Party supported Chifley. No one in its ranks could challenge Chifley's knowledge of economics and government administration nor match his reputation for financial matters. Caucus members also knew that when finances were on the agenda, the Prime Minister gave little away but courtesy.

Caucus also respected Chifley's political skills. He had won the 1946 election and guided the ALP to an unprecedented third term in government. The Party had a majority in the House and dominated the Senate with a 30-member majority. This Government was the longest-serving and most disciplined Labor administration since Federation. While Chifley was Prime Minister there was not a single dismissal, resignation from the ministry or instance of a member crossing the floor.

Being likeable is important in politics and Ben Chifley was surpassingly likeable. He was straightforward, easy to deal with, and used the robust humour of the railyard and the union hall to smooth relationships. "His unfailing cheeriness and good nature enabled him to win the affection of his team."[2] The Prime Minister listened to his associates and respected their opinions but ultimately his ideas mostly prevailed. His colleagues could rely on him to put party interests ahead of his own and knew he would doggedly pursue what he believed was best for Australia. In a profession abundant with egos, Chifley showed no vanity or self-importance.

Notwithstanding the merits of bank nationalisation and Chifley's virtues, the Caucus had little choice but to support the Prime Minister. His press statement backed them into a corner. He had not consulted them beforehand and whether by design or convenience Evatt's task force had worked in secret in Sydney. If the Caucus ordered a rethink or

---

[1] *Border Morning Mail* (Albury), 3 September 1946, p. 6.
[2] *Canberra Survey* (Canberra), 17 June 1948, p. 5.

a halt now, the Prime Minister, the Government and the Party would be supremely embarrassed.

When the Caucus meeting ended, Chifley told waiting journalists the international situation was fraught with uncertainty and the transition from war to peace was not over yet. His Government would introduce legislation designed to promote and protect the welfare of the Australian community. He added somewhat deviously that voters had endorsed bank nationalisation at the 1946 election the year before. This was not true and neither was his suspicion that the private banks might issue fresh challenges to other banking legislation.

Liberal and Country Party MPs saw bank nationalisation as a chance to unite and bury past differences. They began the new parliamentary term with a no-confidence motion in the Government and by demanding an election or referendum on banking. They shouted there was no mandate for any takeover and it was a cynical abuse of power. "For 45 minutes Robert Menzies spoke of dictatorship, tyranny, political fraud, despotism, oppression, serfdom and the invasion of the affairs of private individuals."[1] Labor had a majority in the House and easily defeated the motion. Still the Opposition had shown it would use every parliamentary ploy to stall or kill the Government's plans.

The Prime Minister told Parliament there would be no referendum on banking.[2] That was clever given the deep passions the issue had stirred and because Australians had traditionally shown a reluctance to hand more powers to the Commonwealth. The biggest hurdles to a successful referendum were the constitutional requirement to have a majority of voters in a majority of states vote Yes. And history showed a referendum was likely to fail if the opposition resisted it. The Government's recent record on referendums was also discouraging. The Curtin and Chifley Governments had presented various referendum questions in 1944 and then in 1946 but only one succeeded.

---

1 Duthie, p. 48.
2 *Sydney Morning Herald* (Sydney), 18 September 1947, p. 1.

9 One-Bank Town

"Plans for the conduct of business under nationalisation must developed to the utmost prior to the takeover date."[1]

The Government introduced the 1947 Banking Bill on 15 October 1947. The commercial radio networks offered to broadcast Chifley's and Menzies' speeches live but the Government opted for the ABC, because it guaranteed to broadcast the entire debate – every speech by every member.[2] A massive audience was expected when the Prime Minister spoke and Labor MPs were told to advise their constituents to tune in.

At 8.36 p.m. the House of Representatives was packed as the Prime Minister rose to speak. Every MP was in the chamber. Lobbyists, public servants, union officials and ordinary citizens queued for more than an hour for a place in the small public gallery. Extra seating was laid out for senators, diplomats and VIPs and fifty-seven journalists crammed into the press gallery above the Speaker's chair. Staff clustered around amplifiers in Kings Hall and listened over internal speakers throughout the building. The banks sent representatives with instructions to immediately phone through the key points from the Prime Minister's speech. A car idled outside ready to speed printed copies of the bill to the banks in Sydney.[3]

The Prime Minister began by placing twenty-two typed pages on the ornate despatch box on the long polished table in the middle of the chamber. Robert Menzies sat opposite him. Behind them were their ministers, shadow ministers and MPs. Chifley began nervously but calmed as he went along. For the next sixty-five minutes the House listened in silence to the longest parliamentary speech in Ben Chifley's career.

The Prime Minister said Australia was entering a golden age of national development but to achieve this and steady the country against future instability the Government needed proper financial powers. He recalled Labor's misgivings about the performance of the banks during the Depression and said "the Government is convinced that under public ownership the banking system will have immense opportunities for serving Australia".[4] He outlined how bank nationalisation would work,

---

[1] RBAA: C.3.22.3.24 Research Department – Legislation Nationalisation of Banking 1947–1949, 1947, p. 24.
[2] *Newcastle Herald and Miners' Advocate* (Newcastle), 9 October 1947, p. 1.
[3] *Daily Telegraph* (Sydney), 19 October 1947, p. 27.
[4] Commonwealth, *Parliamentary Debates*, House of Representatives, 15 October 1947, 796 (J. B.

how the Commonwealth Bank would acquire the private banks and at the same time safeguard the rights of customers and the entitlements of private bank staff. The banks and their shareholders would receive fair compensation but the Government would limit drawn-out negotiations and litigation and penalise any bank that resisted the takeover. The Prime Minister did not mention the public servants and parliamentary officers who took his barren press statement and turned it into a twenty-one-page plan.

An estimated audience of one million Australians heard the Prime Minister's speech and Labor MPs cheered and rushed forward to congratulate Chifley when he finished. Some said it was his finest speech. The Prime Minister quietly returned to his office, made a pot of tea and resumed work. Admirers telegraphed their congratulations to Parliament House. Radio personality Cliff Cary wrote, "Being employed in radio I don't very often listen to the radio but last night I heard your address on the ... nationalisation of banking. May I congratulate you on what I consider to be one of the sincerest talks I have heard broadcast. It is good to know that in Parliament we have men prepared to be just to all and give most thought to the little people."[1]

Reaction from Chifley's opponents was as quick as it was predictable. McConnan said Chifley's bank grab was a misuse of government power. Menzies predicted the upcoming debate on the bank bill would be as bitter as any in an Australian parliament. A week later it was Menzies' turn to reply. Again, the House was packed and there was a vast radio audience. Liberal officials had alerted major newspapers to what Menzies would say and some had already published his main points. The Opposition Leader spoke twenty minutes longer than the Prime Minister while Chifley and his ministers listened politely. Some Labor men took notes.

Menzies punched hard from the start. Eloquent and forensic, he occasionally thumped the table or pointed an accusatory finger at those opposite. He declared the banking bill was the "most far-reaching, revolutionary, unwarranted and un-Australian measure in the Federal Parliament's history". It would lead to "a second battle for Australia" and was a giant step towards socialism. The Government had no mandate to dismantle the banking system and only an election or a referendum could settle the issue. Continuing this theme he called on Victorians, who were due for a state election the following month, to "cast a popular vote on this

---
Chifley, Prime Minister).
1   Cary to Chifley, 16 October 1947, L. F. Crisp Papers, NLA, MS 5243/20/63/2.

revolutionary measure".¹ Throughout his speech Menzies defended the performance of the banks. Liberal MPs were delighted with their leader and when he finished, many rushed from the chamber to praise Menzies' performance to journalists. Well-wishers sent telegrams, and morning papers published the speech in full. Some Labor members conceded Menzies had spoken powerfully if a bit too long.

The debate on bank nationalisation was of Wagnerian proportions. It started on 15 October 1947 and ended on 11 December and all but four MPs took part.² Even South Australian MP Edgar Russell, who rarely spoke in the House, gave a 12,000-word speech. Most days the public gallery was packed and visitors booked out hotels and boarding houses for miles around.³ MPs prepared thoroughly for the debate, knowing people back home were tuned to the ABC. They spiced their speeches with facts, statistics, personal stories, anecdotes and inspiring quotes. Fred Daly regarded his bank nationalisation speech as his finest. Chifley penned notes to those who spoke particularly well.

Labor men defended the bank takeover and said a publicly owned banking system was vital for national reconstruction and to maintain full employment, check inflation, and steady the economy as Europe and Asia teetered. The recent High Court banking decision had thrown doubt on the Government's capacity to manage the economy so nationalisation was necessary. Some painted a rosy picture of a future where the Commonwealth Bank would loan money based on the needs of ordinary people and to industries or businesses that contributed to the collective good.

The Commonwealth Bank would advise those on farms and in factories about best practices, new technologies, legal issues and economic trends. Labor members claimed Australians knew about Labor's nationalisation ambitions because they were in the ALP platform for decades and besides voters had re-elected Labor the year before. This was a convenient but misleading pretence. Few beyond the ALP knew about the Party platform and fewer still cared. There was hardly any press coverage that mentioned nationalisation during the 1946 election and only Doris Blackburn the independent MP had publicly supported it.⁴

---

1   Commonwealth, *Parliamentary Debates*, House of Representatives, 23 October 1947, 1273 (Robert Menzies, Leader of the Opposition).
2   Patrick Weller assisted by Beverley Lloyd, *Caucus Minutes 1901–1949*, Melbourne, Melbourne University Press, 1975, p. 429.
3   *Northern Star* (Lismore), 1 November 1947, p. 6.
4   Commonwealth, *Parliamentary Debates*, House of Representatives, 5 November 1947 (Doris Blackburn, Member for Bourke).

An officer from the National Bank was on hand in Canberra to offer material to Liberal and Country Party speakers and senior bank men came to town to brief them.[1] When it came their turn to speak Opposition MPs slammed the bill as dictatorial and socialist and demanded an election or referendum. Many defended the performance of the banks and asked why nationalisation was necessary when the Commonwealth Bank already controlled the currency, foreign exchange and interest rates and managed investment and credit policies.[2] Through the Commonwealth Bank the Government had as much power as it could ever need.

The debate was long and robust, with frequent eruptions. Les Haylen recalled, "The Speaker used his hammer like an auctioneer's gavel; division bells were ringing incessantly; the sergeant at arms was taking out prisoners like a village cop at a dance and points of order flew thick and fast." Three members were expelled from the Chamber and three offered to step outside and fight anyone who would "like a go".[3]

The most inflammatory contribution came from the Speaker of the House, John Solomon Rosevear. He had been the Speaker since 1943 and there were rumours he wanted to replace Chifley when he retired. Opposition members said Rosevear was partisan and inflexible and had a "taste for the grog".[4] At one point Rosevear handed over his duties and descended into the well of the House to speak on the legislation. Usually the Speaker did not participate in a debate unless it concerned the running of the House. Rosevear had spoken from the floor of the House or in committee a few times but what came next was beyond ordinary.

Rosevear accused the justices of the High Court of making a political decision when they delivered their verdict on the 1945 Bank Act. Questioning their capacity he said, "I have a fundamental objection to people in a state of senility due to old age being continued in positions where they can frustrate the will of the people as expressed in a popular vote."[5] On another occasion he accused Menzies of having a "yellow streak". These extraordinary outbursts were not in keeping with the dignity of the Speaker's place in the Parliament and Rosevear was condemned

---

1   A. H. B. Jones, Bank of New South Wales Melbourne to R. R. McKellar, Bank of New South Wales, 16 September 1947, Westpac Group Archives, WGA/Nationalisation of Banking.
2   Commonwealth, *Parliamentary Debates*, House of Representatives, 28 October 1947, 1382, (Dame Enid Lyons, Member for Darwin).
3   Haylen, p. 32.
4   Frank Bongiorno, "Rosevear, John Solomon (Sol) (1892–1953)", *Australian Dictionary of Biography*, National Centre of Biography, Australian National University, https://adb.anu.edu.au/biography/rosevear-john-solomon-sol-11565/text38690, published online 2021, accessed online 4 April 2022.
5   *Age* (Melbourne), 14 November 1947, p. 1.

inside and beyond Parliament. Critics said his behaviour showed Labor's arrogance after so long in office.

The final vote in the House of Representatives was never in doubt and on 11 November the bank nationalisation bill passed. The following night Labor MPs met to discuss ways to counter the press campaign that had enveloped the debate and created a "war of nerves". Caucus considered printing leaflets, radio broadcasts, campaigning in electorates and a propaganda committee to manage communications. Other suggestions were to hire a research officer to help with speeches and to add publicity officers to the Prime Minister's Department. Someone thought releasing more newsprint to papers that supported Labor would be a good idea. Backbenchers were worried about the furore the issue had raised. Still, Chifley deferred the matter and defiantly declared he "would march on and would not falter in the fight".[1] Nothing was done to ease concerns and ways of improving communications were still being discussed a year later.

The *Sydney Morning Herald* described the post-war Senate as a "servile institution" because the ALP held thirty-three of its thirty-six seats. This meant the fate of the bill was never in doubt. The three senators who made up the Opposition were granted extra speaking time but their contributions were no match for the speeches from the Government side. The Senate made some minor amendments, otherwise the bill passed unscathed. The last hope to save Australia's private banks now rested with the Governor-General who had to provide royal assent to the legislation on behalf of the Sovereign. Only then the bill would become law.

William John McKell was only the second Australian to be Governor-General.[2] From a working-class background and with a broad accent, McKell was a footballer, boxer, boilermaker and union secretary before he was elected as a Labor MP to the New South Wales Parliament. Eventually he became a successful Premier and worked closely with Chifley during the war. In 1946 he announced his retirement from politics and very shortly afterwards King George VI, on Chifley's recommendation, commissioned McKell as Australia's twelfth Governor-General.

McKell's appointment was widely criticised. He was seen as too close to Labor politics and critics said the former train driver (Chifley) had appointed the former boilermaker (McKell) to do his bidding. Labor supporters however saw his advancement as "working-class boy makes good". Initially critical, Menzies accepted the situation once McKell was

---

1 Weller and Lloyd, p. 435.
2 Sir Isaac Alfred Isaacs was the first Australian appointed as Governor-General and served from 1931 to 1936.

sworn in. Still some Liberals were not so accommodating and refused to go to Government House.

The new Governor-General became the focus of last-minute attempts to stop nationalisation. The Royal Society of St George, the British Empire Union of Australia and other conservative organisations petitioned him to withhold royal assent. A delegation from Western Australia flew to Canberra to present McKell with a gold pen and a petition with 50,000 signatures damning bank nationalisation.[1] The UBOA (NSW) wrote to the Governor-General asking him to direct the Prime Minister to find out what Australians thought before he moved on the banks. The press canvassed opinions on McKell's constitutional options to delay or block the legislation, although his choices were limited. Since 1901 only one bill had failed to receive royal assent and eleven bills had been returned to Parliament for amendment.[2]

As soon as parliamentary formalities were completed, a courier took the necessary paperwork to Government House at Yarralumla. McKell was not about to buck precedent and at 5.25 p.m. on 27 November he took a black-barrelled fountain pen from his suit jacket and signed and stamped four copies of the bill. At 8 p.m. the legislation was published in a special edition of the Commonwealth Gazette. It was just over a hundred days since Chifley issued his press statement.

The Government had previously agreed it would refrain from acting on the legislation for forty-eight hours to give the private banks sufficient time to lodge an injunction with the High Court.[3] With the ink barely dry on the paperwork the banks lodged an appeal with the High Court which triggered a legal battle that would consume much of the attention and energy of the Chifley Government for the next two years.

With the divisive bill now law the Government should have ended 1947 buoyant and energised. Instead it was battered and bruised. Its handling of the nationalisation issue had been flatfooted, uninspiring and confusing. While the passions of the last four months had shocked Government MPs, they had produced an "electrifying and consolidating effect" for the Opposition".[4] Robert Menzies was expansive at his end-of-year drinks party for the Press Gallery. He had lost in Parliament but

1   *Sydney Morning Herald* (Sydney), 2 October 1947, p. 1.
2   "Bills Reserved for the Sovereign's Assent and Bills Returned by the Governor-General with Recommended Amendments", Parliament of Australia. https://www.aph.gov.au/About_Parliament/House_of_Representatives/Powers_practice_and_procedure/Practice7/HTML/Appendices/Appendix19
3   *Examiner* (Launceston), 28 November 1947, p. 1.
4   Letter: Cox to Murdoch, 12 March 1948.

nevertheless was the man of the hour. The bank fight had revitalised his leadership, repaired relationships with the Country Party and provided an issue to carry the country's conservative forces through to the next election.

The mood at Labor's Christmas drinks was far different. Journalist Harold Cox observed, "The Prime Minister dispensed hospitality with his usual courtesy but he seemed preoccupied and tired. He disappeared before the function ended. There is no doubt the hostility provoked by the banking plan has surprised him." Cox reported to Sir Keith Murdoch, "The PM himself has aged amazingly this session ... He is completely played out and slumped off in appearance and vigour in this last week." Sir Earle Page, a medical practitioner and key Country Party figure, told Cox that Chifley was "far from very well".[1] As the year ended Chifley headed to New Zealand for his first holiday in seven years.

After the Banking Bill passed the next step was to develop the details of dismantling the private banking system. The Government wanted a smooth takeover with minimal disruption and inconvenience. The most damaging outcome would be a messy process marked by years of delay and legal obstruction. The new legislation was controversial enough for Australians but what if a ham-fisted grab of the three British-owned banks scared off foreign investors? And the situation in New Zealand was of special interest. Australian banks controlled 35 percent of that country's banking business, so what would happen to the New Zealand industry once those banks disappeared?[2]

Historically Australians were happy for their governments to supply essential services like electricity, water and sewerage. Only the state had the finances to build such expensive infrastructure and manage it in the public interest. However they were less certain when the state competed with the private sector and operated enterprises such as coal mines, timber mills, shipping services and trawler fleets. Such state-run businesses usually lost money.

In the past the Commonwealth had operated a shipping line but sold it off in 1928 after losing millions of pounds. The government-run Trans Australian Airlines operated at a loss despite lucrative government contracts for mail and passenger services. The Post Office was the most significant state enterprise but since it had no competition who could tell if it was efficient.

---

1 Letters: Cox to Murdoch, 27 October 1947 and 10 December 1947.
2 *Wanganui Chronicle* (NZ), 2 October 1947, p. 4.

There were a few success stories. The New South Wales State Brickworks made an 80 percent profit. Government butcher shops lowered beef prices in Queensland and the Commonwealth Clothing Factory made suits for returned soldiers at half the price of private factories. Would a government-run banking system benefit the country or would it create a nation of angry customers, farmers, factory owners, merchants, exporters, bank officers and shareholders?

Nationalizing an entire industry would be complex and confusing, so a key consideration was to make it gradual, consistent, and as easy as possible for everyone to understand. Nationalisation would start with a notice in the Commonwealth Government Gazette and instructions to each private bank from the Treasurer. At first the public would see only subtle changes. Customers would still bank at the same branch as before and deal with familiar managers and tellers. Passbooks, forms and paperwork would be identical except for an overprinted reference to the Commonwealth Bank. Outside their branches would be new brass nameplates and repainted signage but otherwise the banking experience would be as before. Importantly customers could expect their financial affairs to remain confidential, and if they were unhappy they could take their grievances to a special tribunal.

Each private bank would become a division of the Commonwealth Bank. The Bank of New South Wales would be the Bank of New South Wales Division of the Commonwealth Bank, the Union Bank would be another division of the Commonwealth Bank and so on for each private bank.

Banks would be told to hand over critical documentation to the Commonwealth Bank which would manage nationalisation on behalf of the Federal Government. This documentation would include their share registers, staff lists and reports on deposits, liabilities, assets, securities, investments, reserves, loans and advances and a stocktake of the coins, notes and bullion in their vaults.[1] The Government and the Commonwealth Bank would use this data to calculate compensation for each bank which would then have sixty days to agree to a compensation package. Or the private banks could appeal to a special federal court of claims established under the legislation. If all else failed the Commonwealth Bank would simply take over unwilling institutions.

The boards of the private banks would be replaced by Treasury officials and senior bank executives chosen by the Government. The

---

1 RBAA: Secretary's Department; S-d-152, Secretary's Department – Banking Legislation – Banking Act 1947 – Section 54 – Nationalisation Plans – July 1949, 1949, p. 56.

former directors were to be paid up to two years' remuneration for their unexpired terms. The new boards, being government appointed, were unlikely to fund lawsuits against the Government and they would not have the old boy links private bankers had enjoyed with their peers in other parts of the economy.

The thousands of men and women who worked for the private banks would go to work as usual but as well as their normal duties they would be obliged to help with the dismantling of their banks. Things would quickly unravel if bank officers resisted the takeover, so the legislation provided heavy punishments for those who did not cooperate. The Government might tolerate industrial disruption by coal miners, wharf labourers or train drivers but a bank officer could be held in contempt of court and his defiant bank penalised £10,000 a day for obstruction.

Bank officers would need to make critical career decisions before their employers ceased to exist. They could be absorbed into the Commonwealth Bank, seek employment in one of the smaller state banks that were exempt from nationalisation or they could quit banking altogether. A transfer to the Commonwealth Bank came with a guarantee that existing seniority, salary, leave, pension and other entitlements would be preserved. Arguably junior bank officers would be better off because the Commonwealth Bank paid lower grades marginally more and the benefits were better. A three-person committee in each private bank would monitor the entitlements of emigres to the Commonwealth Bank which would gain a sudden windfall of highly experienced bank officers.

How long these safeguards would last was anyone's guess. During the Depression the State Bank of New South Wales had been forced to merge with the Commonwealth Bank and the promotion prospects of many transferees had withered over time. John Dedman's wartime rationalisation program had closed branches and redeployed staff, but in 1947 some former bank managers, accountants and specialists still waited for their seniority to be restored.

A small cadre of managers in each private bank would remain as a rear guard to safeguard the interests of shareholders. There were fifty thousand investors and many relied on their annual dividends to boost their income or provide a pension. The Commonwealth Bank was said to have spent £100,000 to purchase bank shares under dummy names before Parliament passed the legislation but this was not successful and criticised when it became public.

The Government planned to buy shares for what they were worth the day before the Prime Minister's press statement, and the Commissioner of Taxation proposed that shareholders would pay no tax if they cashed in their shares within an agreed timeframe. Hopefully this would motivate them to sell and spare the Tax Office the monumental effort of calculating the tax liability of tens of thousands of shareholders.[1] Once an investor agreed to sell, the mechanics were straightforward. The private banks would send out a letter informing shareholders of their rights and advise they had sixty days to sell their shares. Investors would hand in their share certificates at their local branch or Commonwealth Bank and receive an interim payment within three months. The final settlement would follow shortly afterwards. Australian investors could be paid in cash or the equivalent amount in government bonds. English shareholders could be paid in pounds sterling.[2] Despite these inducements most investors watched warily and waited before they committed to a course of action.[3] Government lawyers anticipated there would be numerous court cases from angry shareholders claiming they would have divested earlier if they had known the Government's intentions or from those who would not accept the August 1947 valuation.

There were even greater challenges in dealing with the private banks. They would never agree to be part of anything that resembled a fire sale. They would demand premium price for their projected earnings, brand equity, goodwill and the estimated £20 million they had locked away in real estate, vehicles, safes, furniture, firearms, typewriters and teapots throughout Australia, the United Kingdom, New Zealand and the Pacific.

Calculating the value of the assets of the private banks would be an immense task and involve valuers, solicitors, photographers, title searchers, inspectors and tax examiners. The Government planned to use officers from the Commonwealth Bank and the government teams in each capital city that had been responsible for acquiring land and equipment during the war and managing compensation claims. Those teams were still in place, handling the disposal of surplus military equipment and assessing battle damage to the New Guinea and South Pacific economies. No one knew how long the valuation process would take but all agreed there would be endless litigation if it was mismanaged. The private banks had no intention of letting the Commonwealth determine their worth. Immediately after Chifley's press statement they retained the services of some of the country's

---
1 Memo: Income Tax Acquisition of Private Trading Banks by the Commonwealth Bank, 1 September 1947, Donald K. Rodgers Papers, NLA, MS 1536/Box 5.
2 RBAA: Secretary's Department; S-d-151, Secretary's Department – Banking Legislation – Banking Act 1947 – Section 53 – Nationalisation Plans – July 1949, 1949, p. 56.
3 Letter: Cox to Murdoch, 27 October 1947.

best commercial valuers, estate agents and auctioneers who were only too willing to help.[1] The Bank of New South Wales poached and appointed one of the Commonwealth's most senior valuers as its Chief Valuer. Mr J. F. Murray had fourteen years' experience and had written the *Principles and Practice of Valuation*, then the bible for Australian valuers.[2]

When the Commonwealth offered a compensation package to a private bank, it had sixty days to accept or appeal the figure to a Federal Court of Claims. This newly created body would have equivalent status to the Federal Arbitration Court and its decisions could not be appealed to the High Court. Critics claimed this was an unconstitutional arrangement and likely to face an early legal challenge if nationalisation went ahead.

The Commonwealth Bank plans for nationalisation were elaborate and ran to thousands of pages. Yet there was no communications strategy among this mountainous paperwork There were pious statements that the Bank must "reach as many persons in Australia as possible" and a folder of drily worded press statements, circulars and letters ready for release. But there were no master campaign plan, media schedules, division of responsibilities or budgets for advertising and public relations.[3] Apparently the Commonwealth Bank had no communications specialists to advise on such matters and perhaps expected the three-hundred strong Department of Information to win public support for its grand takeover. By 1947 the Department was a well-oiled bureaucracy and had executed some of the Government's most effective promotional campaigns during and after the war. Yet there is no record to suggest these experienced practitioners would be involved.

Although planning was as complete as it would ever be by April 1949, the Governor of the Commonwealth Bank recommended that any takeovers should wait until after the election later that year. It was sound advice. The private banks were still fighting nationalisation in the courts and had no incentive to cooperate until they knew the outcome of their legal challenges and the election results. If Labor lost the election the threat of nationalisation would disappear. But if the Government was returned the private banks would be little choice but to surrender.

Early in the planning process the Governor of the Commonwealth Bank said, "the current negotiations about nationalisation should

---
1 Bank of New South Wales letters to estate agents and auctioneers, 20–22 August 1947, WGA/Nationalisation of Banking.
2 *Mercury* (Hobart), 11 December 1947, p. 20.
3 RBAA: Secretary's Department; S-d-152, Secretary's Department – Banking Legislation – Banking Act 1947 – Section 54 – Nationalisation Plans – July 1949, 1949, p. 203.

not affect the cordial relationship between the Central Bank and the trading banks".[1] This was achieved and despite their profound policy differences, relations between the banks remained friendly. Yet as staff in the Commonwealth Bank toiled diligently on their plans, the men and women of the private banks worked as hard to make sure their efforts would never see the light of day.

---

1 RBAA: Research Department; C.3.6.19.2, Banking Section – Conferences with Private Banks, October 1946–November 1951, p. 205.

10 Banks Raise the Stakes

"The principles outlined by the Prime Minister, whatever form they ultimately take ... will deceive no one." [1]

The defence of Australia's banks was never a single or coordinated campaign. Rather, it was based on collaboration, loose networks and exploiting opportunities as they arose. The bankers in Melbourne and Sydney were obvious frontline warriors but others joined the fight for their own reasons.

Before Christmas 1947, the Bank of New South Wales and the Commercial Bank of Sydney mailed over half a million circulars to their customers and shareholders warning about a government banking monopoly and predicting nationalisation would end democracy in Australia. The Bank of New South Wales also sent a memo to its 600 branches instructing staff to "convince the public this [nationalisation] was the threat of a socialist revolution striking at the very roots of individual freedom". [2] Both banks advertised. One Commercial Bank newspaper ad screamed, "What more power does the Government want?" and asked readers to "protest to your Federal member now against the seizure of the Banks by the politicians". [3] A Bank of New South Wales ad warned that the socialization of banking threatens the freedom of every man, woman and child in the community, and an image of a black clenched fist dramatised the text.

Claud Victor Janes worked in the Economics Department of the Bank of New South Wales and was a key architect of the campaign. Janes, a long-serving and often cantankerous manager, had written three books on economics and was given remarkable latitude to discuss economics and finance in public. He published articles in Sydney newspapers and addressed service clubs, women's organisations and protest groups. [4] Janes directed the industrial-scale manufacturing of letters and material for the press and brought 2,000 subscriptions to the conservative magazine *Current Problems Digest*, which published page after page of anti-nationalisation editorials in each issue. [5]

1 *Barrier Miner* (Broken Hill), 18 September 1947, p. 3.
2 Reginald Frank Holder, *Bank of New South Wales: A History*, Sydney, Angus and Robertson, 1970, p. 26.
3 *Maryborough Chronicle* (Maryborough), 1 September 1947, p. 5.
4 A. G. L. Shaw, "Claud Victor Janes", *Australian Quarterly* 31, no. 2 (1959), p. 49.
5 Warwick Eather and Drew Cottle, "'The Mobilisation of Capital behind 'the Battle for Freedom':

The Sydney banks enlisted the support of organisations which opposed the Government's plan such as the Institute of Public Affairs (NSW) and the Australian Women's Movement Against Socialism (AWMAS). The Bank of New South Wales was particularly generous with the AWMAS, helping to pay for rent, rallies, staff and publications.[1] The Bank also helped lesser-known organisations like the Country Traders' Association with advertising and the printing and distribution of literature.[2]

There was support for Liberal and Country Party pamphlets, flyers and brochures and at the end of 1949 over half a million copies of third party literature were stored in the Bank's warehouse. The Bank also supported individuals like W. C. Wentworth, who was a zealous anti-Communist.[3] It printed and distributed 100,000 copies of a Wentworth pamphlet and, for a time, paid him to speak at protest rallies.[4]

Both Sydney banks sent organisers into the field to help towns and suburbs establish protest committees and allowed bank officers to join these organisations. Bank of New South Wales officers filled the secretary positions in half the protest organisations in the Riverina. By the end of 1947 the banks were spending so much money on local groups it was hard to distinguish between genuine community outrage and the machinations of bank staff at head office.[5]

The Melbourne banks seconded economists, administrators and a public relations officer to a central committee tasked with promoting the anti-nationalisation case, educating the public and coordinating campaign efforts. By the end of September 1947 the Committee had spent over £6,000 (around $500,000 today) on activities including dispatching officers to set up protest groups in marginal Victorian electorates.[6] The Freedom League in Warrnambool was the first of these groups and became a model for other areas.[7] There was also a strong focus on working with the press and funding talks by Leslie McConnan, Richard Casey and Archdeacon O'Donnell on radio stations throughout Victoria, Queensland, Tasmania and Western Australia.[8]

The Sydney Banks, the IPA and Opposition to the Australian Labor Party 1944-49", *Labor History*, no. 103 (November 2012), p. 177.
1 Eather and Cottle, "Sydney Banks and the IPA", p. 179.
2 Eather and Cottle, "Sydney Banks and the IPA", p. 177.
3 W. C. "Bill" Wentworth was a Liberal MP from 1949 to 1977.
4 Eather and Cottle, "Sydney Banks and the IPA", p. 178.
5 Eather and Cottle, "Sydney Banks and the IPA", p. 180.
6 Summary of Activities of The Banks' Central Committee, 10–27 September 1947, NABA/Bank Nationalisation, p. 5.
7 *Herald* (Melbourne), 23 September 1947, p. 8.
8 Summary of Activities of The Banks' Central Committee, 10–27 September 1947, NABA /Bank Nationalisation, p. 2.

The committee contracted a writer from the Melbourne *Herald* to produce articles for country papers and paid £200 a month (near $14,000 today) to the British Commercial News agency for media relations work that involved supplying pro-bank material to Australian and foreign newspapers.[1] There were posters, pamphlets, radio scripts, talk of a film and overtures to respected organisations such as the Country Women's Association, the Victorian Chamber of Commerce and Manufacturers and the Royal Automobile Club of Victoria. Around £56,000 (over $3.2 million today) was funnelled to the Liberal and Country Parties and bank officers were trained in public speaking to address community meetings.

The Bank of Adelaide was the smallest private bank so there was speculation it might be abolished first and then serve as the takeover model for the larger banks. Oscar Isaachsen was the General Manager and a colourful personality with a fondness for fine food, good cigars and racehorses. The energetic "Ike" was as committed to the anti-nationalisation fight as his peers in the eastern states. He established a "constitutional committee" of thirty eminent South Australians to advise on anti-nationalisation activities and fostered twenty-two citizen protest committees which received support with printing and advertising.[2]

The Melbourne and Sydney banks financed campaigns in Queensland, Western Australia and Tasmania. Queensland got about £50,000 and smaller amounts went to other states. An all-bank committee in Brisbane employed a former newspaper editor and worked with the Liberal and Country Parties. The Queensland banks were ready to fund anyone who could help their cause though there was less emphasis on sponsoring citizen protest groups.

Those who gained the most from the banks' efforts were the printers of Australia. The bank nationalisation episode was a "peerless season" for them as batch after batch and millions upon millions of protest booklets, circulars, flyers, letters, pamphlets and posters rolled off their presses.[3]

Traditionally, bank officers were politically neutral. It made little business sense to alienate customers by staff voicing their own opinions. Immediately after the Government announced its banking plan, the banks encouraged staff to "publicly or privately, personally or politically campaign against nationalisation".[4] Officers needed little urging. Though

---

1 A. H. B. Jones, Bank of New South Wales Melbourne to Thomas Heffer, General Manager Bank of New South Wales, 19 August 1947, WGA/GM102/30.
2 *Smith's Weekly* (Sydney), 26 February 1949, p. 19.
3 May, p. 25.
4 *News* (Adelaide), 20 November 1947, p. 2.

the vast majority were political novices, they were soon among the most zealous and best-organised activists in the country.

People in the lower echelons of the banks were generally the type of workers the ALP represented: clerks, juniors, machine operators, cleaners, drivers, messengers, night watchmen and typists. Yet staff at all levels overwhelmingly resisted nationalisation because it threatened their jobs. This was despite Government promises their entitlements would be safeguarded if they transferred to the Commonwealth Bank. One staff member noted, "The Government's promise is that officers shall not be employed under nationalisation at a disadvantage but there is no guarantee about future increments."[1] Opposition in the bank ranks was inflamed when Calwell and other ministers said managers were pressuring, bribing or tricking staff to protest.

The United Bank Officers' Association (UBOA) was the registered trade union which represented bank workers and had branches in each state. The Australian Council of Trade Unions (ACTU) and other unions were uneasy about the UBOA's ties to the banking industry so it sat on the fringes of the labour movement. The union and its members knew they could not expect the moral and industrial support other workers received when their jobs were endangered.

The UBOA head office in Melbourne managed national affairs and union business in Victoria and Tasmania. From the outset the national headquarters wanted no part in any anti-nationalisation campaign. It wanted to be able to lobby the Government and feared Canberra would stop listening if it organised protests. However the national body agreed that individual members and state bodies could speak out.

Stan Card was the General Secretary of the United Bank Officers' Association of New South Wales (UBOA NSW) which had 7,500 members in cities and towns across the State. New South Wales was the biggest and best-organised body mainly because of Card's years of banking and industrial relations experience, energy and his flair for public relations. The middle-aged, round-faced Secretary had started his banking career after the First World War and ended as a valuer for the Rural Bank. He relished his role as a full-time union official and would later boast he was the only union secretary to ever stand up to Ben Chifley.[2]

Card was adding the finishing touches to the latest edition of the Association's magazine when the Chifley press statement came out. He

---
1 *Press* (NZ), 5 November 1947, p. 6.
2 Stan Card received the Order of the British Empire in 1967 for his contribution to industrial relations.

immediately called the printers and ordered them to stop the presses. Then he sat down to write what may have been the first scathing editorial condemning the move. Within days he offered support to the Associated Banks and the Sydney banks and set up a "Nationalisation of Banking Sub Committee" to coordinate protests.[1] The Commercial Bank provided rooms for the new body at its George Street headquarters.

The Bank of New South Wales released Harry Jago to run this new committee on a full time basis. An Army veteran but a relative newcomer to banking, the thirty-four-year-old Jago had little experience with politics or public relations. Yet he and Card formed a most effective partnership. It seems that Card remained the principal union spokesperson while Jago was responsible for grassroots campaigning.[2] Jago led a small team of officers, also released from bank duties, that helped to establish citizen committees around the State, encouraged union members to be involved in protest activities and produced literature for members, kindred associations, newspapers and anyone else who could help.

The Sydney banks bankrolled Card and Jago and probably paid for the American ad agency J. Walter Thompson to help them. Certainly the ad agency was involved with the production of *The Way the Wind Blows*, a newsletter that provided information to the public and campaign updates to union members. When word got out that Card had money, other advertising and public relations agencies flooded him with offers to help with advertising, press relations, printing and signage.

Union members sent their own suggestions to the tireless Card. One put forward an ad calling on Australian men to protect their women from the humiliations women in Nazi Europe had suffered. A member from Manly suggested Card lampoon Dr Evatt because "ridicule is the handmaiden of justice". Others said bank officers should refuse to cash cheques for Chifley lovers and the Commonwealth Government. Others sent in ideas for banners, bands, freedom marches and talks in cinemas and dance halls.[3]

Card's earliest success was a "monster rally" in Sydney. The Moreton Bay figs, colonial pines and flowering palms in the Domain parklands were a popular backdrop for political gatherings. Card planned to use the rally to pressure Labor MPs to carefully consider what Chifley was

---

1 *Sydney Morning Herald* (Sydney), 12 February 1949, p. 3. From 1947 to 1949 the UBOA (NSW) protest machinery had several names: the Nationalisation of Banking Sub Committee, the Trading Banks Staff Central Organising Committee and the Bank Employees Committee.
2 *Sun* (Sydney), 4 September 1947, p. 2.
3 Australian Bank Officers' Association (NSW Division) General Correspondence, 1947-1948, N112-262, Noel Butlin Archives Centre (NBAC).

up to, and scheduled the event for the day before politicians returned to Canberra for the spring session of Parliament. The Association spent £250 on radio and newspaper advertising and printed 10,000 fliers which a plane would drop over the rally crowd.[1]

There was a tense lead-up to the rally. Two thousand bank staff met in the Bank of New South Wales foyer in Martin Place and were urged to attend the rally. Outside, UBOA members invited passers-by to sign a petition. Several Communists arrived for a confrontation but were quickly seen off. A day later twenty Communists picketed the Bank and there were rumours they planned to "do over" the bank officers collecting signatures.[2] An angry crowd gathered to heckle the Communists before police intervened. Two days before the rally an anonymous telephone caller warned Card to be careful and not to cross other unions that supported nationalisation. Card immediately told reporters about the threat and insisted his weekend rally would go ahead. He added that many UBOA members were veterans and were prepared to show their fighting spirit if necessary. Card seemed to enjoy the ballyhoo and was unconcerned the Communists had planned a rally in the Domain on the same day.

On Sunday bank officers from across Sydney and trainloads from the country made their way to the Domain. The veterans among them formed up and marched as a group "ready for the Reds". Forty police constables were on duty to separate the bankers and the Communists and plainclothes men mingled with both crowds. Patrol vans and police reinforcements stood ready.[3] Card had invited newsreel operators, photographers and reporters to cover the event and the 10,000-strong crowd.

At 3 p.m. Card and three union leaders clambered onto a small, raised platform to address the gathering. A loudspeaker van boomed their speeches across the Domain, drowning out the occasional heckler. Those on the platform said they spoke as bank officers and fellow Australians. They demanded a referendum and said the destruction of private banking would be a national calamity. Card's motion for a people's vote on nationalisation met with an ear-splitting "Aye". The bank men and few women in the crowd quietly dispersed when the meeting was over though some wandered across to see what was happening at the much smaller Communist rally. There was no trouble between the groups and the only mishap on the day was a sudden gust of wind which blew Card's

---

1 UBOA (NSW Division) Memorandum, 12 September 1947, NBAC N112-262.
2 *Otago Daily Times* (NZ),11 September 1947, p. 5.
3 *Sun* (Sydney), 13 September 1947, p. 1.

air dropped leaflets into Sydney Harbour.[1]

The rally was the biggest anti-nationalisation event and among the most significant gatherings in the Domain for many years. Card and Jago organised other events but none matched the size and drama of the demonstration in the Domain. The rally showed bank officers could organise, earn extensive and favourable press coverage and were prepared to confront the roughest of agitators. It inspired bank staff across the country.

Congratulations flowed into UBOA (NSW) headquarters but Card did not rest. The next day he reported the rally to the banks, union members and the other state associations and fired off telegrams and letters with details of the Domain resolution to the Governor-General, the Prime Minister and the Labor ministry. In the afternoon he farewelled a three-car convoy headed for Canberra which carried a petition bearing hundreds of thousands of names.

When the National Office of the UBOA refused to be part of an anti-nationalisation campaign, Victorian and Tasmanian officers were left without a platform for their protests. They responded by setting up the Bank Employee Protest Committee (BEPC) to coordinate their activities in both states. The Bank of New South Wales released G. W. Sneddon to serve as its full-time chairman and other banks detached officers. The ES&A Bank provided offices at its Collins Street headquarters.[2] In September the BEPC organised a mass petition with more than 300,000 signatures. When Labor senators claimed most bank officers supported nationalisation, Sneddon responded with another petition which showed 90 percent of Victorian and Tasmanian officers opposed state control.

In October the BEPC planned a rally in Melbourne and ran ads in the city's papers asking the public to bank early so staff could attend the meeting. The mood before the rally was grim. Days before, a bank officer in Ballarat was brutally bashed. The man was walking with his wife when three men taunted him over nationalisation and then attacked him. The bank veteran felled two assailants but the third bashed him with a piece of timber and he fell to the ground. It was the campaign's first instance of violence, and people worried there would be more trouble.[3]

On the afternoon of 13 October 2,000 bank officers (two-thirds of Melbourne's banking community) packed Princess Theatre in Spring Street. Women employed by the banks were there and wives, concerned about the

---

1 *Sydney Morning Herald* (Sydney), 15 September 1947, p. 1.
2 Letter A. H. B. Jones, Bank of New South Wales, Melbourne, to Chief Inspector Bank of New South Wales, Sydney, 30 August 1947, WGA/Bank Nationalisation Files.
3 *Telegraph* (Brisbane), 14 October 1947, p. 7.

impact nationalisation would have on their families, sat with their husbands. An overflow crowd listened to loudspeakers in the street outside.

The language inside the theatre was confrontational. Sneddon and three speakers told the audience Chifley had sentenced the trading banks to death and said bank officers could expect more physical threats. Conditions would deteriorate if bank officers were press-ganged into the Commonwealth Bank and some would be shanghaied to the backblocks to work in prefabricated shacks. The speakers had three simple messages. Be suspicious of Labor, oppose nationalisation, and use the forthcoming Victorian state election to oppose a bank takeover.[1]

Bank unions in other states did similar things. The UBOA (QLD) formed a committee with the banks to plan a state-wide campaign. The Committee President, H. C. Wood, said his organisation was a trade union and had the right to protect the industrial conditions of its 2,500 members. Western Australian officers formed an anti-nationalisation committee which said bank legislation threatened every Australian. It held a 600-strong meeting in October, approached employers around the state and formed a delegation to call on Chifley when he visited Perth. The contingent came away with no concessions or promises. The UBOA (SA) was divided. A vocal minority was keen to protest but the majority wanted the association to stay out of politics and focus on industrial issues. However individual South Australian members were free to protest.[2]

Commonwealth plans explicitly excluded state banks from nationalisation but those banks followed developments with keen self-interest. They stood to gain tens of thousands of new customers and a phalanx of experienced officers forced to leave their old banks. The Liberal governments in Victoria, South Australia and Western Australia saw a chance to use their state banks to checkmate Chifley.

The Western Australian Government allowed its Rural and Industries Bank (R&I) to capture any business the private banks might surrender. Premier Ross McLarty boasted that the R&I Bank could have more branches and staff and altered the bank's credit policies to support new customers from the mining industry. South Australian Premier Thomas Playford was prepared to amalgamate his two state banks to compete with the Commonwealth Bank. In Victoria a new Liberal Government said the state might create an entirely new bank to compete with the

---

1 *Argus* (Melbourne), 14 October 1947, p. 1.
2 Geoffrey H. Manning and Haydon R. Manning, *Worth Fighting For: Work and Industrial Relations in the Banking Industry in South Australia*, Adelaide, Australian Bank Employees Union, South Australia and Northern Territory Branch, 1989, p. 52.

Commonwealth Bank and there was talk of making the private banks agents of the State Savings Bank of Victoria. Tasmanian Labor Premier Robert Cosgrove had no plans for his state bank or the two small banks in Hobart and Launceston.

New South Wales Labor Premier James McGirr publicly supported bank nationalisation.[1] Nevertheless in December 1947 "Big Jim" introduced a bill that allowed the State's Rural Bank to expand its customer base beyond country people and agricultural organisations.[2] The Bank President had bolder ambitions. Should the private banks disappear he would buy up their branches, corral their customers, recruit their best officers and absorb their most lucrative accounts. The Rural Bank would become an escape tunnel for people fleeing the Commonwealth Bank.

Chifley was nearly speechless when he heard about these plans but the Premier reassured him that his government was only responding to community demand. "Big Jim's" motives however were more opaque. McGirr resented the fact that when William McKell resigned as Premier of New South Wales, some Chifley supporters tried to block his election as premier. As well McGirr believed the states would be more dependent than ever on Canberra if bank nationalisation went ahead and criticised Commonwealth imperialism at Commonwealth–State conferences. McGirr had little to lose since public sentiment in New South Wales was firmly against bank nationalisation.

---

1 David Clune, "McGirr, James (Jim) (1890–1957)", *Australian Dictionary of Biography*, National Centre of Biography, Australian National University, https://adb.anu.edu.au/biography/mcgirr-james-jim-10957/text19473, published first in hardcopy 2000, accessed online 4 April 2022.
2 *Otago Daily Times* (NZ), 6 December 1947, p. 8.

Ben Chifley was Treasurer during the Second World War and Australia's Prime Minister from 1945 to 1949. The driving force behind the post-war plan to take over the private banks, Chifley never wavered in his push to nationalise Australian banking.
Image courtesy of the National Library of Australia

At the onset of the Second World War, Robert Menzies was Australia's Prime Minister but he spent most of the war years in opposition. He capitalised on the public outcry over bank nationalisation to regain power in 1949. After successive election victories, Menzies became the country's longest-serving Prime Minister.
Image courtesy of the National Library of Australia

In 1947 Herbert 'Doc' Evatt served as Minister for External Affairs and Attorney-General. He assured the Labor Government that bank nationalisation was within the scope of the Australian Constitution. However, he was unsuccessful in defending the Government's legislation before the High Court of Australia and the Privy Council. Following Chifley's death, Evatt became Leader of the Federal Parliamentary Labor Party.
Image courtesy of the National Library of Australia

Richard Casey was the Federal President of the Liberal Party of Australia from 1947 to 1949. A tireless organiser and prolific fundraiser, he introduced American-style advertising and public relations into Australian politics. He served as a minister in the Menzies Government after 1949 and was the 16th Governor-General of Australia.
Image courtesy of the National Library of Australia

Leslie McConnan was the Chief Manager of the National Bank of Australasia, and from 1947 to 1949, was the Chairman of the Associated Banks. He directed the opposition of the banking industry to the Government's nationalisation plans with great energy. Known at the time as 'the man who saved the banks', McConnan's contribution to the battle of the banks was soon forgotten.
Image courtesy of the State Library of Victoria

The Head Office of the Bank of New South Wales was located in Martin Place, Sydney. Bank buildings conveyed authority, power and prestige and occupied prominent sites in cities and towns throughout Australia.
Image courtesy of the State Library of New South Wales

Millicent Preston Stanley led the Australian Women's Movement Against Socialism, which was pro-Empire, anti-Labor and opposed bank nationalisation. Although she was an excellent organiser, strong campaigner and a nationally recognised figure, the Liberal Party overlooked her as a Senate candidate in 1949.
Image courtesy of the State Library of New South Wales

Bank officers delivered protest petitions to Parliament House in Canberra in September 1947. They became energetic political activists from 1947 to 1949 and helped to defeat the bank nationalisation legislation and the Chifley Government.
Image courtesy of the State Library of New South Wales

The Australian banking industry engaged Garfield Barwick to challenge the bank nationalisation legislation in the High Court of Australia and the Privy Council. Barwick later served in the Menzies Government for eight years and became the Chief Justice of the High Court of Australia in 1964.
Image courtesy of the National Archives of Australia

Opposition Leader Ben Chifley was seen arriving at Parliament House in Canberra in 1950, accompanied by his press secretary, Don Rodgers. A very effective Prime Minister, Chifley had difficulties leading the Labor Party in opposition. He died 18 months after his government lost the 1949 election.
Image courtesy of the National Library of Australia

11 Allies and Opportunities

"Katanning Freedom League asks you to nominate speakers to put the case for the nationalisation of banks ... the League to arrange speakers for the case against."[1]

In September 1947 the Australian Congress of Trade Unions (ACTU) held its biennial congress in Melbourne. It was the biggest union gathering since the war and what was decided at the Congress would affect over a million unionists.

The Trades Hall in Melbourne was packed as delegates unanimously agreed to support nationalisation and passed a fulsome motion that said, "The proposal of the Federal Government to nationalise the banking system is one of the most progressive steps ever taken in the interests of the Australian people. It will give small farmers and business people protection from a small group of financiers, who exercise a monopoly control over large sections of the economic life of the community and will give the Government greatly added power to ameliorate the effects of the economic crisis and depression."[2] A delegate from the milk and ice-carters union said the coal and steel industries should be nationalised next and the congress agreed to ask the Government to broaden the nationalisation effort. The ACTU executive was instructed to develop a publicity campaign to support bank nationalisation.

The Trades and Labour Council (TLC) in New South Wales planned a £10,000 promotional effort funded by levies on unions and individual donations. The plan was to dispatch union officials throughout the state to arrange meetings, organise a mass petition and whip up support for the Government's program. The Australian Journalists Association was asked to help with media and publicity. In early October 300 union officials crowded into the TLC's Goulburn Street headquarters for a campaign launch where two pro-nationalisation bank officers addressed the crowd.[3]

The first event was a week later when the annual "Six Hour Day" procession was given a bank nationalisation theme. Unionists marched from Sydney Town Hall to the Sydney Showgrounds led by the Labor Premier and his Cabinet, three federal ministers and the Speaker of the House of Representatives. They were followed by unicycles, lorries, bands

---
1 *West Australian* (Perth), 27 September 1947, p. 16.
2 *Tribune* (Sydney), 24 September 1947, p. 7.
3 *Sydney Morning Herald* (Sydney), 3 October 1947, p. 4.

and marching contingents. On one float, unionists acted as portly bankers in top hats sitting around a table of food and wine while hungry workers looked on. A banner on the side of the truck said "Remember 1929-33 and support nationalisation". Arthur Calwell told a cheering crowd after the march, "We are in the process of plucking the fowl (with bank nationalisation) and not one feather will be put back."[1] Those present relished Calwell's colourful language but elsewhere in the community there was a fear that things would never be the same if the Government killed off the banks.

Fifty thousand unionists were expected at that procession but only a tenth of that number turned out. The largest contingent was 142 ironworkers and the *Sydney Morning Herald* pointed out the high ratio of marching bandsmen to marching unionists. Plainly the union numbers were below those at the bank officers' Domain rally a few weeks' earlier.[2] Days later Minister John Dedman launched the New South Wales campaign in favour of bank nationalisation but the event did not go well. The venue was in uproar as half the crowd cheered and the other half jeered Dedman. A hoax call brought three ambulances and a motorcycle police squad, further disrupting the meeting.

After this inglorious start the New South Wales union campaign seemed to limp long except in the Hunter Valley. There, the Newcastle Trades Hall Council arranged public and factory meetings, talks on the radio, coverage in its own newspaper and a petition that circulated in the centre of Newcastle on Friday and Saturday nights.[3]

The Queensland TLC committed to a propaganda campaign to which affiliated unions were asked to contribute £5 for every 1,000 members. Speaking notes were distributed to shop stewards for factory meetings, union officials toured the State, there was a radio campaign and special leaflets were planned for different communities. Like New South Wales the Queensland effort seemed to shuffle ahead with little serious effort to engage audiences beyond union members. Trades and Labour Councils in other states passed motions, planned events and called for donations but with few results to show. This was perhaps understandable in Victoria where unions suddenly found themselves in an unexpected state election.

Some individual unions were active. Chifley's alma mater, the Australian Railways Union, published a pamphlet, circulated petitions and held railyard and workshop meetings. Unions in Port Pirie held

---

1 *Queensland Times* (Ipswich), 6 October 1947, p. 1.
2 *Advertiser* (Adelaide), 4 October 1947, p. 1.
3 *Newcastle Morning Herald and Miners' Advocate* (Newcastle), 26 September 1947, p. 2.

meetings and Sydney waterside workers staged rallies as did textile workers in Goulburn and cabinet makers in Perth. Unions in Broken Hill told their members, with a hint of menace, that nationalisation was ALP policy and it would be unwise for anyone to oppose it. One union refused to take part. The Bridge and Wharf Carpenters' Union represented the painters on the Sydney Harbour Bridge, who had never been on strike. Its members were happy to paint the Bridge and for their union to mind its own business.[1]

Overall the effort of the union movement was ineffective. The ACTU's entire expense budget was £9,000 for 1947. The Melbourne banks spent nearly that amount in the first three weeks of their campaign and the banking industry could easily outspend the union movement.[2] While bank officers were fighting to save their jobs, nationalisation threatened no other union jobs. Could rank and file unionists see any personal benefit in abolishing the banks and where was the urgency to take to the barricades when a union-backed Labor Government was behind this radical change? Union excitement for bank nationalisation faded further when the Prime Minister told the unions to be careful what they did when his bank legislation came before the courts. The banks however felt no such inhibition at campaigning while the courts considered their case.

The organisational wing of the ALP had no serious plans to take the case for bank nationalisation to the people. Labor councils and branches passed motions and discussed campaigns but delivered little. Labor newspapers lauded nationalisation, but they had small readerships and little influence in the wider community. The attitude of Labor politicians was to let opponents fire off their ammunition in the hope they would soon exhaust their rage.[3] Only two small organisations on the fringes of the Labor movement made a compelling case for nationalisation.

The Fabian Society of New South Wales was formed after the war to present an independent view on topical issues and draw attention to socialist policies. The society did not represent the ALP or the Labor Government but thought along similar lines. The Fabians produced *The Case for Bank Nationalisation*, a thirty-two-page booklet which was by far the best explanation of the takeover. Mostly written by acclaimed economists Heinz Arndt and Noel Giblin, it translated the Government's Banking Act into simple language and chopped up the arguments the

---

1 *Argus* (Melbourne), 22 September 1947, p. 1.
2 Summary of Activities of The Banks' Central Committee, 10–27 September 1947, NABA /Bank Nationalisation, p. 5.
3 *Workers Star* (Perth), 17 October 1947, p. 6.

banks were making. It explained why state banking would create cheaper credit, help fund national development and result in better services. Chifley was so happy with the booklet he paid for 40,000 copies. Some copies were put on sale and but most were sent to public servants, supporters and unionists.[1]

The Henry Lawson Labor College in Sydney made the other creditable contribution. The college trained unionists in economics, politics, public speaking and other subjects. Its four-page *Questions on Bank Nationalisation and the Answers* was a masterpiece of clarity. It argued a referendum was unwarranted because the Government had acted with constitutional authority. Yet, as good as the Fabian and Henry Lawson documents were, they were no match for the volume of bank circulars, pamphlets and leaflets being stuffed into Australian letterboxes by opponents such as Millicent Preston Stanley.

One newspaper described Preston Stanley as a woman with "a pencil, a phone and a brain".[2] Another described her as a plump (woman) with a fair complexion and a rich contralto voice.[3] A better characterisation was that Preston Stanley was an arch-conservative feminist, an uncompromising crusader and the inspiration for a popular and unique anti-socialist movement.[4]

Preston Stanley's first foray into political organising was during the Great Strike of 1917 when she recruited women as cooks, tram drivers and fare collectors to help break the strike which threatened to cripple New South Wales. In 1925 she became the first woman elected to the New South Wales Parliament where she championed education, housing and legal rights for women. She worked briefly as a journalist, was active in conservative causes during the Depression and recruited women to volunteer for the war effort.[5]

Chifley's bank nationalisation press statement disturbed Preston Stanley and in league with sixty prominent women she organised a protest rally at the Sydney Town Hall. Three thousand women attended and two Liberal parliamentarians, Dame Enid Lyons and Senator Annabelle Rankin, spoke at the event. Preston Stanley took the energy of the rally

1 May, p. 52.
2 *Sun* (Sydney), 28 July 1949, p. 18.
3 *Telegraph* (Brisbane), 29 October 1947, p. 4.
4 Millicent Preston Stanley was variously known as Mrs Preston Stanley Vaughan or Mrs Crawford Vaughan after her marriage to former South Australian Premier Crawford Vaughan.
5 Heather Radi, "Preston Stanley, Millicent Fanny (1883–1955)", *Australian Dictionary of Biography*, National Centre of Biography, Australian National University, https://adb.anu.edu.au/biography/preston-stanley-millicent-fanny-8107/text14153, published first in hardcopy 1988, accessed online 18 April 2022.

and launched the Australian Women's Movement Against Socialism (AWMAS). She was the driving spirit behind an organisation that became a platform to inform Australian women that socialism posed a threat to "the future of our children".[1] She set up branches in South Australia, Western Australia and New South Wales and helped Dame Mabel Brookes, a respected Melbourne socialite to start a similar organisation in Victoria. Bank nationalisation was the first AWMAS cause but soon the Movement was campaigning on housing, taxation, rationing, shortages, strikes and other issues that exasperated Australian women.

Preston Stanley was skilful at recruiting prominent women like aviator Nancy Bird Walton, Sydney obstetrician Dame Constance D'Arcy, and Eleanor Donaldson, the Advertising Manager for David Jones. The heartland for her movement was in the wealthier inner suburbs of Sydney where mature, upper-class doyennes disapproved of socialism and dropped large donations into enamel bowls. The Movement was also popular with country women, though Preston Stanley made sure it did not compete with established rural organisations like the Country Women's Association and the Women's Auxiliary of the RSL. Female bank staff and the wives of branch managers were quick to join the AWMAS when it launched in the Riverina.

An early success for the AWMAS came in October 1947 when Preston organised the largest ever women's rally in Canberra. It was a mass protest against bank nationalisation and a thousand women from all parts of the country attended including several who flew from Western Australia.[2] Canberra did not have the cafes to cater for such a crowd and those attending were instructed to bring a picnic basket and ninepence for a cup of tea. The rally began in Albert Hall which was a short distance from Parliament House. After stirring speeches the women marched on Parliament House where they filled Kings Hall, ambushed politicians and forced Labor MPs into hiding because they feared being waylaid.

Dame Enid Lyons and Preston Stanley led a small delegation to see the Prime Minister in his office. They reminded him more women were enrolled to vote than men and pressed him to hold a referendum. Chifley sucked his pipe, listened quietly and told them he could not meet their demands. He had timed the meeting for mid-afternoon and "promptly disarmed and charmed the women by serving afternoon tea".[3] Queensland delegate Mrs T. R. Groom said, "Mr Chifley told us his grandfather had

1 *Daily Telegraph* (Sydney), 27 September 1947, p. 9.
2 *Courier-Mail* (Brisbane), 22 October 1947, p. 1.
3 *Age* (Melbourne), 14 June 1951, p. 2.

suffered when the banks closed on him in 1890. He said he was only a small boy then but he would always remember it ... the man was shy, but his tenseness when he refused to agree to our proposal for a referendum showed that nothing will sway him."[1]

The protesters claimed excellent results though they failed to even dent the attitude of the Government. This was the first time women had formally protested against bank nationalisation and in doing so served notice that many Australian women were against socialism. The rally achieved positive press coverage and led to the formation of more AWMAS branches including one in Canberra.[2] For the next two years the Movement held rallies and meetings and women energetically and earnestly campaigned against Labor and socialism.

Not everyone liked the idea of women expressing their opinions. The Liberal Party never sought to cultivate the Movement because it regarded the AWMAS as a competitor for prospective members. One columnist in the *Australian Women's Weekly* wrote, "The trouble always with women's demonstrations is that the girls are likely to be treated 'as the ladies God bless em', an attitude that is pleasant enough but mars [their] effectiveness." The writer urged women who wanted change to join a broader movement.[3]

Eric Butler, a lean former artillery sergeant, was as passionate about fighting socialism as Preston Stanley. And his organisation was equally opposed to the Chifley bank takeover. The League of Rights began in Adelaide in 1946 and within a year there were branches in all states except New South Wales. It claimed to be non-political and non-sectarian but no Labor supporters could be found in its ranks. It was right-wing, pro-British, pro-Christian and anti-Semitic. It was fiercely for private enterprise and individual ownership and fiercely against Communists and those in high places seeking to impose alien laws on Australia.

Butler was the League's Victorian director and its best-known figure. He established a profile in Melbourne after the *Argus* published his letters and invited him to write on national and international affairs. Old Army mates introduced him to prominent people in business and the law and Butler claimed he knew Oscar Isaachsen of the Bank of Adelaide.[4] The League of Rights saw bank nationalisation as an opportunity to grow its influence and set out to educate Australians about the adverse implications

---

1 *Courier-Mail* (Brisbane), 24 October 1947, p. 1.
2 *Telegraph* (Brisbane), 29 October 1947, p. 4.
3 *Australian Women's Weekly* (Sydney), 7 November 1947, p. 10.
4 Eric Butler, Australian League of Rights, Undated https://alor.org/Storage/navigation/Library4.htm, accessed 3 January 2022.

of government-run banking.¹

In September 1947 the Melbourne banks gave Butler £250 (today around $17,000) which seems to have gone to hiring a secretary and improving his weekly newsletter.² The Sydney banks also supported the People's Union in New South Wales which was affiliated with the League. The Bank of Adelaide possibly helped the League in South Australia with advertising. Previously the League had advertised six times in South Australian newspapers but there were forty ads in the three months after the press statement on bank nationalisation.

Butler launched the League's anti-nationalisation campaign in September 1947 before 500 people in the Princess Theatre in Melbourne. He told the audience that political gangsters were trying to tyrannise the community but the League would fight for liberty and the British way of life.³ Then followed meetings in regional Victoria, discussion groups, a short-lived radio show, print material and the first anti-nationalisation comic book. *Open the Door, Richard!* told the story of sly socialists and wily bureaucrats who tried to trick honest citizens.⁴ In December the League and the People's Union launched the *Defend the Constitution* program which pressed for an Australian bill of rights and greater voter control over Parliament. Butler's other proposals included asking Opposition MPs to resign their seats so the ensuing by-elections would give electors a chance to vote on nationalisation.⁵ He also called on the Governor-General to dissolve Parliament since the Government had lost the confidence of the people.⁶

Butler later claimed bank nationalisation was one of the most critical campaigns in Australian history and it appears the League of Rights was at its most influential during this period. It received good press coverage and Butler claimed he was asked to train bank officers in finance and economics ahead of the 1949 election.⁷ The League's influence waned once banking was no longer an issue, and it became increasingly marginalised for its anti-Jewish and anti-immigrant policies. The *Argus* stopped taking Butler's articles when the paper changed owners.⁸ The League still exists but perhaps the Institute of Public Affairs in Victoria is the most influential

1   *Horsham Times* (Horsham), 13 December 1949, p. 2.
2   Summary of Activities of The Banks' Central Committee, 10–27 September 1947, NABA /Bank Nationalisation, p. 5.
3   *Argus* (Melbourne), 1 September 1947, p. 3.
4   Victorian League of Rights, *Open the Door, Richard!*, Melbourne, Ruskin Press, 1947.
5   *Mercury* (Hobart), 20 September 1947, p. 2.
6   *Sydney Morning Herald* (Sydney), 22 December 1947, p. 3.
7   *New Times* (Melbourne), League of Rights Vol 59 no 10, October 1995.
8   *Labor Call* (Melbourne), 26 August 1949, p. 7.

survivor from this time.

In 1943 prominent Melbourne businessmen including Sir Keith Murdoch and Leslie McConnan put up £18,000 ($1.2 million today) to establish the Institute of Public Affairs (IPA). Similar but smaller institutes were established in other states. The Institute's 13-member council recognised that a sizeable part of the population believed a patrician elite ran the economy for the benefit of the wealthy and felt big business had let them down during the Depression. The Melburnians knew the war had changed the political and economic landscape and things would never return to the unfettered days before 1939. They wanted their new organisation to build trust between the business community and the public, advocate for democracy and economic freedom and to oppose state control and socialism.[1] The new body was never intended as a mass organisation rather one that engaged influential people who could sway the opinions of others. Labor supporters regarded the new organisation as a secret club for wealthy men.

In 1945 the Victorian IPA published *Looking Forward*, a blueprint for full employment and industrial relations and the future development of governments and business. By 1947 a small, well-paid team of economists was regularly publishing research on business investment, taxation, productivity and other contested topics. The Institute's magazine had 10,000 subscribers and was a platform for this research. Its articles were often reprinted in other publications extending the IPA's influence beyond its immediate membership.[2]

The IPA and Liberal Party argued that a vigorous and competitive banking industry was essential for Australia.[3] Opposition MPs borrowed ideas from IPA material and a treatise on bank ownership published by the Queensland Institute. The Sydney banks helped the New South Wales Institute with a £20,000 anti-Labor campaign directed at clergymen, doctors and other influential figures in the community.[4] While these Institutes added to the intensity of the banking debate, smaller protest groups were springing up like mushrooms across the nation.

These hometown outfits resembled the community organisations formed during the Depression by middle-class Australians frustrated by the country's desperate economic circumstances. Author Matthew Cunningham has written that these Australians advocated for the "sane

---

1 *IPA Review* (Melbourne), November-December 1948, p. 1.
2 *IPA Review* (Melbourne), November-December 1948, p. 29.
3 IPA press statement, 27 August 1947.
4 Eather and Cottle, "The Sydney Banks and the IPA", p. 175.

and honourable" management of the nation's finances, smaller government and fewer MPs.[1] They formed groups that tended to attract middle-aged men, often First World War veterans, and who were anti-Communist, pro-British and for free enterprise.[2] The best remembered organisation is the New Guard, a paramilitary body whose members stood ready to resist by force a socialist revolution. At their peak the collective membership of these organisations was probably in the hundreds of thousands yet despite being visible and vocal they never evolved into a significant political force.

In 1947 the private banks set out to rekindle the spirit that had motivated these Depression-era movements. Bank officers went into the field to tap into the resentment local people felt about losing their banks.[3] The Melbourne banks sponsored a citizens' rights group in Warrnambool which later became the blueprint for similar groups. By December the Sydney banks had encouraged nearly 200 citizens' rights committees and the banks helped groups in other states. It is hard to estimate the financial support the banks gave. Some organisations received money while the banks helped others with advertising and printing expenses and encouraged their staff to support them.

A citizens' rights committee gave a sense of solidarity to people troubled by bank nationalisation and provided a framework for them to circulate literature, arrange petitions, talks on the radio, lobby MPs and help conservative candidates at election time. Some groups were particularly adventurous. A citizens' protest committee in Sydney commissioned an Avro Anson twin-engine plane to drop thousands of leaflets on the shops in Mosman while housewives did their Saturday shopping.[4]

Nearly all citizens' rights committees staged protest meetings in town halls, local parks or other municipal spaces. These were often formal affairs with a prominent person chairing the proceedings and a bank manager, respected merchant or a state or federal MP addressing the crowd. Sometimes a political celebrity like Richard Casey came to talk. Crowds hooted and applauded when speakers used humour and sarcasm to denounce bank nationalisation and attack the Government. As the meeting closed, the chairperson called for a vote of thanks for the speakers, and put a motion that demanded the Government hold a referendum before anything happened to the banks. Typically

---

1 *Argus* (Melbourne), 20 February 1931, p. 8.
2 Matthew Cunningham, *Mobilising the Masses: Populist Conservative Movements in Australia and New Zealand During the Great Depression*, Canberra, ANU Press, 2022.
3 *Tribune* (Sydney), 17 December 1947, p. 1.
4 *Sun* (Sydney), 31 August 1947, p. 3.

motions passed unanimously and the meeting would finish with tea and refreshments or people heading to the pub to continue the conversation. The next day organisers sent a telegram or letter expressing local feelings off to Canberra and the town paper would report the event.

These local committees were animated but never subversive. Nevertheless there were concerns they might become fascist paramilitaries like the New Guard. In December 1947 the New South Wales Police Commissioner ordered his superintendents in Tamworth, Parkes, Wagga Wagga, Goulburn and Dubbo to quietly investigate what local groups were doing.[1] A police inspector cross-examined bank officers and solicitors in Cowra, and a plainclothes detective arrived in Gundagai to question the wife of a bank manager about her participation in Preston Stanley's rally in Canberra. The Commissioner gave a report to the State Premier but its findings were never made public.

Australia's banks were happy to support these fragmented and often small community groups because they added to the cacophony of protest and gave the impression of widespread resistance.

---

1 *Daily Telegraph* (Sydney), 3 December 1947, p. 4.

12 Fantasy Fighters

> *"I am wondering what happened to Bob and Betty Freeland and John Henry Austral. No doubt they are enjoying a holiday at the expense of big business."*[1]

The fiercest critics of bank nationalisation were Bob and Betty Freeland, their two children and John Henry Austral. All were fabrications and forerunners of the fictitious characters who have popped up in Australian election advertising ever since.

The Freelands were the centrepiece of a very expensive press campaign created by Frank Goldberg for the Melbourne banks. The *Australian Way* campaign ran from November 1947 to December 1949 and promoted the values and attitudes which Australia's bankers considered important. The Freeland family members were "Honest to goodness Australians just like you and me" who wanted a life free of government interference.

Thirty-something Bob was all square-jawed, clean cut masculinity and carried himself with confidence. He could easily have been a veteran. He drove a baker's van but over the course of the two-year campaign achieved his ambition of becoming a manager. Bob worked hard, encouraged everyone else to do likewise and was never afraid to challenge the boss. At home in comfortable suburbia he was a devoted husband, model father, helpful neighbour and enthusiastic gardener. His attractive wife Betty was the idealised post-war woman. She was an accomplished housekeeper and a good cook, a dutiful mother who aspired for her two-year-old daughter Jill to have "as much freedom as men in planning their lives".[2] Ten-year-old Tom looked up to his father as the model of Australian manhood. A late-model sedan sat in the driveway of their neat suburban bungalow which was filled with modern appliances.

The first *Australian Way* ad was published the day after the Governor-General signed the Banking Act into law. It was a quarter-page black-ink drawing of a romanticised country town with text underneath. In the illustration was a cannery to represent industry, a general store standing for commerce and late-model cars representing modernity. The Star

---
1 *Daily News* (Perth), 11 May 1950, p. 8.
2 *West Australian* (Perth), 19 October 1948, p. 10.

Hotel symbolised mateship and beyond the town were well-tended fields to cover agriculture. Absent were a police station, court house, town hall or anything else which implied the state. A few tight, crisp paragraphs said Australians had fought for liberty in two world wars and now "The Government could take all you produced." The call to action was simple. "Tell your elected representative to preserve the Australian Way." The ad was authorised by "Your Trading Bank".[1]

The ads that came next were parables about free enterprise or grim warnings about socialism. Bob and Betty and their friends and workmates believed Australians had the right to "say what we feel, choose our own jobs, make our own decisions and learn from our own mistakes". There were often hints of a sinister force which wanted to control "every phase of our existence and threaten [our] freedom".[2] The Freeland circle was all-white, middle-class, hard workers and nice people. There was no room for slackers or dreamers, working women, Indigenous Australians or non-English migrants. Early ads mentioned values but rarely banking, Chifley or Labor. Nationalisation became a theme as the 1949 election approached and Bob and Betty discussed the merits of private banking. The final ad, the day after the election, showed the couple with "a little spare cash", rejoicing that Labor had lost.

The format of Goldberg's campaign never really changed. Each ad was an eighth or a quarter page placed in the early section of a publication. The illustrations were finely drawn and the text was crisp and emotive. The Melbourne banks shared the campaign costs and rotated their logos through the ads. The Freelands appeared more than 2000 times in newspapers across the country and in magazines like the *Australian Women's Weekly*. They rarely ventured into New South Wales because the Sydney banks did not support the series.

Using surrogates in advertising was not new. From 1909 to 1920 a boot polish company called Blythe and Platte paid artist Lionel Lindsey to create the character Chunder Loo of Akim Foo. The oriental Loo had adventures with a talking dog and a big-eared koala and used each exploit to promote shoe wax. The Chunder Loo ads were popular and published in a book for soldiers during the First World War.[3]

The *Australian Way* had some critics. One reader said the average person would be "naive, a knave or nuts" to believe Bob Freeland.[4] A

---

1 *Mercury* (Hobart), 29 November 1947, p. 4.
2 *West Australian* (Perth), 16 November 1948, p. 6.
3 Ernest O'Farrall and Lionel Lindsay, *The Adventures of Chunderloo*, Sydney, Blyth & Platt, 1916.
4 *Daily News* (Perth), 1 October 1949, p. 7.

Geraldton reader described Bob as Simple Simon and Betty as a woman with natty hats and a "say cheese" smile. Someone said the series was a hangover from the Stone Age.[1] Professor Robert Crawford of RMIT University has written that the *Australian Way* campaign helped shape public opinion on bank nationalisation and added to the general anti-Labor clamour ahead of the 1949 election: "While the campaign was not responsible for changing the face of Australian political advertising, it nevertheless deserves recognition for its contributions to the Liberal campaign and indeed the commercialisation of Australian political campaigning."[2] When Labor was defeated and the banks were safe, Bob and Betty retired into the 1950s, never to return. The cost of the campaign remains a mystery but whatever the banks invested the Freeland family repaid them handsomely.

John Henry Austral was the other invented bank warrior. He was the star of a radio soap opera that ran for more than 250 episodes to lash Labor and champion the vision of the Liberal Party. Austral was born out of Sim Rubensohn's belief that politics could be presented in an entertaining way.

John Henry Austral made its first appearance in January 1948 at a Liberal Party public relations conference. With Federal President Casey's blessing, Rubensohn had prepared eight pilot episodes to be played for the conference delegates. Initially, they thought the show was too provocative but relented when Casey agreed to give the states some control over the content of the program.[3]

John Henry Austral was broadcast in prime time from February 1948 until December 1949 on eighty-one stations nation-wide. Twice a week for fifteen minutes the stentorian-voiced lead actor Richard Matthews put a conservative spin on topical issues. Episodes were a melodramatic parable of good versus evil, weak versus strong. The "Low Down on Communism" episode was about unscrupulous trade union officials. In "Places Where They Sing" Chifley's socialist ambitions were said to be silencing the song in Australian hearts. "Who Owns Big Business" was a defence of business owners and investors and a warning that nationalisation would shoot profitable enterprises into incompetent hands. Austral was supported by a roster of colourful characters such as the scheming capitalist Sir Barcome Enderby, Joe Pendleton the Communist agitator, and newlyweds Elsa and Jim. Satan made guest appearances.

---
1 *Daily News* (Perth), 12 May 1949, p. 5.
2 Robert Crawford, "Supporting Banks, Liberals and The Australian Way: The Freelands and the 1949 Election", *History Australia* 2, no. 3 (2005), pp. 84.1–84.23.
3 Letter Casey to Menzies, 18 January 1948, NLA MS 4936/14c/418/30.

The show opened with a rousing rendition of "Waltzing Matilda", which was Richard Casey's idea, and musical interludes punctuated the dialogue.[1] There were Christmas and Anzac Day specials and once or twice Matthews interviewed Menzies and a Liberal state premier. Other actors impersonated and mercilessly mocked Labor politicians. Each show ended with the line, "This program is presented for your thought and consideration by the Liberal Party of Australia."

The series was a major, and no doubt, profitable undertaking for Rubensohn's agency. Each week creative director Pip Cogger and his staff identified topics, drafted scripts and got the approval of each State Division of the Liberal Party to proceed to production. The agency then assembled Matthews and other members of the cast to record an episode onto vinyl discs in a single run-through. The discs were dispatched to stations around the country and the agency advertised the latest episode in local papers with a special focus on advertising in states with Labor governments. The first-year budget for *John Henry Austral* was over £40,000 (over $2.5 million today). Casey was happy to spend because, as he told his diary, nearly a third of Australians enjoyed the show.

The idea of mixing entertainment, radio and politics came from North America. In 1928 a specially produced radio program dramatized the life of US presidential candidate Governor Al Smith of New York. With 20 Broadway actors, a chorus of newsboys and a shiny orchestra, the show presented Smith's journey from stripling newsboy to Democratic hopeful.[2] Then came a Canadian political soap opera which aired during that country's election campaign in1935. In the runup to the election *Mr and Mrs Sage*, imaginary figures on an imaginary front porch, opined each week about politics and poked fun at the Liberal Party in Canada. The couple caused such an uproar that the Liberals, on winning office, introduced regulations that banned such broadcasting.[3]

Like his Canadian cousins *John Henry Austral* upset many people. A Tasmanian writer said the program was childish prattle and a Labor minister said the real purpose of the program was to undermine democracy.[4] The Government became increasingly snappish over the program's criticisms and duly amended the Broadcasting Act in December 1948. One section read, "neither the ABC nor the licensee of a commercial broadcasting station shall broadcast any dramatisation of

---

1 Scripts: *John Henry Austral* – 1948-1949, NLA MS 4936/14(c)/418/32.
2 *New York Times* (New York), 20 October 1928, p. 36.
3 *Barrier Miner* (Broken Hill), 31 December 1948, p.4.
4 *Brisbane Telegraph* (Brisbane), 24 November 1948, p. 7.

any political matter which is current or was current at any time during the last five preceding years".[1] This meant *John Henry Austral* or future shows were forbidden to cover current or recent events like bank nationalisation or to satirise politicians.

The Government said the change was for the public good, but in reality it did not enjoy being the subject of biting satire each week. The Opposition said, "When this legislation becomes law the Government will be able to bring a censorship of opinion and expression into every home in which there is a radio set."[2] Rubensohn said the Government gagged *John Henry Austral* because it could not answer its criticisms.[3] Pip Cogger delighted in seeing how far the Government was willing to go to silence his fabricated figures. Station managers, concerned for their broadcasting licences, reacted by pulling the show off the air, replaying older, less polemical programs, or by insisting on reviewing scripts before they were produced.

Rubensohn's agency re-cast *John Henry Austral* who now limited himself to interviewing Liberal politicians and other conservatives. He could still jab and punch but his bite was gone and the show hobbled towards the 1949 election. Australian political scientist Stephen Mills credits *John Henry Austral* as a pioneer in modern political campaigning in Australia. It was emotional, expensive and relentless in how it applied modern advertising techniques to politics.[4] The Liberal Party funded the show but the banks were happy to watch from the sidelines as *Austral* and his colourful colleagues alerted Australians to the dangers of Labor.

As *John Henry Austral* was being restructured, Sim Rubensohn's agency introduced a second radio program. *Country Quiz* was for rural audiences and based on a successful American format. It ran from September 1948 to July 1949 and was the first commercial program for a nationwide country audience. The show was broadcast for thirty minutes each week on fifty country and some metropolitan stations in the Macquarie Network. *Country Quiz* drew on the popularity of quiz shows after the war. The Liberal Party funded the show and used it to connect with wheat farmers, dairymen, orchardists, graziers, sugar growers and other primary producers, the types of voters the Country Party usually courted.[5]

---

1 *Brisbane Telegraph* (Brisbane), 27 October 1948, p. 4.
2 *Northern Star* (Lismore), 24 November 1948, p. 1.
3 *Daily Examiner* (Grafton), 16 November 1948, p. 3.
4 Stephen Mills, "Campaign Professionals; Party Officials and the Professionalism of Australian Political Parties," PhD Thesis, University of Sydney, p. 92.
5 The Country Party did not participate in the program although a minor party official appeared in one episode.

In each episode contestants competed for prizes and used their knowledge of local farming practices to answer questions which ranged from pigs to pineapples depending on the district. Contestants were mostly men although there were a few women. A quick-witted and comical quiz master peppered them with questions.

Country Quiz moved from one country town to the next and from the eastern states to the west. Local winners advanced to zone finals and originally there were plans for state and national finals though these never proceeded. There was a buzz when *Country Quiz* came to town. The Macquarie Network sent an advance man to scout a town, select contestants, hire a venue and book local musicians. The show would then follow once arrangements were in place.

The Liberal Party influence on the show was generally subtle but sometimes obvious. A Liberal liaison officer might encourage local members to get involved and occasionally a luminary like Richard Casey would be a guest. The winner in each show got a couple of minutes to speak about a pet topic which often fitted nicely with a Liberal Party policy. The program always declared its Liberal sponsorship.

Country Quiz was technically complex and expensive. Few country stations could stage a live show so a technician from the Macquarie Network accompanied each production. He sent the live quiz down telephone lines to be copied on to vinyl records which were then mailed out to affiliate stations. Wages, travelling expenses and prize money added to the costs though Rubensohn and his agency made sure publicity was usually free.[1] Stations and newspapers in the district were happy to promote the show and local contestants as a matter of community pride. For a time *Farmers and Settlers* magazine printed quiz questions and advertised the show to its New South Welsh readers.

Country Quiz was politics frocked as entertainment. It portrayed rural Australians as resourceful and independent people who had little need for socialism. As a precautionary measure, the show was taken off the air when the Labor Government introduced its restrictive broadcasting regulations.

Bankers also used radio though not on the same scale as the Liberal Party. Bank officers in New South Wales sponsored but masked their involvement in a show called *Ask Peter Barry* which aired in New South Wales and Victoria from April to October 1949. The format seemed innocent enough. Listeners were invited to write to host Peter Barry (a

---
1   *Sun* (Sydney), 31 August 1948, p. 8.

former war correspondent) and tell him the problems they were having in dealing with the Government. Barry would approach the authorities and intercede for his listeners.[1] In reality it was a set up to allow Barry to highlight Government shortcomings.

The Government suspected the show was more political than public-spirited and asked the Australian Broadcasting Control Board to investigate. The Board reported that *Ask Peter Barry* did not comply with broadcasting regulations and unmasked the UBOA (NSW) as the sponsor of the program. The union abandoned the program and 2GB, which produced it, was forced to apologise for breaching broadcast regulations.[2]

Ask Peter Barry was not an isolated subterfuge. The *Bush Telegraph* column was a light-hearted newspaper item full of jokes, gossip and barbs aimed at the Government. It was published by eighty country papers in New South Wales from May to December 1949. Max Bryant wrote *Bush Telegraph* for the *Muswellbrook Chronicle*, C. Henderson was the author at the *Jerilderie Herald* and John Lane did something similar at the *Gloucester Advocate*.[3] Readers of these newspapers never knew that what these fictitious correspondents wrote, came from bank union headquarters in Sydney and that local bank officers customised it for each newspaper. In November 1949 the ALP exposed the bank officers' involvement but the UBOA (NSW) cheerfully admitted responsibility and continued on.

The Bank of New South Wales sponsored *Hear These Actual Interviews*, the first radio show devoted to bank nationalisation. It ran on stations nationwide for six weeks. The format was simple. The show's host interviewed men and women about the banking issue. He claimed to be an independent businessman but was really an ad man employed by the Sydney banks.[4]

The Bank of New South Wales had marginally more success with *The Mantle of Greatness*. This radio docudrama ran from 1947 to mid-1950 and cost almost £17,500 a year (more than $1 million today).[5] The show profiled the lives of historic figures who succeeded in life despite hard times, bad laws and incompetent or corrupt governments.

The explicit purpose was to highlight the rewards of persistence and resourcefulness. The implicit message was that if these people could succeed without being socialised or nationalised so could the listener. The program was pompous and moralizing and lacked the flair and creativity

1 *Glen Innes Examiner* (Glen Innes), 6 May 1949, p. 6.
2 *Sydney Morning Herald* (Sydney), 15 September 1949, p. 4.
3 May, p. 107.
4 *Western Star and Roma Advertiser* (Roma), 7 November 1947, p. 4.
5 Casey diary entry: 2 December 1947.

Rubenshon and Casey brought to the Liberal Party productions. In 1948, the Bank of New South Wales turned the scripts from the show into a book, and Western Australian bank officers apparently used some of this material in a press campaign.[1]

In Melbourne the banks were becoming more adventurous with radio. They sponsored *Random House*, a humorous and sometimes moving saga of family life, and the *Musical Comedy Show* which featured well-known singers and emerging artists.[2] The banks also supported *The Watchman*, a weekly fifteen-minute, right-wing monologue on topical issues.[3]

While the Government had the authority to regulate radio, its effectiveness as a broadcaster was limited. Labor could not match the artistry and innovation of its opponents and instead saw radio as another platform for making speeches. Chifley was never a good speaker but eventually a reluctant Prime Minister was persuaded to do a weekly broadcast about what his Government was doing.[4] The original intention was for a nationwide hook-up of commercial stations but Labor balked at the production costs of £550 each week (around $37,000 today.) The Government accepted an unsolicited offer from the Macquarie Network of free time on selected stations.

Chifley's first *Report to the Nation* was on 12 September 1948. It and the talks that followed aired for five minutes after the seven o'clock news on Sunday evenings. The Prime Minister spoke on topics like the economy, exports, shipping, national security, industrial affairs, coal strikes and Anzac Day. Never did he address banking or nationalisation. Supporters said his talks were like US President Franklin Roosevelt's fireside chats during the Depression. Chifley however was no Roosevelt. The late President was a master communicator who projected a reassuring presence into the lounge rooms of America. Chifley's raspy voice, clunky wording and data-heavy content was difficult listening even for his keenest supporters. His sixty broadcasts over fifteen months probably did little to sway sceptical Australians that his government had their best interests at heart.

---

1 *Mantle of Greatness*, Sydney, Publicity Press, 1948, p. 2.
2 *Murray Pioneer* (Renmark), 6 January 1949, p. 6. Sunday Mail (Brisbane), 3 July 1949, p. 7.
3 Memo to Chief Manager: Opposition to Bank Nationalisation List of Activities, 22 September 1949, NABA/Bank Nationalisation, p. 1.
4 *Daily Mercury* (Mackay), 23 August 1948, p. 1 .

13 Wigs at War

"It's a rare piece of hypocrisy because in the Banking Case the Government is doing exactly what the party platform says it is opposed to."[1]

Fifty-year-old Norman Lethbridge Cowper managed the Bank of New South Wales account for the Sydney law firm of Allen, Allen and Hemsley, then Australia's oldest law practice. Cowper had closely followed the nationalisation issue and correctly guessed it would end in the courts. Immediately after Chifley's press statement he recruited some of Australia's top barristers to act for the Bank of New South Wales. At the same time the Melbourne banks began adding eminent King's Counsellors (KC) to their legal rosters. These early bank moves to enlist accomplished silks denied the Government access to some of the best legal minds in the country.

Garfield Edward John Barwick KC was possibly the best appellate advocate of his day. He had a photographic memory, an encyclopaedic knowledge of the law and an uncanny feel for the personalities in a courtroom.[2] Barwick was "one of a handful of counsel for whom there is always a dive when big issues are involved".[3]

Maurice Byers, the Commonwealth Solicitor-General in the 1970s and 1980s, recalled seeing Barwick perform in action. "I remember as if it were yesterday, the face vibrant with life and vitality, the restless brown eyes, the questioning slightly amused face and above all the powerful, winning and magnetic personality ... his fertility of illustration was unrivalled, his ability to support his own argument or to ridicule his opponent's by apt and telling examples enabled him to present his case in its most seductive garb. When to this was added the force and charm of his personality his power as an advocate at this time was unrivalled in Australia."[4]

Barwick believed in free enterprise and during the war represented clients who tested Commonwealth wartime regulations before the High Court. Even so, years later when asked if he would have represented the Commonwealth in the nationalisation case he said, "I'd have taken it if I hadn't already a [bank] retainer."[5]

1 *Sydney Morning Herald* (Sydney), 27 September 1948, p. 1.
2 Garfield Barwick, *A Radical Tory: Garfield Barwick's Reflections and Recollections*, Leichhardt, Federation Press, 1995, p. 63.
3 *Bulletin* (Sydney), 25 August 1948, p. 11.
4 Maurice Byers, "Obituary: The Right Hon Sir Garfield Barwick AK, GCMG, QC", *Australian Law Journal* (1997) 71(9), p. 723.
5 Sir Garfield Barwick interviewed by the Hon. Clyde R. Cameron, 30 January–1 December 1981, NLA Oral History TRC 1045.

Choosing Barwick was an easy decision for the banks. He had represented Melbourne City Council in its successful challenge to Section 48 of the 1945 *Banking Act*, and his legal skills were admirably suited to what would be the first chance to forensically examine bank nationalisation free of politics and special interests.

Cowper quickly sought an injunction to restrain the Commonwealth from proceeding with nationalisation until the High Court could decide its constitutionality. The injunction was to prevent a midnight strike by the Government to decapitate the boards of the private banks and replace their directors with its own officials. The Victorian and South Australian governments were also concerned the Commonwealth would move swiftly before they could appeal. The threat of an injunction persuaded the Government to agree to alert the banks and the states before it acted. The High Court cleared its calendar for a challenge from the banks and the states early in the new year. Instead of holidays, lawyers on all sides spent the summer preparing their cases. Deputising once more for an absent Evatt, Senator McKenna told Caucus he hoped the legal challenges would be finalised within nine months.[1]

The newspapers reported the case but none picked up on the mysterious company the banks set up to continue their fight should they disappear. Hampden Pty Ltd was a front organisation that would allow the banks to contest nationalisation if they were suddenly absorbed into the Commonwealth Bank.[2] The company's public charter said it was to "provide opportunities for the consideration and discussion for all questions affecting the interests of the community or the alteration and administration of the law."[3] Hampden conveniently shared a postal address with Allen, Allen and Hemsley. The five directors were from manufacturing, construction, legal and real estate backgrounds, all of which could be affected by bank nationalisation. The President of the Employers Federation in New South Wales was a director and a well-known opponent of nationalisation. He and his fellow directors had a £20,000 war chest (nearly $1.6m today) for their contingency mission.

Battling bank nationalisation in the courts involved many parties with large budgets yet the essential arguments were simple. The banks planned to argue the new Act contravened section 92 of the Constitution, which guarantees "absolutely free trade and commerce" between the states. Barwick and his colleagues would maintain nationalisation would

---
1 Weller and Lloyd, p. 436.
2 May, p. 77.
3 *Dun's Gazette for New South Wales* (Sydney), Volume 78, No. 17, 24 October 1947, p. 252.

effectively remove the banks' freedom to trade across state borders. Since Federation individuals and organisations had used section 92 to resist attempts by Commonwealth or state governments to expand their powers. The banks would also argue that any Commonwealth takeover would not be on just terms. The South Australian, Victorian and Western Australian Liberal governments joined in the bank case, claiming nationalisation would force them to deal with the Commonwealth Bank thereby violating their sovereignty. Furthermore it would upset the Commonwealth-state arrangements set out in the Constitution.

The Government was confident it had the constitutional authority to determine under what circumstances a party could conduct the business of banking in Australia. It maintained any compensation it offered the private banks would be fair and was adamant the new Act would not upset Commonwealth-state relations.

Barwick was to be the public face of the bank challenge, and at first glance, it seemed obvious Evatt as Attorney-General should lead for the Government. His legal credentials were impeccable. He was a Doctor of Laws, had written scholarly books on law and history, and was among the most outstanding constitutional scholars in the British Commonwealth. In 1930, he was the youngest person appointed to the High Court of Australia and in his ten years there he had heard several Section 92 cases.

Evatt was the best-educated man in the ministry and his colleagues trusted his legal judgment. Ministers no doubt assumed because Evatt was responsible for drafting the nationalisation legislation he had closed off all avenues of challenge. Evatt assured Chifley he could win the case in the High Court and if necessary win an appeal to the Privy Council in London.[1]

There was no doubt about Evatt's qualifications and experience, but was he the best choice for the Government? His workload as Attorney-General and Minister for External Affairs was punishing, and he was frequently overseas representing Australia in the significant international forums set up after the war. Evatt, however, liked to involve himself in important affairs and maybe sensed a victory in such a landmark case would make him the logical successor to the Prime Minister when Chifley retired. He also knew his appearance in the High Court would make legal history being the first time a former Justice had pleaded a case before his former colleagues. Outwardly Attorney General seemed undaunted by the additional workload and pressure the case would bring.

---

1 *Daily Telegraph* (Sydney), 1 November 1947, p. 14.

Evatt however had private reservations about the road ahead. He did not share these with his colleagues but was happy to discuss his misgivings off the record with a reporter. He told Harold Cox that government officials were alarmed because a win in the bank case would "involve the greatest difficulties in implementing [nationalisation] and they did not know how they could carry it out". He also confided he needed a good win in court because the public had lost confidence in the Government.[1] Other Labor MPs had doubts and mused privately that they would be happy for a quick High Court decision that favoured the banks. That would end the matter and they could concentrate on the next election.[2] They estimated Chifley's "brainwave" had already cost 200,000 votes.

Even though "Doc" Evatt had spent ten years on the High Court and knew each of the seven Justices, that association granted him no favours. Melbourne-born Justice Sir Owen Dixon believed that Evatt's appointment to the High Court in 1930 had come about because of political scheming. Both respected the other's talents but Dixon thought Evatt was essentially dishonest.[3] In 1942 Dixon accepted the post of Envoy Extraordinary and Minister Plenipotentiary to the United States on condition he report to Prime Minister John Curtin and not to the Minister for External Affairs. In 1944 Dixon resigned his post, reputedly dismayed by Evatt's persistent interference, and returned to the High Court.[4]

Curmudgeonly Justice Sir Hayden Starke had a poor opinion of most people including Evatt. The two were a combustible combination and at times Starke and Evatt communicated only through curt notes.[5] Sir George Rich was the oldest Justice and had served on the Court for thirty-four years. He was known for humour, wit, a humane interpretation of the law and sometimes letting other judges write his judgments.[6] There was speculation he stayed on the Court to deny Attorney-General Evatt the chance to appoint his replacement. Justice Edward McTiernan came to the High Court at the same time as Evatt. From a Catholic and working-

---

1 Letter: Cox to Murdoch, 6 May 1948.
2 *Daily Telegraph* (Sydney), 4 February 1948, p. 1.
3 Philip Ayres, *Owen Dixon*, Carlton, Miegunyah Press, 2003, p. 59.
4 Grant Anderson and Daryl Dawson, "Dixon, Sir Owen (1886–1972)", *Australian Dictionary of Biography*, National Centre of Biography, Australian National University, https://adb.anu.edu.au/biography/dixon-sir-owen-10024/text17671, published first in 1996, accessed online 4 April 2022.
5 J. D. Merralls, "Starke, Sir Hayden Erskine (1871–1958)", *Australian Dictionary of Biography*, National Centre of Biography, Australian National University, https://adb.anu.edu.au/biography/starke-sir-hayden-erskine-8629/text15077, published first in hardcopy 1990, accessed online 4 April 2022.
6 J. D. Merralls, "Rich, Sir George Edward (1863–1956)", *Australian Dictionary of Biography*, National Centre of Biography, Australian National University, https://adb.anu.edu.au/biography/rich-sir-george-edward-8191/text14327, published first in hardcopy 1988, accessed online 4 April 2022.

class background, McTiernan had been a Labor MP in the New South Wales and Commonwealth Parliaments and was thought to have lingering Labor sympathies.

Justice Dudley Williams replaced Evatt on the Court in 1940. Williams was quiet and pragmatic and took a legalistic approach to constitutional matters. In 1948 the remaining Justice, Sir William Webb, was presiding on the International Military Tribunal in Tokyo and did not return for the banking case. Chief Justice Sir John Latham had a deep understanding of politics. He had been a federal MP, Leader of the Opposition and Deputy Prime Minister in the Lyons Government. Before Pearl Harbor and while Chief Justice, Latham had been Australia's minister to Japan.[1]

In post-war years the High Court held its hearings in different cities.[2] In February 1948 the High Court sat in Melbourne for the bank nationalisation case. On a fiercely hot morning as bushfires ringed the city, six justices in heavy black robes and heavy wigs convened in the classically designed and ivy-covered court building in Little Bourke Street. As the Justices entered, they took their places along an elevated concave bench and the Chief Justice sat in the middle under an ornately carved coat of arms.

Advocates for the Government, the private banks and the three state Liberal governments sat at tables below the bench. Those in attendance included Attorney-General Evatt, the Commonwealth Solicitor-General Kenneth Bailey and a phalanx of barristers and solicitors who would later become Attorneys-General and Supreme, Federal and High Court judges. A barrister and a solicitor from London represented the English banks. Behind this galaxy of legal notables sat stenographers and court reporters and a group of "well dressed and splendidly hatted ladies" filled the small public gallery.[3] Outside the courtroom two constables supervised a crowd of people eager to gain entry.

Things did not go well for Evatt that first day. The day before, a Sunday, Solicitor-General Bailey had visited the homes of Justices Hayden Starke and Dudley Williams apparently at the behest of Evatt and the Prime Minister. The highly respected Bailey, who previously headed the Faculty of Law at the University of Melbourne, had a strained relationship with Evatt and was known for being above politics.[4]

---

1 Stuart Macintyre, "Latham, Sir John Greig (1877–1964)", *Australian Dictionary of Biography*, National Centre of Biography, Australian National University, https://adb.anu.edu.au/biography/latham-sir-john-greig-7104/text12251, published first in hardcopy 1986, accessed online 4 April 2022.
2 *Argus* (Melbourne), 2 November 1945, p. 20. The High Court did not have a permanent home in Canberra until 1980.
3 Barwick, *A Radical Tory*, p. 66.
4 Jack E. Richardson, "Bailey, Sir Kenneth Hamilton (1898–1972)", *Australian Dictionary of*

The Solicitor-General arrived unannounced at the respective front doors of the very surprised Starke and Williams. Bailey told them the Government knew they had close relatives with bank shares, nevertheless it had confidence in them. Justice Starke's wife had small investments in the National Bank and the Bank of Australasia and Justice Williams managed a parcel of bank shares for a sister in Paris. The motive for Bailey's house calls was unclear. Was it a veiled claim that Justices could not be trusted to be independent or a clumsy attempt to incline them to the Government's position. Melbourne's legal fraternity was abuzz when it heard of Bailey's unusual mission.

The next morning as the case began, the two Justices told an amazed courtroom about their encounter with Bailey. Both confirmed they had relatives with bank shares but declared they would not recuse themselves from the case. The Chief Justice supported their stance and noted that Justices, like many Australians, had bank accounts and bank shares but this was not a sufficient reason for them to step aside. Evatt was invited to pursue the matter further but petulantly declined.[1] Henceforth the irascible Starke took every opportunity to bait the Attorney-General.

Over the next three months the Court heard from the Government, the three state governments and the private banks. Barwick eloquently made the bank case and refuted the Government's arguments with polish and precision. He took the Justices through the new Act in detail, highlighting its flaws along the way. He patiently answered questions, cited examples, statistics and case law and used occasional sarcasm. Each morning he summarised the previous day's arguments to refresh the Court's understanding. He deftly avoided the politics around nationalisation and made his case to the High Court, not the court of public opinion. From February to April 1948 he spoke for a total of seven days, impressing everyone with his knowledge and oratorical skills.

Evatt on the other hand was rambling, repetitious and sometimes testy. It was obvious his courtroom skills were rusty and Barwick's sarcasm distracted his focus at times.[2] The Attorney-General spoke for eighteen days including four days on Section 92. Barwick's performance was like an alpine stream gathering force as it moved to its final and predictable appointment with the sea. Evatt's presentation meandered like a billabong with no clear destination.

Biography, National Centre of Biography, Australian National University, https://adb.anu.edu.au/biography/bailey-sir-kenneth-hamilton-9404/text16529, published first in hardcopy 1993, accessed online 4 April 2022.
1 *Argus* (Melbourne), 10 February 1948, p. 1.
2 Letter: Cox to Murdoch, 10 March 1948.

All sides were relieved when on 15 April 1948 the Chief Justice took the Court into recess and ended the drawn-out, exhausting hearing. It was the longest hearing in High Court history, lasting thirty-nine days and generating a 2,000-page record of proceedings. In early August the High Court reconvened in Sydney to deliver its judgment. Public interest was intense and the gallery in the Darlinghurst Courthouse was packed. People queued outside along the colonnades and on the lawns. At 10.30 a.m. the six Justices filed into the courtroom and announced their findings. Chief Justice Latham then summed up.

The majority of the Justices held that the Banking Act contravened Section 92 of the Constitution which mandated free trade between the states. This was the third time since the war that Section 92 had frustrated Commonwealth attempts to create a government monopoly. As well the majority said the Act failed to provide just compensation for the private banks, and the Court of Claims proposed in the legislation was unconstitutional because its decisions were unappealable to the High Court.

Chief Justice Latham and Justice McTiernan dissented. They said the legislation did not violate Section 92 and, with the majority, ruled the Act did not interfere with Commonwealth-state arrangements.[1] Nevertheless the Commonwealth had lost the case and the Government was ordered to pay £75,000 ($5.5m today) in costs and given fourteen days to seek leave to appeal to the Privy Council.

As the Justices filed from the court room, people rushed outside to shout the news. A Salvation Army officer ran out crying, "It's five to one for the banks! Say hallelujah!"[2] Traders at the Sydney and Melbourne stock exchanges cheered. Bank shares held firm but there was a modest rise on the London and Wellington stock exchanges. A press statement from the National Bank said banking was no longer a political football and the ES&A Bank declared the Constitution had protected Australians. The Bank of New South Wales praised the winning legal team. In the days that followed, major newspapers published analyses, commentary and transcripts of what each Justice had said.

Bank staff were jubilant. Nearly every branch manager of the Bank of New South Wales in the state contrived to be in Sydney on the day of the verdict. When they heard the announcement they crowded into Martin Place to cheer. ES&A staff held an impromptu party and in the afternoon bank officers from across Sydney celebrated at the newly opened Bankers' Club on King Street. Even men from the Commonwealth Bank joined in.

1 *Argus* (Melbourne), 12 August 1948, p. 8.
2 *Sydney Morning Herald* (Sydney), 12 August 1948, p. 1.

Normally status-conscious senior executives got behind the bar to pour the beers.[1] Almost every bank in Adelaide hoisted an Australian flag and the Bank of New South Wales office in Hobart flew flags all day. The decision was the talk of Perth and crowds at the Royal Queensland Show cheered when the news came over the radio. Some senior public servants in Canberra discreetly called their bank managers and congratulated them.

Calls from well-wishers jammed the switchboards of the Melbourne banks. Staff at the head office at the National Bank gave Leslie McConnan a hero's welcome when he arrived at work. The ordinarily taciturn general manager beamed as he walked through a six-deep crowd in his marble foyer. Menzies was in London when the news came through. He hailed the ruling as a political and legal landmark that showed the limits of Commonwealth power. The Liberal premiers welcomed the decision. Monsignor O'Donnell said the High Court had dropped "an atomic bomb on the evils of Communism and the totalitarian state" and declared the Justices had shown more commitment to social justice than Chifley's Catholic Ministers.[2]

Chifley was visiting Melbourne and only said, "The matter is one for Senator McKenna, the Acting Attorney-General, who will report to Cabinet." The news was cabled to Evatt in Geneva. He gave reporters a terse "no comment".[3] Some in Labor's ranks secretly welcomed the decision, hoping it laid to rest further thoughts of a bank takeover. In Canberra government officials and political pundits examined the 322-page High Court ruling to determine the Government's options.

The Commonwealth could abandon nationalisation completely. It would be a humiliating backdown but might help restore Labor's waning popularity and ease the anxiety of Labor MPs in marginal seats. The Government could amend its Act or introduce fresh legislation which would overcome judicial objections. It could hold a referendum on bank nationalisation or appeal the High Court ruling to the Privy Council in London, which was the ultimate court of appeal for Commonwealth countries.[4] No option was especially appealing. Chifley was unlikely to abandon nationalisation and he had consistently refused to hold a referendum. Going to the Privy Council ran counter to sentiment within the ALP that the High Court should be the final arbiter of all things

---

1 *Daily Telegraph* (Sydney), 12 August 1948, p. 6.
2 *Argus* (Melbourne), 12 August 1948, p. 1
3 *Argus* (Melbourne), 12 August 1948, p. 1.
4 *Sunday Herald* (Sydney), 20 March 1949, p. 8.

Australian. Yet encouraged by the dissenting judgments of the Chief Justice and Justice McTiernan, Chifley and Evatt considered the Privy Council as their last legal hope.

The Prime Minister consulted his ministers who agreed on an appeal but he did not consult the Labor Caucus. It was left in the dark as it had been on bank nationalisation the year before. When the decision to appeal to London was announced Chifley's admirers saw it as the Prime Minister's strong commitment to Labor principles. Opponents saw it as "notorious pigheadedness".[1] Leslie McConnan said it was a last throw by a desperate government.

The English solicitors Coward Chance and Company acted for the Australian Government in the United Kingdom. In 1947 they had warned the Government that Australian banks were retaining some of Britain's foremost barristers in the event bank nationalisation ended up before the Privy Council. They had forwarded a shortlist of names and recommended who the Commonwealth should hire. The Attorney-General's Department equivocated so by the time the Government decided on an appeal to the Privy Council, the Australian banks had already recruited three eminent KCs and other highly regarded English counsel to their cause.

Barwick had won for the banks in 1945 and again in 1947 so the private banks were keen to have him for London. Initially Barwick was reluctant to take on the case. His law practice was growing and taking more time, and he knew a Privy Council case would take him out of Australia. Leslie McConnan however was determined to get him and as an inducement McConnan booked the vice-regal suite on the ocean liner *Strathnaver* so that Barwick and his wife Norma could travel to the United Kingdom in comfort. Barwick relented. He and his wife thought they would be overseas for three months so the couple arranged for relatives to look after their two small children.

McConnan had set the Barwicks up grandly. The *Strathnaver* had air-conditioned suites, an elegant dining room, a well-stocked library, a tiled swimming pool and uniformed stewards who attended to the passengers' every need. Barwick described the voyage to England as "parties, games, swimming and plenty of relaxing amusement".[2] His shipmates were other KCs and solicitors retained by the banks, some of whom sailed with their wives. Norman Cowper was also aboard, charged by the banks to be part-bodyguard and part-batman so no misfortune would befall Barwick

---

1 Letter: Cox to Murdoch, 16 August 1948.
2 Barwick, *A Radical Tory*, p. 67.

before the hearings began in London.

There was a welcome reception at Claridge's Hotel when the Australian party landed in England. The evening was a great success, with leading figures from the City of London inviting the new arrivals to stay at their country estates. The next morning the group set to work with the English barristers and solicitors retained by the Australian and English banks and those acting for the three Liberal state governments.

There was a more modest reception for Evatt, Bailey and the other Government lawyers when they arrived in London. The Australian High Commissioner and former Labor Minister Jack "Stabber" Beasley greeted them and provided office space and two stenographers to handle "a good deal of typing". Coward Chance had arranged for three English barristers to join Evatt and promptly invoiced Canberra for £10,000 ($500,000 today) for services rendered so far.[1]

After the war hearings of the Privy Council involved two stages. The first involved a hearing by the Judicial Committee of the Council to grant or deny the Australian Government leave to appeal. It was doubtful the Committee would reject a Commonwealth application because the case had serious constitutional consequences and the recent High Court ruling was not unanimous. Once leave was granted the second stage involved a full hearing by selected Privy Councillors. Their decision would have far-reaching consequences. A victory for the Commonwealth meant the Government could proceed with ending Australia's century-old system of banking. If the banks won, nationalisation would be dead.

On 25 October 1948 Lord Robert Wright and four law lords presided over the preliminary hearing at 9 Downing Street. Their Lordships wore lounge suits and sat around a table looking more like directors at a board meeting than one of the highest appellate bodies in the world.

That first morning eighteen barristers in wigs and gowns packed the small courtroom. The Victorian and South Australian premiers had arranged to be in London and the Australian High Commissioner, Commonwealth officers and bank officials were also present. The London manager of the Bank of New South Wales was delegated to report developments back to his head office in Sydney, and English and Australian reporters leaned against the back wall.

A bewigged Evatt opened by requesting permission for the Australian Government to appeal to the Privy Council. He argued the recent High

---

1   NAA: Australian High Commission, United Kingdom (London), A2910, Coward Chance and Company – Bank Nationalisation Litigation, 412/1/25/52, Crown Solicitor's Memorandum, 6 October 1948.

Court decision denied the Commonwealth "the legislative power to an extent that could not reasonably be regarded as flowing from the Constitution". Following Evatt, the brilliant English barrister Sir Cyril Radcliffe took the floor, and in a polished and clear performance, energetically argued the High Court's ruling was right and disputed the Commonwealth's case to appeal.

The first stage hearing ended in early November 1948 when the Commonwealth gained approval to proceed. Evatt pressed for an early hearing of the Privy Council because the Government did not want events in London to overlap the federal election due the next year. A hearing was scheduled for the following March which left both sides five months to finalise their arguments.

Evatt's department shipped twenty-eight volumes of documents to London for his preparation while Barwick and his team prepared a case book that some at the English Bar said was as fine as they had ever seen. Both sides submitted depositions and documents which were bound into five weighty appeal books their Lordships could refer to. The next stage of the appeals process was expected to take six weeks and cost around £200,000 ($14.5m today).

In mid-March seven law lords took their places to hear the case. Among them was Baron Augustus Uthwatt, who was born in Australia.[1] The Chairman was Baron Samuel Lowry Porter, a seventy-two-year-old bachelor who enjoyed books, classical music and steamed fish. Porter was known for his cool demeanour, fastidious regard for detail and as a jurist who would slash through loose language with industrial precision.[2] Every day precisely at 11.45 a.m. an attendant in white tie and tails ceremoniously placed a pot of tea and a China cup before the Chairman, who poured his tea with a theatrical flourish and surveyed his courtroom with lynx-like intensity.

Initially Barwick thought the Committee would be predisposed to Evatt because of his renowned legal credentials and status as a former Justice of the Australian High Court. Barwick thought seven right-minded Englishmen would hardly believe a Westminster government like the Commonwealth of Australia would act without proper authority.[3] As the days in the tiny courtroom passed Barwick became more comfortable and confident, engaging their Lordships with logic, well-timed humour

---
1 Uthwatt was born in Ballarat and studied at Melbourne University. He left Australia to study at Oxford and went on to have a distinguished legal career in Britain.
2 *Herald* (Melbourne), 15 March 1949, p. 8.
3 Barwick, *A Radical Tory*, p. 75.

and forthright responses. His performance guiding them through the controversial Section 92 of the Australian Constitution was masterful.

Evatt's performance however was even worse than his appearance before the High Court in Melbourne. His explanations and arguments were verbose, exhausting and often repetitious. Moreover his unwillingness to delegate to others in his team meant there were long delays when their Lordships asked questions. Evatt's tortuous approach tried the patience of their Lordships, who at one point wagered among themselves that whoever asked Evatt a question should forfeit a pound. Legal scholar Geoffrey Sawer contrasted the performances by Evatt and Barwick. "Evatt lectured their Lordships for 22 days, glowered at them, read them interminable passages from decisions, and never presented a clear theory about Section 92. Barwick, who took nine days, followed his High Court technique of careful, patient and amiable explanation and reduced case-reading to a minimum."[1] Other aspects of Evatt's personality came through and the Englishmen in the courtroom disapproved of the imperious way the Australian Attorney-General treated his subordinates in public.

In fairness, Evatt was undoubtedly distracted by his other ministerial duties and constant calls and cables from Canberra. He was also, to Australia's great pride, then President of the United Nations General Assembly, and actively involved in drafting the Universal Declaration of Human Rights. The Committee appreciated Evatt's responsibilities and his need to travel. When his absences became so frequent, Porter would only allow adjournments if the Commonwealth met the cost of delays. When the Judicial Committee was not meeting, Evatt buried himself in multiple tasks while Barwick and his wife took their leisure by hunting, skiing and touring the Continent.

The hearing lasted three months and the final transcript ran to over a million words. Two Lords died during the proceedings. On 26 July 1949 the Judicial Committee, accommodating the Government's request for an early decision, delivered a bare judgment. It simply said the High Court's decision was upheld and the Government's appeal was dismissed.

News of the verdict was immediately telegraphed to Canberra so the Prime Minister was prepared for questions in Parliament and from the press. A cable also flashed to the boardroom of the Bank of New South Wales in Sydney where bankers and lawyers nervously waited. That cable

---

1 G. Sawer, "Absolutely Free Man: Sir Garfield Barwick Looks Up an Old Constitutional Battle", *Nation*, 4 June 1960, p. 164.

simply said "appeal dismissed" but was enough to trigger celebrations by bank officers around the country.

In late October 1949, weeks before the Australian federal election, the Privy Council published its full decision. Once again Section 92 of the Constitution had brought the Commonwealth case undone. Nevertheless the judgment left a sliver of hope for Chifley and Evatt. The Privy Council said cryptically that while bank nationalisation was not acceptable in the current environment, it might be right in other circumstances in the future.

After the Privy Council dismissed the Government's appeal, the Commonwealth was ordered to pay costs. Canberra instructed Coward Chance to settle as quickly and quietly as possible. The private banks also wanted a speedy settlement. They hinted that if there were delays they would seek compensation for the expenses they incurred during Evatt's frequent absences from London. The banks eventually received £55,000 sterling (over $3 million today). The Victorian Government recovered its expenses but Western Australia and South Australia did not press for costs. Of more consequence than the money was the two years eaten up by the High Court and Privy Council cases which had robbed the Government of any chance to implement its nationalisation plans.

Most people felt the Privy Council decision would finally end the matter. Evatt declared nationalisation was dead at least as an election issue. Chifley never explicitly abandoned nationalisation but said his Government would always act within the Constitution.[1] Opponents were cautions about the London verdict. McConnan warned Australians the decision meant only that the banking system was safe for the present. The General Manager of the Bank of New South Wales said the "Government could, if returned to power, use freeze and squeeze tactics to reduce the business of the trading banks to stagnation".[2] Menzies was willing to bet "a guinea to a gooseberry" the Government would try something else to get its way.[3]

Barwick returned to Australia celebrated as the man who saved the banks. In the years that followed he argued several Section 92 cases before the High Court and appeared at various times before the Privy Council. In the 1950s he was elected to Parliament and later appointed as Attorney-General in the Menzies Government. From 1964 to 1981 he served as Chief Justice of the High Court of Australia.

---

1 Don Rodgers interviewed by Mel Pratt, 29 April 1971.
2 *Gisborne Herald* (NZ), 28 October 1949, p. 5.
3 *West Australian* (Perth), 6 August 1949, p. 8.

Evatt returned from London beaten but unapologetic. He had directed the drafting of the banking acts the Government deemed essential for its post-war plans. He assured his Party both were constitutionally sound and then performed poorly when forced to defend them before the High Court and the Privy Council. Though he was responsible for the Government's humiliating legal losses, his standing within the ALP at this stage was relatively unscathed. Evatt was elected Labor leader when Ben Chifley died.

14 Collingwood versus Canberra

"The by-election was the contest of the year."[1]

In September 1947 the inner Melbourne suburb of Collingwood became the first place in Australia where voters could express their feelings about bank nationalisation. Collingwood had been a Labor stronghold for generations and the workers in its breweries, factories, warehouses and workshops always supported ALP candidates. For twenty-five years they had elected Tom Tunnecliffe to the Victorian Parliament. The ALP veteran was so entrenched he ran unopposed at some elections.

Shortly after Chifley's press statement on bank nationalisation, illness forced Tunnecliffe to resign from the Victorian Parliament. A by-election to elect his successor was called for 20 September 1947. The Liberal Party knew the seat was unwinnable but believed that Collingwood voters were just as incensed at the prospect of losing their banks as the rest of the country. The Liberal Party framed the by-election as a test of public opinion on nationalisation and hoped a reduced Labor vote would show the banking measure was unpopular. Normally the by-election would have been unremarkable, but now the press called it "Collingwood versus Canberra".

In Victoria Premier John Cain led the Labor Government which had been in office for two years. Cain was moderate, generally well regarded and a capable administrator. He actively campaigned for the Party's Collingwood candidate, and Commonwealth Minister John Dedman flew in from Canberra to help. The Liberal Party lined up Menzies, Dame Enid Lyons and other prominent Liberals for their candidate and Melbourne's major newspapers threw their weight behind the Liberals. Victorian business interests spent an unprecedented amount to defeat a Labor candidate in a by-election. Both sides argued the merits of the bank takeover in a boisterous campaign.

The results on election night allowed both sides to claim victory. Despite a ten percent swing against the ALP, the Party managed to keep Collingwood. Yet some wondered that given the significant swing against it, whether Labor could afford to keep winning seats like Collingwood. Menzies was satisfied with the result. His supporters said if the swing was

---

1   *Telegraph* (Brisbane), 5 September 1947, p. 1.

repeated at the next federal election the Chifley Government would be driven from office.¹ Two months later Victoria had another but far more dramatic election.

The Victorian Constitution provided for two legislative chambers. The Legislative Assembly was elected through a near-universal franchise and the party with the most seats in the Lower House formed government. In 1947 Labor governed with the help of three independent MPs. On the other hand the Legislative Council, the house of review, was elected by only about one-third of Victorian voters who included property owners, teachers, doctors, those in the law, retired military officers and university graduates. With such a narrow voting base it was easy for critics to claim the Legislative Council was a citadel for the privileged classes.

In the aftermath of the Collingwood by-election the Labor Government presented a budget or supply bill to the Legislative Council for approval. This was standard parliamentary procedure yet this time the Council refused to pass the bill. This deprived the Government of the necessary funds to pay its 25,000 workforce of public servants, policemen, teachers, firemen and contractors. The rejection of supply was exceptional, with few precedents in Australia or even in the British Commonwealth.

The rationale for blocking supply was that Premier Cain had failed to protect the state from industrial anarchy and stop the imminent destruction of private banking in Victoria. Even though the future of the banks was a Commonwealth and not a state issue, the Upper House declared it would pass supply only if Cain called a state election so Victorians could pass judgment on bank nationalisation.

The President of the Legislative Council, Sir Frank Clarke, was the architect of the "Black Friday coup." Clarke was a thirty-four-year veteran of the Victorian Parliament and a former minister. He was also Vice Chairman of the Board of the National Bank. "Sir Bank Clarke", as Arthur Calwell called him, had foisted this manufactured parliamentary crisis on Victoria as Chifley was introducing the nationalisation legislation into Parliament and the banks were accelerating their campaigns.

With supply blocked, Victorian public servants and policemen were not being paid. In a surprising offer the Melbourne banks promised interest-free loans to public servants who were not drawing wages and to honour State Government cheques until the budget drama was settled.² Few could remember the banks being so generous to people without incomes.

---
1 *Argus* (Melbourne), 22 September 1947, p. 1.
2 *Age* (Melbourne), 3 October 1947, p. 3.

Cain was forced to call an election and the Legislative Council swiftly passed the supply bill. The four-week election campaign was as trenchant as Victorians had ever seen. Liberal and Country Party candidates made bank nationalisation the main issue and took every chance to slam Canberra's bank grab. Key Opposition leaders flew to Melbourne. Robert Menzies addressed packed halls around Melbourne night after night and Arthur Fadden spent his weekends rallying support in the Victorian countryside.[1] ALP candidates tried to shift the focus away from banking to the need to reform the Legislative Council and Cain asked voters to consider the merits of his government. The Victorian ALP got some support from Canberra and from ministers like Arthur Calwell but Chifley stayed away.

The State election was held on 8 November 1947 and once the polls closed it was clear that voters had clobbered Cain. Forty-one years old Liberal leader Tom Hollway became one of the youngest premiers in Victorian history. Labor lost almost half its seats, including those of three ministers. The result was such it became major news across the country. Tasmanian Monsignor O'Donnell commented, "On Saturday the free people of Victoria again routed the tyrants … they dealt a deadly blow to the evil forces of socialism and Communism which seek to bind the people in chains."[2] Leslie McConnan, speaking for the banks, said the result was a marvellous win.

Victorian bank officers were active in the election campaign even if the extent and nature of their involvement was unclear. Nevertheless a spokesperson for the newly formed (Victorian) Bank Employee Protest Committee said "the election provided the first effective platform on which we were able to state our case. It demonstrated we could be a decisive political force. It provided us with practical experience in political organisation and platform work and expedited the development of our organisation."[3] Labor's loss caused a sensation in Canberra and Sir Frank Clarke's political intrigues earned him the lasting enmity of the ALP.[4] The Victorian result encouraged jubilant Liberal and Country MPs to believe they could beat Labor at the next election. Stunned Government MPs offered excuses. The election was about local issues they said and

---

1 *Courier-Mail* (Brisbane), 23 October 1947, p. 2.
2 *Argus* (Melbourne), 10 November 1947, p. 6.
3 May, p. 38.
4 R. J. Southey, "Clarke, Sir Francis Grenville (Frank) (1879–1955)", *Australian Dictionary of Biography*, National Centre of Biography, Australian National University, https://adb.anu.edu.au/biography/clarke-sir-francis-grenville-frank-6316/text9581, published first in hardcopy 1981, accessed online 4 April 2022.

besides, the electoral machinery in Victoria was biased against the ALP. Voters lacked the opportunity to properly consider the arguments for nationalisation and would not be concerned about the bank takeover if they just knew what the Government knew. Chifley made no comment about Victoria but the Opposition said he was committing slow suicide if he pushed forward with his bank plan.[1]

A month after the Victorian result there was a by-election for the seat of Hartley in the New South Wales Parliament. Chifley's federal electorate took in part of Hartley. The ALP had held the seat for twenty years, and so tight was its grip, sometimes the major parties did not bother to run candidates at election time. This time was different. The fight in Hartley was sharp and aggressive as the Liberal and the independent candidate bashed bank nationalisation from dawn to dusk. Labor retained the seat but by its smallest margin in decades.[2]

In April 1948 there was a by-election for the seat of Coogee in the New South Wales Parliament. The Liberal candidate pounded away at "the barren freedom-destroying policy of socialism" and beat a well-known and popular Labor woman.[3] In July the Liberal Party won another by-election in the seat of Kogarah which took in Evatt's federal electorate. Bank officers actively campaigned in both by-elections.[4]

In July 1948 the Tasmanian Legislative Council threatened to block supply unless the Labor Government called a state election. This was similar to what Sir Frank Clarke had done the year before in Victoria. Premier Robert Cosgrove had only recently been cleared of bribery and corruption allegations. The Liberal Opposition accused his Government of bad administration and said Tasmanians should have the opportunity to pass judgment on Labor. Banking was not as important as it had been in Victoria but a key Opposition promise was to establish a state trading bank should the private banks disappear. The election results were inconclusive and both sides claimed a victory of sorts. Against "the full power of the press and money" Labor gained three seats while the Liberal Party achieved a 3.5 percent swing in its favour.

The most significant setback for the Chifley Government came in 1948 with the defeat of the Commonwealth referendum on rents and prices. During the war the Government had regulated prices and rents to keep inflation in check. Labor wanted to continue these arrangements

---

1 Letter: Cox to Murdoch, 10 November 1947.
2 *Lithgow Mercury* (Lithgow), 15 December 1947, p. 2.
3 *Sydney Morning Herald* (Sydney), 22 April 1948, p. 3.
4 Harry Jago interviewed by Peter Coleman, 22 March 1987, NLA ORAL TRC 2606.

to stabilise the economy and allow domestic production to increase in a sustained and orderly way. The High Court was increasingly less likely to endorse the indefinite use of wartime powers, so the Government needed a referendum to secure the constitutional authority to continue its wartime regulatory regime.

A referendum was long planned for 28 May 1948. It proved unfortunate timing for the Government. The High Court was in the last stages of hearing the bank nationalisation case so there was a feeling that in pressing for a referendum to increase Commonwealth powers, the Government was again over-reaching. Many Labor MPs knew the mood in their electorates was against the Government and Evatt privately told Harold Cox the referendum was doomed because of community feeling on bank nationalisation. Roy Morgan and his pollsters predicted the Government would lose. Still Chifley and his ministers pushed ahead calculating the public would support the referendum once the Government made its case.[1]

Labor's message to voters was straightforward. Prices and rents would go up unless Australia voted Yes.[2] The unions strongly urged a Yes vote and claimed only racketeers, the wealthy and the unscrupulous would vote No. The Communist Party produced and screened a hard-hitting documentary film to persuade people to vote Yes.[3] Menzies and Fadden advocated a No vote arguing state governments should be responsible for prices and rents because they understood local conditions better and were closer to the people.[4] Furthermore they pointed out there was no expiry date for any controls the Government might impose in future. Conservative newspapers attacked the Referendum as a green light for socialism, a wretched excrescence, a Canberra booby trap and arrant trickery.[5]

Labor spent more money and effort promoting the Yes vote than it had ever done for bank nationalisation. The Party allocated around £3,000 (over $200,000 today) and the Government spent around £150,000 on advertising (over $10m today.) Even so, Labor's advertising was unconvincing and messy while Opposition advertising was dramatic and prominent. Opposition spokesmen spoke on prime-time radio while Labor spokesmen spoke whenever radio stations could spare them time. The Liberal and Country Parties produced a very sophisticated campaign, which the ALP claimed cost £500,000 ($36m today)and involved two

---

1 Letters: Cox to Murdoch, 19 April 1948 and 26 May 1948
2 *Sun* (Sydney), 11 May 1948, p. 7.
3 *Tribune* (Sydney), 3 September 1949, p. 2.
4 *Sun* (Sydney), 24 May 1948, p. 6.
5 Commonwealth, *Parliamentary Debates*, House of Representatives, 27 November 1947, (John Lang, Member for Reid).

advertising firms. And this did not account for support from the banks, the AWMAS and the Institute of Public Affairs.[1]

The 1948 Referendum was the largest in Australian history and the result was a decisive No in every state. Critics said this latest attempt to expand Commonwealth powers had been crushed and common sense had prevailed over woolly socialist theories. The *Bulletin* said if the voting pattern was repeated at the next federal election, Chifley and his ministers would lose their seats and the ALP would be reduced to a shadow.[2] Leslie McConnan said Australians had shown they did not wish to surrender their democratic way of life to an out-of-touch government. Richard Casey said the country's political boundaries were not between Labor and non-Labor but between those who wanted socialism and those who valued freedom.[3] A wag poet penned, "There's this about Ben that as plain as a steeple. He'll never again put it over the people."[4]

The defeat jolted the Government. Chifley blamed the press for misleading voters while some Labor MPs privately blamed bank nationalisation.[5] The Prime Minister took responsibility for the outcome. He briefly considered resigning but the prospect of Evatt as party leader stopped him. Responding to the referendum result, the Government cancelled subsidies worth millions of pounds and returned responsibility for prices and rents to the states, hoping voters would blame them for future price hikes.

Labor's critics had pinned a socialist label on the Government and the Referendum decision suggested Australians had come to accept it. Furthermore powerful interests had spent vast sums to prevent the Government carrying out its plans. For a time ALP MPs considered imposing spending limits on future referendums and elections, but nothing happened.[6] They may have been more diligent in their efforts if they had known the exorbitant sums their opponents would spend at the next election. The most personal setback for Ben Chifley however was not in a federal or state election but in a rural shire most Australians had never heard of.

Ben Chifley had returned to Bathurst after he was defeated in the 1931 federal election. Two years later, he was elected as a councillor on the Abercrombie Shire which took in the farming country around Bathurst. It was a sharp descent from being a minister of the Crown to serving in a

---

1 *Sydney Morning Herald* (Sydney), 26 May 1948, p. 2.
2 *Bulletin* (Sydney), 2 June 1948, p. 14.
3 *Argus* (Melbourne), 31 May 1948, p. 5.
4 *Bulletin* (Sydney), 9 June 1948, p. 10.
5 Letter: Cox to Murdoch, 7 June 1948.
6 *Queensland Times* (Ipswich), 31 May 1948, p. 1.

little-known rural shire. Nevertheless Chifley liked local government and served on the Abercrombie Shire for fourteen years including a period as Shire President. When a change in electoral boundaries put his Bathurst home outside Abercrombie's borders, he purchased land in the district so he remained eligible for Shire elections.[1]

Chifley continued as a shire councillor when he re-entered Parliament in 1940 and then after became Treasurer and Prime Minister. The voters in the Shire liked Ben Chifley and it was handy to be able to complain to the Prime Minister about local roads, rabbits, sewerage and stray stock. Several times during the war Chifley arranged for an upgrade of roads in the district and additional petrol coupons for local farmers to get their wool to market. Abercrombie gave Chifley an understanding of country people and their issues and he said, "I know a lot of people are surprised that I still remain a member [of the Council] having risen to the position of Prime Minister. Besides finding an atmosphere of harmony here, I am helped by it to keep in contact with the everyday affairs of the man in the street and to understand his problems."[2]

Even as Prime Minister, Chifley was punctilious in his shire duties and attended council meetings, which were held one Saturday morning each month. Chifley's driver chauffeured the Prime Minister from Canberra in his official black Buick with the C1 numberplates. They arrived ready for the 9.30 a.m. meeting after which Chifley toured the small villages in the Shire and spent the rest of the weekend catching up with constituents, party members and old mates from his railway days. He would make time for family and relax at home with wife Lizzie and her elderly mother. Late on Sunday afternoon, Councillor Chifley would drive back to Canberra to become Prime Minister Chifley.

In 1947 the New South Wales Government introduced compulsory voting for local government elections and the Abercrombie election was set for Christmas. Chifley stood for re-election but this time his responsibilities as Prime Minister kept him in Canberra. He relied on friends to campaign on his behalf against his opponent, a thirty-two-year-old grazier and political novice. His opponent did not attack bank nationalisation but suggested Chifley was too busy in Canberra to care for local interests. Despite years of helping Abercrombie's farming families, the voters handed Chifley a mortifying verdict and elected the young grazier. Chifley came third in a field of three and only one polling place in the Shire recorded a majority for him. Of the councillors seeking

1 *National Advocate* (Bathurst), 13 July 1945, p. 1.
2 *National Advocate* (Bathurst), 15 April 1946, p. 2.

re-election he was the only won to be defeated.

The ALP downplayed the election result and said it was about shire not national issues. The President of the Bathurst branch of the Liberal Party however said bank nationalisation had beaten Chifley.[1] *The Land* newspaper said the result showed country people did not want to follow Chifley down the path to Communism.[2] The *Sydney Morning Herald* said Australians were uneasy with "Labor's creeping conquest of individual liberties".[3]

The Prime Minister was gracious in defeat, saying only that he had enjoyed his years as a councillor. He then flew off for a long-planned New Zealand holiday. The rout in Abercrombie cast a melancholy over Labor supporters. Some wondered who was next if their famous leader could lose so badly.

Liberal President Richard Casey was too busy thinking about money to care for Chifley. Weeks after the Abercrombie defeat, Casey and his wife flew to London to raise money for the Liberal Party ahead of the 1949 election. His reported goal was to raise £100,000 (over $6,000,000 today) for Party coffers.[4] The couple stayed at Brown's Hotel in Albemarle Street, a five-star establishment patronised by the wealthy and royalty. They intended to be away for a month but Casey became seriously ill and a bout in hospital forced them to extend their stay.

British investments were worth around £400,000,000 in post-war Australia. Casey wanted to alert the London business world to the threat Chifley posed to their antipodean interests and encourage them to donate to Labor's defeat. He networked tirelessly, meeting with wartime acquaintances, Conservative Party officials, the boards of English banks, general managers of conglomerates, government heavyweights and civil servants in the Foreign Office. He appeared on BBC Television and discussed public relations trends with the British movie mogul J. Arthur Rank. It is unclear how much money Casey raised but the highlights of the trip undoubtedly were dining with Sir Winston and Lady Churchill and tea with the Royal Family.

---

1 *Daily Telegraph* (Sydney), 8 December 1947, p. 4.
2 *Land* (North Richmond), 12 December 1947, p. 4.
3 *Sydney Morning Herald* (Sydney), 8 December 1947, p. 2.
4 *Inside Canberra*, (Canberra), 22 Jan 1948, p. 1.

15 Menzies Roadshow and a Coal Strike

"The Leader of the Opposition, Mr. R. G. Menzies, said ... he intended to make extensive political tours in various States, beginning with New South Wales."[1]

In January 1949 the Prime Minister left for a two-week vacation at the Lufra Hotel near Port Arthur in Tasmania. It was to be a holiday before the hectic election year began. He was accompanied by staff carrying official documents in thick black binders and a specially installed telephone to keep in touch with Canberra.

Chifley's idea of a holiday was to work eight hours a day not the punishing sixteen-hour days he worked in Canberra. He relaxed at Lufra by reading in the morning, mostly histories and biographies, and then worked in the afternoons. In between he wandered the hotel gardens in shirtsleeves, puffing his pipe. Mrs Chifley stayed in Sydney to shop, attend the opera and play bridge with friends.

The Lufra Hotel was in the federal electorate of Wilmot, which was held by Labor MP Gil Duthie. Chifley had arranged with Duthie to tour his electorate incognito to find out what issues people were concerned about. The Prime Minister and Duthie motored unannounced around the Tasmanian countryside for two days, meeting locals at shops, post offices, pubs, council chambers, homes and over farmyard gates. Chifley caught people by surprise but he made a great impression and people filled his car with fresh bread, jams, vegetables and other edibles. Duthie took photos along the way figuring it would do him no harm if the mantelpieces of Wilmot displayed pictures of "Mum, Dad and Chifley". The visit was kept quiet but made national news when a local reporter unexpectedly came upon the Prime Minister.

Chifley was impressed with Duthie. The first term MP was an ordained Methodist minister with a reputation as a good campaigner. Duthie relished meeting voters face-to-face and carried himself like a winner. Later Chifley pointed to Duthie's work ethic and campaign style as an example for other MPs to emulate.

After the Tasmania the Prime Minister returned to Canberra. The

---

1 *Sydney Morning Herald* (Sydney), 12 March 1949, p. 3.

press reported "his pre-holiday pallor was gone, his eyes were clear and his manner jovial."[1] Chifley was rejuvenated and ready for the election year.

Chifley and his ministers had a lot to be proud of at the start of 1949. Despite the turmoil around bank nationalisation, they had a record of significant achievements to present at the next election. They seemed to have a solid political base too. The ALP had won the last two federal elections and the Curtin-Chifley Government had been in office twice as long as any Labor government.

Under the Chifley Government gross national product, national earnings and personal income had increased and living standards had improved. Australians enjoyed a forty-hour working week, higher wages and record levels of employment. Yet the Labor ministry had not rested. Haunted by the spectre of the Depression, the Government had drafted contingency plans to build houses, hospitals, irrigation works, power stations, schools, railways and roads to stimulate the economy in the event of a downturn. Nation building projects were underway including the Snowy Mountains Hydroelectric Scheme which was the largest construction project in Australian history. The new £2 million General Motors factory in Melbourne was rolling out the first mass-produced cars designed for Australian conditions.

Export prices for agricultural products were three times their pre-war levels and the world clamoured for what the Australian farmer produced. Wheat and wool prices hit historic highs and markets for eggs, meat, dairy products, tinned vegetables and dried fruits grew. South-East Asia clamoured for Australian flour, cheese, butter, jam, milk and clothing.

Australia's transport networks had undergone a remarkable transformation during the war. Australians could now fly and move goods to regional centres and capital cities on government-run airlines at some of the world's lowest freight and passenger charges. The Flying Doctor Service ensured sick and injured patients in the outback were within a day's flying time of a hospital. There was a national shipping line, the Commonwealth and State governments were building thousands of miles of roads and there were moves to standardise the country's different rail gauges.

During the Second World War Australians paid some of the highest rates of income tax. Plus there were sales taxes on everything from amusements to xylophones. After 1945 the Government gradually reduced or eliminated sales taxes and reduced income taxes for lower- and middle-class workers. By 1949 eighty percent of Australians were paying

---
1   *Sun* (Sydney), 23 January 1949, p. 30.

less income tax than they paid ten years ago and less than Americans, Britons or New Zealanders. Simultaneously the Government increased age and invalid pensions, maternity and child allowances, unemployment and sickness benefits and eliminated or eased assets and means tests. In the four years since the war, Chifley had balanced the Commonwealth budget in two of those years.

The resettlement program for veterans had successfully reintegrated nearly half a million ex-servicemen and women back into civilian life and was a vast improvement over the scheme after the First World War. Arguably, Labor's most enduring policy was the post-war immigration program, which laid the foundation for today's multicultural Australia. It began in 1945 when the Commonwealth began to provide free or assisted passage to Australia for British migrants. This soon expanded to include people from other parts of Europe. By 1950 a quarter of a million British and European migrants had settled in Australia. This was a remarkable influx for a country with a small population, and experts predicted the country would have a population of twenty million within the lifetime of young Australians.

Internationally Australia was a respected middle power in the global community. The country contributed £450 million to aid war-ravaged Britain and played a major role in the British Commonwealth. Australian diplomats and Evatt helped to promote global cooperation and to establish the United Nations and other international organisations.[1] An Australian general commanded the British Commonwealth Occupation Force in Japan. RAAF aircraft helped break the Berlin Blockade and Australian officers were helping to resolve conflicts in Kashmir, Indonesia and Palestine.

Despite the often bitter polemic over bank nationalisation, the Labor Party could point to a record of success in many areas which explained why opinion polls showed the Party was recovering popular support.

If the coming election was important for Ben Chifley, it was critical for Robert Menzies.

1949 was the last chance for Menzies to regain the prime ministership he had relinquished eight years earlier. He had created the Liberal Party from the ashes of the UAP, reduced Labor's majority in the 1946 election and been re-elected as party leader. Still there were whispers in the party ranks that "You can't win with Menzies."[2] No one doubted the Opposition

---
[1] *Donald K. Rodgers Papers*, NLA MS 1536/Box 2. These papers give a detailed account of Chifley Government achievements from 1946 to 1949.
[2] Howard Beale interviewed by Mel Pratt, 20–21 October 1976.

Leader was gifted yet some viewed him as a cold and aloof politician with little interest in ordinary people. The Labor Party took every opportunity to label him as a failed wartime leader.

In March 1949 Menzies declared he would embark on a nationwide tour to listen to the "real voices" of Australia and spread the Liberal gospel.[1] The true purpose however was to "sell" Robert Menzies to Australians.

The idea of promoting Menzies was not new. Before the 1946 election Charles Meeking, then Menzies' press secretary, proposed a £3000 advertising campaign (nearly $250,000 today) to "build up Menzies". Eric White, the Liberal public relations officer, suggested something similar.[2] White believed the public needed to see Menzies as a talented, fearless leader who cared about their problems. White hoped promoting Menzies would end party squabbling about his leadership. The public relations officer drafted a campaign to portray Menzies as a politician but also as a father, husband, raconteur, sports fan and art lover. He even suggested featuring Pattie Menzies in the *Australian Women's Weekly* talking about her husband.[3] The idea languished when White quit his job, but Sim Rubensohn resurrected it after he started with the Liberal Party. Rubensohn proposed Menzies should undertake a national roadshow to introduce his policies and himself to Australia.[4] These travels would be different than touring during an election campaign because Menzies would have time to meet people and share his hopes for Australia's future.

The inspiration for Rubensohn's proposal may have come from America and President Harry Truman. In the 1948 US Presidential Election Truman had embarked on a transcontinental train tour, "whistle-stopping" through prairie towns, midwestern cities and southern centres. Along the way, his seventeen-carriage train stopped at country crossings and small stations where Truman addressed locals, and then took him on to large cities for appearances in crowded arenas. Truman's staff travelled ahead to liaise with police, encourage local reporters and mingle with track-side spectators to encourage applause.[5] The Menzies version was less grand but there were similarities. Menzies would visit Labor and Liberal strongholds in each state, deliver speeches, stroll through country towns, inspect mills and factories, meet local personalities and gee up party faithful. Mrs Menzies would go with her husband when she could.

1 Daily Telegraph (Sydney), 12 March 1949, p. 5.
2 Ian Hancock, National and Permanent? The Federal Organisation of the Liberal Party of Australia 1944–1965, Carlton, Melbourne University Press, 2000, p. 74.
3 Eric White to Menzies, 29 July 1947, NLA MS 4936/13/413.
4 Rubensohn to Menzies, 1 March 1949, NLA MS 4936/14C/413/31.
5 *Daily Telegraph* (Sydney), 18 Oct 1948, p. 6.

Opponents sneered that Menzies was to "be sold like condensed milk, breakfast food, soap, or even cheese".[1]

To manage such an ambitious adventure, the Liberals needed an organiser who Menzies could trust, who understood public relations, had strong media skills and who had the stamina for such an undertaking. Rubensohn put forward forty-six-year-old W. S. (Stewart) Howard, a graduate from Sydney University and qualified accountant.[2] Howard had worked for the *Daily Telegraph*, *Sydney Morning Herald*, *Smith's Weekly* and the *Australian Women's Weekly* and was a public relations officer for New South Wales Premier Bill McKell. After the war, he established a public relations agency in Sydney and his clients included conservative organisations like the Graziers' Association and the Melbourne City Council. He was committed to Liberal values and believed in Menzies. He had proclaimed in 1946 that there was a "need for leadership, inspired and inspiring, capable of reviving in the people that living faith in the democratic ideal which is now dormant".[3] Casey described Howard as a "capable, resourceful and experienced public relations man of a type that is rare in Australia".[4] Critically Menzies and Howard got along from their first meeting.

Howard's title was "special public relations adviser to Mr Menzies" and his salary package reflected the significance of that role. He was to receive £5,000 a year (or $300,000 today) plus travelling allowances. The Party relocated him to fashionable inner-city lodgings in Melbourne and paid for his Sydney-based wife to visit him three times a year.

Casey, Rubensohn and Howard developed an itinerary for the Menzies' roadshow which the Opposition Leader approved with only minor changes. The tour ran from March to September 1949 and recognised Menzies' need to be in Canberra when Parliament was sitting. Menzies was to do a trans-continental circuit that took in coal mines, ports, farms, machine shops, meatworks, packing sheds, shopping centres and steelworks. Reporters from major newspapers would accompany Menzies when he was in their state and parochial journalists would get the chance to interview him when he came to town. Howard predicted it would be an arduous affair.[5]

---

1 *Advocate* (Burnie), 12 May 1949, p. 6.
2 Bridget Griffen-Foley, "Howard, William Stewart McPhee (1903–1983)", *Australian Dictionary of Biography*, National Centre of Biography, Australian National University, https://adb.anu.edu.au/biography/howard-william-stewart-mcphee-12659/text22813, published first in hardcopy 2007, accessed online 4 April 2022.
3 Stewart Howard, "The State of Democracy", *Australian Quarterly* 18, no. 2 (1946), p. 15–22.
4 R. G. Casey to W. H. Hooper, 14 February 1949, NLA MS 5000/5/116.
5 S. Howard to R. G. Casey, undated, NLA MS 5000/5/116/File Mr Stewart Howard.

New South Wales was the first state and the Small Arms Factory in Lithgow was the first stop. The factory manufactured rifles and machine guns during the war but had since re-tooled to produce refrigerators and appliances. Menzies chatted with machinists and Mrs Menzies swapped gardening tips with a worker with a large African marigold on his workbench.[1] In Kurri Kurri, on the coalfields, miners gathered at the town rotunda to hear Menzies denounce Communism. These same men had booed him in 1941 when he had visited the town as prime minister. Now they applauded and laughed at his jokes. In Gilgandra he chatted with shoppers and storekeepers and Menzies and his wife enjoyed morning tea with members of the Country Women's Association.

After roadshow stops in Gulargambone and Singleton there were large rallies in Newcastle and Dubbo. The final event in New South Wales was in Sydney at the Rushcutters Bay Stadium where 8,000 people cheered as Menzies delivered a powerful speech about Communism. The speech was broadcast live and listeners at home could hear the commotion in the hall as demonstrators continually interjected and hurled abuse. Menzies engaged all comers. A recording of Menzies' address was later edited and played on radio in Sydney and Melbourne.[2] Liberal organisers said Menzies' resilience in the stadium demonstrated their leader was unafraid to take on the Communists. They calculated his performance and the recording that subsequently aired were worth thousands of votes.

Menzies was used to boisterous audiences like the one at Rushcutters Bay. He would rely on his quick wit and colourful turn of phrase to turn around troublesome crowds. Future MP and Governor-General of Australia, Paul Hasluck said, "In political campaigning Menzies had great skill with a crowd and better than anyone I have observed. He could overcome a rowdy opposition and get them to the point where they were waiting to hear what he would say next instead of trying to stop him from saying anything. He was never frightened of his fellow Australians."[3]

Two weeks and 2,000 miles later the New South Wales leg of the Menzies' roadshow ended in triumph. The State Liberal Council was told Menzies had been a great success. The *Daily Telegraph* observed, "Famous for his biting wit and acid retort, Mr Menzies showed mellowness throughout the tour. He pulled no punches, but rammed home his points with a sincerity that impressed his audiences."[4] A letter in the

---

1 *Lithgow Mercury* (Lithgow), 30 March 1949, p. 2.
2 *Sydney Morning Herald* (Sydney), 8 April 1949, p. 4.
3 Sir Paul Hasluck, *Sir Robert Menzies*, Carlton, Melbourne University Press, 1980, p. 22.
4 *Daily Telegraph* (Sydney), 25 March 1949, p. 8.

Cootamundra Herald declared the tour "should certainly dispel once and for all the legend of Menzies' aloofness".[1]

ALP pundits initially thought it was foolish to send Menzies to factories, wharves and mining areas. These were their political hunting grounds. However they became less certain as workers in one industrial area after another welcomed the Liberal leader. The President of the Northern Miners' Union lamented, "Our friend Bob Menzies is putting on a good act. We must do something to counteract it. Bob is getting far too good a hearing from people like us."[2]

The next stage of Menzies' travels was six days in Victoria visiting factories, mills and mines. The crowds were generally friendly although there were rowdy scenes on the Melbourne waterfront and at the University of Melbourne. In Tasmania Menzies inspected timber mills, butter factories and canneries and strolled the Launceston port. Harold Cox reported, "Menzies has had a very useful effect in his country tours and his prestige is definitely higher than it has been for a very long time."[3]

The Liberal Party in South Australia was fiercely independent and some of its members thought Menzies was getting too much attention. They also queried the money Stewart Howard was making and said it could be better spent promoting local candidates. Premier Thomas Playford took personal charge of the South Australian leg and drove Menzies on a 1500-mile odyssey around his state. South Australian reporters were encouraged to feature both Menzies and the Premier in their coverage.[4]

The Queensland roadshow was the most extensive tour of the state undertaken by a major political leader outside of an election.[5] Dubbed the "Think It Over Tour" Menzies invited Queenslanders to compare what Chifley had promised and what he had delivered. The Opposition Leader spoke at street rallies, factories, foundries, oil installations, waterfronts, cafes and theatres in twenty regional centres. Fadden and Menzies shared a stage in Toowoomba in their first joint appearance since 1941. They declared their aim was "to rid Australia of socialism and its twin brother Communism".[6] Menzies travelled 2,000 miles around Queensland drawing large, attentive crowds and curious Labor supporters.

Life on the road for Menzies and Howard was unrelenting. Mornings began with a major speech followed by a car or plane trip to the next

---

1 *Cootamundra Herald* (Cootamundra), 27 April 1949, p. 2.
2 *Sydney Morning Herald* (Sydney), 7 April 1949, p. 1.
3 Letter: Cox to Murdoch, 22 May 1949.
4 *News* (Adelaide), 12 August 1949, p. 1.
5 *Townsville Daily Bulletin* (Townsville), 16 June 1949, p. 2.
6 *Courier-Mail* (Brisbane), 2 August 1949, p. 1.

town for an afternoon address. In the evening there were big rallies and town hall meetings. Street walks, civic receptions and talks to local party members were squeezed in somehow. While Menzies met people and mingled with crowds Howard was busy confirming arrangements for the next town, briefing city pressmen and canoodling with local reporters to ensure coverage of Menzies' time in their town. Each day was as gruelling as the next apart from when Menzies had to be in Canberra to attend Parliament. The roadshow was to end in Western Australia but was cancelled as an exhausted and sick Menzies was forced back to Melbourne to rest at home.[1]

While Menzies and Howard were away Rubensohn was in Sydney overseeing a well-funded advertising and media campaign that wrapped around the roadshow. There were ads in small papers such as the *Gosford Times* which announced Menzies was in town and was happy to chat with anyone.[2] The *Morning Bulletin* in Rockhampton advertised a free lunch for anyone who wanted to meet the Opposition Leader.[3] Large ads in metropolitan papers echoed the points Menzies was making on the road. Rubensohn arranged an evening radio show so Menzies could reiterate what he was telling his roadshow audiences. "The Liberal Leader Speaks" aired nation-wide from July to December 1949 and covered topics like bank nationalisation and Communism. In another image-building effort Howard recruited three well-known Sydney journalists, his "Sydney bureau," to write favourable articles on Menzies and his policies. These appeared as independent reports in newspapers.

The final part of the Menzies' makeover was *How Well Do You Know This Man?* an eight-page pamphlet that depicted Menzies as a fighter, family figure, self-made man and sports enthusiast.[4] Twenty-five thousand copies were printed and distributed for £700 (nearly $50,000 today.)[5] The ALP parodied the pamphlet and used isolated and selected quotes from past Menzies speeches to discredit the Liberal leader.

The roadshow was estimated to cost £25,000 ($1.5 million today.)[6] This was a significant investment but it brought good returns. Menzies spoke to thousands of people across the country and challenged the

---

1 *Sun* (Sydney), 6 April 1949, p. 17.
2 *Gosford Times and Wyong District Advocate* (Gosford), 18 March 1949, p. 4.
3 *Morning Bulletin* (Rockhampton) 22 July 1949, p. 8.
4 *Truth* (Sydney), 6 November 1949, p. 50.
5 Rubensohn to McClelland, 17 November 1949, NLA MS 5000/1949/ 217, PR files on press, broadcast, finance general correspondence.
6 Bridget Griffen-Foley, *Party Games: Australian Politicians and the Media from War to Dismissal*, Melbourne, Text Publishing, 2003, p. 35.

notion only Labor politicians could stir the interest of working people. Rubensohn and Howard earned a wealth of mostly free and positive publicity for Menzies whose opinion poll ratings were very favourable. Crucially Menzies energised his Party ahead of the election and was now their unquestioned leader. There is no evidence the private banks supported the roadshow but they would have been delighted Menzies had so perfectly framed the upcoming election. It was to be a choice between servitude and state control or personal liberty and free enterprise.

When the roadshow ended Stewart Howard wanted to work for Menzies, Casey or the Liberal Party campaign and even offered to take a substantial cut in pay. Neither Menzies, Rubensohn or the Liberal election machine had a further need for his services. Casey expressed regret he could not find a place for Howard so he went back to his small Sydney agency. Stewart Howard was never again prominent in Australian politics. It was a sad end for the man who did so much to recast the public image of Robert Menzies.[1]

As Prime Minister, Chifley aimed to visit the major centres in each state at least once a year. But in 1949 his duties largely kept him in Canberra and in April he attended the Commonwealth Prime Ministers' conference in London. When he returned, Chifley travelled to South Australia and Western Australia to confer with ALP officials and encourage supporters. However these trips were short and lacked the creative touch of a Rubensohn-Howard itinerary. But even if the Prime Minister had wanted to travel more that year, he was soon distracted by one the nastiest strikes in Australian history.

On 27 June 1949 coal miners in the Hunter Valley of New South Wales and other areas went on strike for better wages and to protest their working conditions. Coal mining in post-war Australia was dirty and dangerous. Miners worked in cramped, poorly ventilated mines with the constant threat of cave-ins, explosions, gas leaks and "dusted lung" disease. No mine in New South Wales had an underground facility to treat an injured worker. In 1948 twenty-five men were killed in mining accidents and nearly 600 were injured. The Miners' Federation, a union dominated by Communist officials, pressed for improved worker safety, shorter working weeks, better wages and long-service leave for miners in the Hunter Valley. Negotiations and arbitration over these demands between the Union, mine owners and the government-appointed Joint Coal Board went on for almost a year. The Miners' Federation abruptly

---

1 Letter Casey to Howard, 25 October 1949, NLA MS 5000/116, Miscellaneous File: Advertising Agency File.

ended discussions and took its members out on strike. This resort to industrial action was unsurprising, since ninety per cent of strikes in New South Wales in 1949 were connected to one degree or another with the coalfields.[1]

What happened on the country's coalfields rippled throughout the nation since coal was the energy source that powered factories, foundries, brick kilns, chemical plants, textile mills, water works, farms, shops, steelworks and smelters.[2] Nearly every system of transport depended on coal and families needed it to cook, heat and light their homes. The *Lithgow Mercury* estimated Australia had only three to five weeks of "coal at grass" which were the above ground supplies which could be readily accessed in an emergency. Historically miners were reluctant to let reserves build up believing surpluses weakened their bargaining power.

Just weeks after the strike started nearly a million people had been laid off or sent home as manufacturers shut down or reduced production. Menzies described this ricochet effect as "One coal miner's freedom to strike means ten other men in factories are denied their freedom to work."[3]

Nearly every aspect of Australian life was affected. State governments shut down public transport on weekends, closed or limited the hours of theatres, cinemas and dance halls, and restricted radio broadcasting.[4] Mail services slowed. Train services were in disarray. The sharp drop in the number of cattle trains meant abattoirs in Western Australia could not slaughter so butcher shops and cafes in Perth were forced to close. Bank branches were forced to limit trading hours and restrict their electricity usage. There was a drop in deposits and an increase in withdrawals in mining towns as small shopkeepers and miners used up their savings. In some areas the Commonwealth Bank loosened its lending policies to help small businesses survive the strike.

Families were hit hard because it was the coldest winter in years and no coal meant no heat and no electricity. People in Sydney lit candles for light and cooked with Bunsen burners in the backyard.[5] A South Australian woman complained, "For a stove I have six broken bricks and three iron rails in this modern age. My fingers are burnt and four of my new saucepans are black with smoke."[6] The *Adelaide Advertiser* said "every home robbed

---

1 *New South Wales Industrial Gazette*, No. 3, vol. 92, p. 840.
2 *Daily Telegraph* (Sydney), 6 November 1948, p. 9.
3 Robert Menzies, "Election Speech: 20 August 1946", Museum of Australian Democracy, electionspeeches.moadoph.gov.au/speeches/1946-robert-menzies, accessed 4 April 2022.
4 *Sydney Morning Herald* (Sydney), 1 July 1949, p. 1.
5 Fred Daly interviewed by Mel Pratt, 26 August–25 November 1976.
6 *Adelaide Advertiser* (Adelaide), 6 July 1949, p. 1.

of gas, heat and electricity became a centre of discomfort and discontent".[1]

Chifley knew the mining communities well because his electorate took in part of the Hunter Valley. While he sympathised with them he knew a protracted strike would damage the economy and a coal strike in winter would do little for Labor's election prospects.[2] The Prime Minister cancelled an overseas trip and urged the miners to return to arbitration to settle their claims. The Government would do no backroom deals with Communist-run unions or yield to their demands. When the strike continued the Government enacted emergency legislation to block support for the strikers. The Opposition supported this action as did the broader union movement which was as determined as the Government to reduce the influence of the Communists in Australian workplaces.

The National Emergency (Coal Strike) Act made it illegal to give financial support to the strikers or for banks to handle their accounts or those of anyone suspected of supporting them. Union officials could be fined and jailed, funds frozen and records seized. When the strike continued, police raided the Sydney offices of the Communist Party and the courts fined officials and jailed eight union leaders.[3] The Government did not want to set worker against worker and refused to bring in miners from other coalfields. Rather it threatened to send in troops to end the strike.[4] The Hunter Valley miners were increasingly isolated but did not buckle.

As the miners continued their industrial action, the Government launched Operation Excavate which was the first postwar use of troops to break a strike. Almost three thousand army and air force personnel were sent to the open-cut and mechanised mine sites in the Hunter Valley.[5] Police constables from Sydney patrolled mine sites in case miners attacked the soldiers who drove tractors, bulldozers and draggers, blasted drill holes, set explosives, removed rock, broke the coal seam and loaded trucks. On the first shift the Army mined over 2,000 tons of coal for Sydney. In the next first three days troops tripled the daily output at one mine and later smashed the daily record for open-cut production.[6] The miners were amazed at the work rate of the troops. Members of the Seamen's Union refused to crew vessels carrying "Army coal" so the Navy was called in to sail colliers and tugboats.

When Chifley sent the troops to the coalfields, the press expected

---

1 *Adelaide Advertiser* (Adelaide), 15 August 1949, p. 3.
2 *Maryborough Chronicle* (Maryborough), 27 June 1949, p. 2.
3 *Weekly Times* (Melbourne), 13 July 1949, p. 4.
4 *Mercury* (Hobart), 26 July 1949, p. 1.
5 *Brisbane Telegraph* (Brisbane), 3 August 1949, p. 4.
6 *Queensland Times* (Ipswich), 30 July 1949, p. 1.

the military to clamp "an iron wall of security on their plans".[1] However, seasoned reporters were pleasantly surprised when Army intelligence officers briefed them, commanders answered their questions in detail, and cameramen and photographers were escorted to record the troops mining coal.

The New South Wales and Commonwealth Governments established a command post in Sydney that was staffed by union and government officials and political operatives. It coordinated public relations and kept the broader union movement informed of what both Governments were doing. The Commonwealth Government launched an advertising campaign to encourage the miners to end their "Communist-inspired strike" and the topic of the strike featured in three of Chifley's radio broadcasts. Federal and state Labor MPs and union officials were dispatched to mining areas to urge the miners to return to work, and sent into factories and workshops to explain the Government's position. Arthur Calwell told 7,000 unionists at a meeting in Newcastle that the Government would not "let 20,000 stupid men defeat the interests of millions of Australians".[2]

As troops and sailors mined and moved coal, the voices of moderate miners grew stronger. On 15 August 1949 the men voted to return to work.[3] The Prime Minister continued to encourage the miners to rid their union of Communists and in subsequent elections Communist candidates were defeated.[4] Chifley thanked Australians for their fortitude during the strike, ministers thanked the armed services and plans were made to improve conditions in mining communities.

Everyone was relieved when the bitter strike ended but praise for the Government was short-lived. An opinion poll even suggested a swing away from Labor. People wondered why the Government was not as forceful in ending previous strikes. The Liberal Party said the level of industrial action since the war would have halved if the Government had confronted the Communists earlier.[5] Some unionists and ALP supporters believed the decision to use the troops as strike breakers was a betrayal of Labor principles and refused to help the ALP in the 1949 election.

The coal strike had a tangential effect on the bank nationalisation issue. It was yet another reason for Australians to be annoyed with their Govern-

1 *Lithgow Mercury* (Lithgow), 3 August 1949, p. 1.
2 *Newcastle Sun* (Newcastle), 25 July 1949, p. 7.
3 *Chronicle* (Adelaide), 4 August 1949, p. 5.
4 Broadcast 14 August 1949, Prime Minister's "Report to the Nation: 1948–1949," NAA A9790/844/257313.
5 *Herald* (Melbourne), 15 August 1949, p. 3.

ment and highlighted Labor's inconsistent approach to communicating with the public. During the strike the Government effectively communicated its resolve and won. Never did it show the same sophisticated effort or consistency for its banking plan.

16 Election Blueprints

"Australians have a world reputation for fair play ... let us uphold this splendid tradition, by listening without interruption to what the candidates have to say."[1]

In September 1949 Chifley turned sixty-four. Caucus presented him with a pipe and a tobacco pouch and sang "Happy Birthday". An observer noted that Australia's oldest prime minister and the longest-serving Labor prime minister "looked surprisingly unruffled. He is fit and his tail is up."[2]

That same month the Prime Minister set 10 December 1949 as the date for the country's election. Australian elections are always held on Saturdays and that particular Saturday was the last feasible date before Christmas and summer holidays when voters are more interested in family and friends than politicians. It was also forced Parliament to sit late into the year. Opposition MPs were be forced to stay in Canberra and away from the campaign trail and ministers had greater opportunity to boast about their achievements in Parliament.[3] The 1949 federal budget contained tax breaks and other incentives and it was hoped voters would see the benefits of these inducements by the end of the year.

The 1949 election was the largest and most complex since Federation because the Parliament had legislated to increase the size of the House of Representatives and to expand and change the voting system for the Senate. In 1901 the average electorate in the Lower House had around 25,000 people. Five decades later some electorates were four times that size. The membership of the House of Representatives would increase from seventy-four to 121 MPs and the Senate from thirty-six to sixty senators. Electoral boundaries were re-drawn so future MPs would represent around 40,000 voters and henceforth Australians would elect their senators through a complex system of quotas, proportional representation and preferences.[4]

Throughout 1949 there was a surge of construction in Parliament House as staff prepared for these changes. Both chambers received extra seating, offices were expanded, the press gallery was enlarged and kitchens and dining rooms were remodelled.[5]

---

1 *Daily News* (Perth), 16 November 1949, p. 5.
2 *Smith's Weekly* (Sydney), 3 September 1949, p. 7.
3 *Maryborough Chronicle* (Maryborough), 10 October 1949, p. 2.
4 Tasmania was unaffected by the changes and the Australian Capital Territory had a MP for the first time.
5 *Herald* (Melbourne), 10 December 1949, p. 13.

Arthur Calwell was the architect behind these changes and had persuaded his colleagues they would improve Labor's chances of keeping its majority in the Senate and that a larger House of Representatives would favour sitting Labor MPs and the ALP generally. The Liberal Party also thought the reorganisation suited the ALP especially in industrial areas and New South Wales. In public the Government claimed more MPs and Senators would mean better representation for voters, more oversight over a growing bureaucracy and a larger talent pool for future ministries.

The ALP planned to contest every seat in the country except for one Sydney seat considered to be safe Liberal territory. Labor considered New South Wales the must-win state while their opponents believed the ALP was vulnerable in Queensland because of a strong anti-Communist sentiment in the State and a widespread feeling that Labor had neglected the Far North.[1] The presence of anti-Communist voters made Victoria attractive to the Liberals and Tasmania, South Australia and Western Australia also seemed promising.[2] The Liberal and Country Parties agreed not to run candidates against each other, and based on the results of the Referendum and recent state elections and by elections the electoral algebra looked reassuring. The Opposition only needed 110,000 voters in key seats to change their 1946 voting behaviour and it would win.[3]

Wartime issues had dominated the 1940 and 1943 elections, and the 1946 election was about the transition from war to peace. The 1949 election would ask voters what they wanted from the second half of the twentieth century and who should lead them into that future. Labor aimed to leverage what remained of Ben Chifley's popularity and to criticise Menzies' perceived failures as a wartime Prime Minister. They planned to attack the Liberal and Country Parties as ill-disciplined, incompetent and too disunited to govern. The ALP would highlight its achievements in office and present the 1950s as a time to build the nation, create a stronger economy and secure the welfare of working people. It aimed to move past bank nationalisation and other unpopular measures and above all distance itself from the Communist Party in the wake of the coal strike. The Opposition parties planned to paint the Government as arrogant, stale and socialist. It would stress the same themes as the Menzies' roadshow: personal freedom, private enterprise and prosperity for Australian families.

---

1 Liberal Party Research Note, 23 September 1948, NLA MS 5000/Box 114, Redistributions: Miscellaneous Files, 1946, 1948, 1962.
2 *Canberra Survey* (Sydney), 17 June 1948, p. 2.
3 *Westralian Worker* (Perth), 28 October 1949, p. 3.

The major parties completed their campaign strategies once the date of the election was announced. This included selecting candidates, marshalling party supporters, fundraising, finalising media and advertising schedules, organising launches, events and rallies and locking in major speeches by leaders. There were so many changes to the electoral landscape no one could afford to take a single seat for granted. Officials developed detailed plans for each electorate.

In October 1949 the Honorary Treasurer of the Liberal Party reported the organisation was in good shape. It had 1300 branches with over 150,000 members and funds totalling £113,000 ($6.5 million today). More than 200 full-time, paid staff were in the field or working in state and federal offices.[1] The state divisions were confident. The Liberal Party in South Australia reported a sense of good will towards the party and ten percent of its 53,000 members had joined within the last twelve months.[2]

Federal President Richard Casey had amassed a substantial war chest from membership fees, business donations and private contributions.[3] He knew modern public relations and advertising practices were expensive and had spent the previous two years relentlessly and enthusiastically raising funds. Casey later claimed to have raised millions of pounds for the Liberal Party. He solicited donations from businesses, and any social and political networks he could tap into. He mailed letters to thousands of companies and individuals seeking contributions for "a large scale, centrally organised programme of research, publicity and public relations". Casey excelled at speaking to company boardrooms and small groups and encouraging those he dined with to reach for their wallets. At one Adelaide dinner he received pledges worth £15,000 (almost $1 million today) from prominent South Australians with promises of more to follow. Banks were another target. In early 1948 he went to London supposedly to solicit £100,000 from British companies with commercial interests in Australia. Back home he met with all but two of the private banks and received from one a "very satisfactory piece of paper". The National Bank handed over a cheque for £5000 (nearly $300,000 today).[4]

The UAP, the forerunner of the Liberal Party, had been criticised for letting corporate donations influence its policies. Menzies and Casey were determined not to accept money from trade associations and business

---

1 Liberal Party Federal Executive Minutes, 10 October 1949, NLA MS 5000/Box 1249, Federal Executive, 1947–1954(2).
2 *Advertiser* (Adelaide) 17 September 1949, p. 11.
3 It was not until 1984 that political parties received public funding for elections.
4 Casey diary entries: various dates in November 1949.

organisations. Menzies said, "An individual or firm who contributed £10 or £100 to the Party could not hope to influence its policy, but groups able to offer £10,000 or £20,000 might consider they had some claim to a say."[1] It was unclear how the Party differentiated the banks from this policy and at least in public Casey seemed keen to police donations. At one stage he rejected an offer of money from the Victorian Chamber of Commerce and returned a cheque written by the Fire Accident Underwriters' Association.[2]

The ALP war chest was lilliputian in comparison. Labor's funds came from party branches, Chifley admirers and large unions. The Clothing and Allied Trades Union contributed £20,000 to the ALP from 1943 to 1949. This was a significant amount for a union but almost pocket change compared to the money Casey was raising. Labor boasted about not accepting money from big business or Communists but by 1949 neither group had much inclination to support Labor.[3]

Serious fundraising for the ALP started only in July 1949 when the Prime Minister launched a £20,000 appeal (almost $1.5 million today) for Labor's Victorian campaign.[4] Every Victorian unionist was expected to donate five shillings, though few workers could afford that much from a single pay. Workers were encouraged to buy a one shilling Chifley stamp for five successive weeks.[5] These looked like Post Office stamps and featured Chifley's portrait sandwiched between the words "Labor" and "Victory Appeal". It is unknown how much the stamps raised but shop stewards peddled them to timber millers, tram conductors, printers, boot makers and other unionists throughout Victoria.

ALP branches in New South Wales received a booklet of "proved money spinners" to spur on their fund raising. Suggestions included bingo nights, fetes, card parties, dances, barbecues, country gymkhanas, an exotically named "American tea party" and having a pretty young woman rattle a donation tin in front of male passers-by. Branches could keep half of what they raised and send the rest to a centralised campaign fund.[6]

Chifley and Evatt controlled a special publicity or leaders' fund to help with advertising and state campaigns. The fund, which started originally in John Curtin's day, brought in money from party ads, unions, Chifley

---

1 *Camperdown Chronicle* (Camperdown), 2 September 1949, p. 10.
2 Casey diary entry: 19 August 1949.
3 *Westralian Worker* (Perth), 28 October 1949, p. 3.
4 *Age* (Melbourne), 1 November 1949, p. 3.
5 *Morning Bulletin* (Rockhampton), 5 September 1949, p. 4.
6 "How You Can Help Your Party Raise a Fighting Fund", Australian Labor Party, New South Wales, 1948, Donald K. Rodgers Papers, NLA MS 1536/Box 12.

followers and solicitations made by Senators and MPs. A few mid-sized companies sent in £100 and David Jones, the Sydney emporium, donated £500.¹ Sim Rubensohn's defection to the Liberal Party probably affected Labor's ability to approach business. In the twenty years Rubensohn had been involved in ALP campaigns he had garnered support from Caltex Oil, Phillips Electrical and other leading companies. When the Party lost Rubensohn, it lost these networks as well as his agency's discounted rates and tolerance for late payments.²

The Prime Minister personally acknowledged contributions to the leaders' fund. He wrote to each donor warning in a schoolmasterly manner that their money would buy no favours in Canberra. Chifley personally donated money, usually £50 (around $3000 today) to candidates struggling with campaign expenses. The money came with a caution, "I'm kicking the tin for a few others as well so you needn't mention this."³

Both major parties speculated how much the other had for the campaign. Casey and Menzies mistakenly believed the ALP could draw on "immense" amounts from the unions and Labor newspapers and radio stations. One or two Liberal candidates said the ALP got money from the Communist Party or used taxpayers' money to publish Labor propaganda.⁴

The ALP thought the Liberal Party campaign fund ran to £1,500,000 (almost $100m today) a third of which came from the private banks. Labor also claimed, correctly as it turned out, that Liberal allies like the Institute of Public Affairs and Preston Stanley's AWMAS were spending heavily to defeat Labor.⁵ Arthur Calwell said, "The Liberal Party has so much money it does not know what to do with it ... it has fallen over itself to hand it out to too many fools to carry out its advertising."⁶ Evatt said the money spent by anti-Labor forces was unparalleled in Australian history. "They have even received money from overseas to influence your vote."⁷

It was clear that Labor lagged well behind the Liberals and the ALP was being swamped on the radio and in the press.⁸ A newspaper reported, "Labor will probably have to fight the campaign on the most restricted

---

1 Uncatalogued election finance papers, Donald K. Rodgers Papers, NLA MS 1536/Box 12.
2 Stephen Mills, "Campaign Professionals: Party Officials and the Professionalism of Australian Political Parties," PhD diss, University of Sydney, 2013, p.125.
3 Haylen, p. 37.
4 *Daily Advertiser* (Wagga Wagga), 1 October 1949, p. 2.
5 *Labor Call* (Melbourne), 4 November 1949, p. 1.
6 Commonwealth, *Parliamentary Debates*, House of Representatives, 28 September 1949, (Arthur Calwell, Minister for Information).
7 *Sydney Morning Herald* (Sydney), 8 December 1949, p. 5.
8 *Sydney Morning Herald* (Sydney), 8 December 1949, p. 5.

finances at its disposal for many a long year."[1] The ALP's new advertising agency estimated that from March to September 1949 the Liberals and their allies spent ten times more on press advertising and even more on radio.[2]

The Liberals had learned from their 1946 campaign. This time they were better organised. In the previous election, the state divisions insisted on tight control of what happened within their borders and jealously maintained their independence. Through diplomacy, negotiation and perhaps because he was the chief fund raiser, Casey got state officials to focus on winning local races and cede more control to the national office especially for public relations and advertising. At the same time Rubensohn was bringing a harder edge to the Party's marketing efforts. When Menzies said advertising should be "free of vituperation", Rubensohn told him the coming campaign was a war and the Liberals needed to attack Chifley as much as to promote Menzies.

Labor's campaign management was less effective. The Lyle Davis agency in Sydney took over the ALP contract when Rubensohn left.[3] Davis was probably as professionally capable as his predecessor although a less colourful and public figure. The Party treated Davis as a hired hand rather than a key strategist. Chifley and selected ministers, state directors and members of the Federal Executive were the creative directors. The men, who failed to deliver a bank nationalisation campaign, were in charge of the most crucial campaign of their careers. They made the major decisions, leaving Davis the advertising expert to draft material, buy newspaper space and radio time and manage freight. The Prime Minister even authorised minor changes to campaign material and vetted invoices.

Sitting MPs of all parties were re-endorsed with a single exception; otherwise, the contrast between the candidates from the major parties was sharp. The Liberal Party recruited strong-minded, younger men, preferably with good war records, and who had experience in business, farming, the professions or local government. Prospective ALP candidates answered an ad in a Labor or union paper, sought support from other party members and pledged to abide by party rules. The central committee in each state then reviewed nominations, and after ruling out undesirables like Communists returned a list of vetted individuals to local branches which selected their candidate. In Tasmania the state executive decided candidates. This system tended to favour party officials and union men,

---
1 *Sunday Herald* (Sydney), 6 November 1949, p. 9.
2 Lyle Davis to Rodgers, 13 September 1949, Donald K. Rodgers Papers, NLA, MS 1536/Box 12.
3 *Newspaper News* (Sydney), 2 May 1949, p. 10.

effectively excluding women and those with different ideas.

The conservative roster included four ex-prime ministers (William Morris Hughes, Sir Earle Page, Arthur Fadden and Robert Menzies) and three future Liberal prime ministers (Harold Holt, John Gorton and William McMahon). The Liberal list also including four bankers, including Stan Card from the UBOA, and many veterans some with distinguished records.[1]

Charles Anderson, the Country Party candidate for the rural seat of Hume, was awarded a Military Cross in the First World War and was a Victoria Cross recipient and a prisoner of war in the Second World War. Thirty-six-year-old Nancy Wake was the most glamorous of the Liberal veterans. The highly decorated Wake had served with the British special forces and the French Resistance during the war. She had rescued downed Allied airmen, spirited Jewish refugees to safety and fought gun battles with the Nazis. Known as the woman without fear, the Liberal Party asked Wake to contest Evatt's Sydney seat when she returned to Australia. Her celebrity was such that older matrons, housewives and young women flocked to help.

Hubert Opperman, a former world cycling champion and an Air Force veteran was a Liberal first-timer. Forty-one-year-old Frederick Osborne, the brother of the General Manager of the Commercial Bank, had been decorated for his service with the Royal Navy in Norway and the Battle of the Atlantic. Western Australian Paul Hasluck had represented Australia at the United Nations and helped draft the UN Charter. He also writing part of Australia's official war history.[2] Richard Casey, older than most candidates, had a Military Cross from the First World War which stood him in good stead as he contested the Victorian seat of LaTrobe. Labor had fewer veterans and they tended to be older men like Defence Minister John Dedman who had been at Gallipoli.[3]

Three months before the election, Liberal candidates from Queensland and New South Wales attended a three-day "boot camp" at Kim's Camp near Gosford. It was a spartan beach resort where guests stayed in rough cabins and ate in a bush dining hall [4] Menzies, party elders and Liberal officials tutored them on campaign craft and party policies. A week later Victorian and Tasmanian candidates gathered for similar training in the

---

1 Hancock, *National and Permanent?*, p. 106.
2 Malcolm Allbrook, "Hasluck, Sir Paul Meernaa (1905–1993)", *Australian Dictionary of Biography*, National Centre of Biography, Australian National University, https://adb.anu.edu.au/biography/hasluck-sir-paul-meernaa-18555/text34447, published online 2017, accessed online 4 April 2022.
3 *Braidwood Review and District Advocate* (Braidwood), 6 December 1949, p. 1.
4 *Argus* (Melbourne), 1 September 1949, p. 5.

bayside town of Mount Martha outside Melbourne. The Country Party had a candidate conference in Canberra where Fadden and his deputy John McEwen outlined national campaign plans, and candidates identified issues that were important in their electorates. Despite a proposal at the Victorian ALP conference to train candidates, there is little evidence Labor hopefuls were formally prepared for the election.

The major parties claimed there was no discrimination against women yet the evidence suggests their interest was limited to the votes of women or appointing them to mundane administrative and fundraising roles within their organisations. Twenty women stood for election in 1949. The Country Party had no female candidates. The Liberals had three women and no Labor woman was preselected for the House of Representatives.[1] Millicent Preston Stanley, the nationally-known ideological warrior, failed to win Senate pre-selection for the Liberal Party. Most women who did stand were either Communists, independents or belonged to minor parties.

The wives of the party leaders were to play different roles during the campaign. Lizzie Chifley stayed clear of the limelight as she had always done. Irma Fadden, a "busy, cheerful [woman] without complexes", preferred home over headlines although a Fadden daughter or son would occasionally join their father on the hustings.[2] Pattie Menzies stood out as an accomplished campaigner. As the partner of an ex-prime minister and President of the Australian Women's Liberal Club she was very used to being in the public eye. Mrs Menzies was comfortable in all settings whether a speaking at a small morning tea or addressing a large audience. Mrs Menzies however never engaged in politics and would say, "That's not my job."[3] People from all backgrounds found Pattie Menzies agreeably normal. She accompanied her husband when she could and sat directly behind him at rallies "trying not to go to sleep".

The wives of lesser-known candidates supported their husbands, though their contributions were generally unrecognised. Minnie Peters, the wife of the Labor candidate for the seat of Burke, handed out leaflets for her husband. Zara Holt assisted her partner and future prime minister Harold Holt in "meetings and with last minute preparations". Val Doube made sure the Labor candidate for Henty got a good breakfast before leaving home.[4]

---

1 Janet Wilson and David Black, *Women Parliamentarians in Australia 1921–2013*, Canberra, Parliament of Australia, 2014. Women representing the Country Party were first elected to the Commonwealth Parliament in the 1970s.
2 *South Coast Bulletin* (Southport), 14 December 1949, p. 22.
3 Heather Henderson in discussion with author, 6 July 2021.
4 *Argus* (Melbourne), 3 December 1949, p. 6.

17 Launches and Vicious Slander

"Mr Lang set out for political revenge."[1]

Around 7.00 p.m. on 10 November 1949, Robert Menzies climbed the stage of the Canterbury Memorial Hall in Melbourne to launch the Liberal Party's election campaign. The hall overflowed with people. Every seat was taken, men and women stood in the aisles, sat on the floor and a line snaked up the stairs. A thousand people stood on the pavement outside and listened to loudspeakers. Hundreds were listening to the radio in cars parked along Canterbury Road. The Leader of the Country Party was present in a show of unity, and the biggest radio hook-up in Australian political history stood ready to broadcast what Menzies said.

Menzies speech lasted an hour and was delivered in clear, forceful terms. He attacked the Government and outlined the Liberal vision for the future. He called the ALP dangerous, pounded Chifley and linked the Government to words like *socialism*, *Communism*, *nationalisation*, *rationing* and *shortages*. He said he would outlaw the Communist Party and seek a constitutional amendment to ban Parliament passing any socialist legislation without a referendum. There were promises of full employment, industrial peace, more manufacturing, better farm prices and national development. He committed to introducing national service.

Car horns honked along Canterbury Road when he promised to end petrol shortages. There was two minutes of thunderous applause when he pledged to stop bank nationalisation and promised to replace the Governor of the Commonwealth Bank with a board of directors. He told women that they had "an unanswerable claim to economic, legal, industrial and political equality" and his government would design "housing and similar schemes" with them in mind. He outlined plans for better education and medical services.

The radio networks had allowed an hour for the speech, so Menzies abruptly sat down when he realised his time was up. The hall erupted in wild applause and shouts of "Good old Bob."[2]

Newspaper reviews the next day ranged from positive to reverential.

---

1 *Argus* (Melbourne), 8 December 1949, p. 6.
2 *Sydney Morning Herald* (Sydney), 11 November 1949, p. 5.

Extra material was sent to editors so they could run special supplements in their papers and 30,000 copies of Menzies' speech were mailed to Party branches. The themes at the launch were condensed into a two-minute cinema ad and screened nationwide.[1]

Evatt reacted to the speech by accusing the Liberals of "manufacturing a synthetic poisonous fear to influence the minds of the electors against the Chifley Government".[2] Minister Eddie Ward said Menzies favoured a bankers' monopoly. A Labor newspaper said Menzies' ideas for the Commonwealth Bank were a back-hander to the banks.[3] Chifley said he did not listen to Menzies because he was in his office working.

Don Rodgers had worked on Chifley's speech for the Labor launch and Menzies' address would have worried him more than he already was. Government departments had swamped Rodgers with data on government achievements but there was nothing really new.[4] Rodgers circulated a draft speech to trusted confidants and asked for suggestions. Whatever came forward went unheeded. The final version of the Chifley address lacked fresh ideas or much else that would excite the public. The Prime Minister boasted there would be no glittering promises and he kept that promise. The speech asked for a blank cheque for another term rather than offering an inspiring vision for Australia's future.

There were no impassioned crowds, party faithful or reporters on hand at the 1949 ALP launch. Instead, Chifley recorded an address in a Canberra radio station and copies of his speech were shipped on vinyl discs to stations country-wide. A backup disc was lodged in Sydney and journalists there and in Melbourne had only an hour to listen to the recorded speech before it aired.[5]

Chifley's address lasted thirty-six minutes. It was the shortest launch in Australian electoral history and among the most tedious.[6] The Prime Minister highlighted his Government's successes in a mix of data and dry language. He rejected charges he had nationalisation plans beyond banking and said recent judicial rulings meant the Government could not exceed its constitutional powers. Nevertheless, the Government was responsible for ensuring "resources of money and credit are used to the

1 *Liberal Party Cinema Advertisement: The House that You Built* (1949), National Film and Sound Archive, NFSA Title No. 52317.
2 *Northern Star* (Lismore), 14 November 1949, p. 1.
3 *Labor Call* (Melbourne), 18 November 1949, p. 3.
4 Don Rodgers interviewed by Mel Pratt, 29 April 1971.
5 *National Advocate* (Bathurst), 14 November 1949, p. 1.
6 Ben Chifley, "Election Speeches, Ben Chifley, 1949", Museum of Australian Democracy, 14 November 1949, https://electionspeeches.moadoph.gov.au/speeches/1949-ben-chifley?highlight=1949.

best advantage of the community".[1] Critics said this showed Chifley had yet to relinquish his idea of state-controlled banking.

By pre-recording his address, the Prime Minister completely controlled his message and avoided the hecklers and technical glitches that often plagued political rallies. It was certainly more convenient for the prime ministerial diary to drive the short distance from Parliament to nearby station 2CA. However, those arrangements robbed Chifley of the opportunity to challenge what Menzies had said days earlier, and the chance to feed off the energy of a live audience. The launch did little to inspire voters, and some said Chifley had been dismissive by making his case over the radio rather than facing his fellow Australians.[2] Fadden said the speech was barren and casual.

Two days later Fadden launched the Country Party campaign in Boonah in his electorate and a few hours from Brisbane. It was the first time a major party had launched its campaign in a rural area. Boonah was buzzing on launch night. Farmers came in from nearby properties, cars lined the streets and a band played. Two thousand people packed the Teviot Theatre and Menzies was there to support his colleague.[3] Fadden's speech was relayed by amplifiers to the overflowing crowd outside and a nationwide radio audience.

For an hour Fadden hammered away at socialism and Labor. He questioned whether Australians wanted the hammer and sickle to be on their coat of arms and asked if "the emu shall be murdered and the kangaroo massacred".[4] He detailed the shortcomings of the Chifley era: chronic shortages, crippled production, bad roads and rural industries that struggled.[5] He promised a referendum on banking and to end petrol rationing. When he finished, the audience stamped and cheered and sang "For he's a jolly good fellow."

The three launches by the leaders started their parties' national campaigns. A RAAF aircraft flew the Prime Minister to Central Queensland to start a four-week whirlwind national tour. Rockhampton was the first stop. It was in the electorate of Capricornia which had elected Labor stalwart Frank Forde for two decades. Forde was briefly Prime Minister when John Curtin died and then Deputy Prime Minister under Chifley. Though Rockhampton was a Labor stronghold, Forde lost his seat in 1946. Ben Chifley arrived to show the ALP could win it back. The

---

1 *Age* (Melbourne), 15 November 1949, p. 3.
2 *Queensland Times* (Ipswich), 18 November 1949, p. 2.
3 *Beaudesert Times* (Beaudesert), 18 November 1949, p. 7.
4 *Sunday Herald* (Sydney), 27 November 1949, p. 10.
5 *Daily Mercury* (Mackay), 8 November 1949, p. 6.

Prime Minister was full of fight as he addressed a good-natured crowd of men in shorts and women in summer frocks.

No audience was keener during Chifley's travels than the 2,500 voters who heard him speak in Adelaide. The venue was full fifty minutes before he arrived and the pavement outside was jammed. There was frequent applause when Chifley talked about the banks. "The High Court has said the Commonwealth's power to socialise is very small. We have said very clearly that where a public utility is not giving the best and most efficient service to the community or is exploiting the people it should be nationalised." When the rally ended, supporters surrounded Chifley's car forcing him to walk back to his hotel. Fans followed behind cheering.[1]

The 17 November was a typical campaign day for Menzies. He rose before dawn and took a chartered flight from Sydney to Newcastle. After breakfast he spoke to 200 people at an open-air meeting and then drove fifty miles in sweltering heat to speak from the back of a truck in Dungog, a small farming and timber town of 2,000 people. In Maitland he spoke at the Town Hall to 1,000 people and then drove to Newcastle to attend a dinner. The next day he flew to Brisbane where the pattern of activities was repeated.[2]

Menzies usually made two or more campaign speeches a day, often sparring with hecklers among the crowd. The Opposition Leader was a skilled orator and had a knack of handling interjections. If an audience looked hostile he would confidently stride in, make a joke or two to lower tensions and continue without notes. Once the first interruption was out of the way Menzies would sally forth in his call for an Australia free of Chifley and socialism.[3]

During the campaign Chifley and Menzies found themselves in the same town twice. In Ballarat they addressed crowds on the same evening. A circus was performing in Ballarat that week so an offbeat cast of jugglers, clowns and pirates wandered between the Chifley meeting and the Menzies rally.[4] In Brisbane the two nodded when they met in a hotel lobby by chance.

The 1949 campaign was intense. Menzies, Chifley and Fadden each averaged five rallies a day and together travelled over 50,000 miles. They parried interjections, battled faulty microphones and dodged the occasional missile. Between meetings there were plane flights and car rides, quick meals, catnaps and solitary walks to clear the mind. Journalists reported the

---

1 *Sydney Morning Herald* (Sydney), 1 December 1949, p. 5.
2 *Courier-Mail* (Brisbane), 17 November 1949, p. 6.
3 Heather Henderson in discussion with author, 6 July 2021.
4 *Sydney Morning Herald* (Sydney), 26 November 1949, p. 4.

Menzies' entourage was confident, almost triumphant. Menzies' daughter Heather recalled, "The Liberal side was all on a high because they felt they were going to win because the election had been handed to them on a plate by Chifley saying he was going to nationalise the banks."[1] Menzies was weary but in excellent spirits. He was confident of the outcome and so was Fadden even though by the end of the gruelling campaign his voice was hoarse and he had lost a stone (around six kilograms).

In public Chifley appeared calm and confident but the *Sydney Morning Herald* detected signs of strain.[2] Privately, Chifley had reservations about the result of the election. He wrote to his friend Norman Makin, who was the Ambassador in Washington, "All the Party have gone to the country confident that they will be returned but my opinion is that it will be a strain particularly in view of the amount of money the Opposition is able to spend and the violent press opposition."[3] He wrote to another friend, "The Opposition are beating the Communist drum very loudly for the coming election hoping I suppose to have some effect on the religious (i.e. Catholic vote) vote."[4] His ministers were more optimistic. John Dedman thought the ALP would win as decisively as it had in 1943.

In the final days of the campaign the leaders were in their own electorates and making their last broadcast to the nation. Commonwealth electoral laws prohibited political broadcasts within forty-eight hours of polling day. This ban, which did not apply to newspapers, was to give voters a period of calm reflection and prevent opponents making sensationalist last-minute claims. Each leader had fifteen minutes for a final nationwide broadcast two days out from the election.

The Prime Minister used his time to warn voters that the Liberal and Country Parties were too disunited to deserve their trust. He emphasised Labor's unswerving commitment to Australia and urged women to reject Menzies' policy of "conscripting the youth of Australia". He affirmed Labor could only control banking through constitutional means. Menzies told voters they had to choose being their own masters or allowing the state to be their master.[5] Fadden said the Government was socialist.

Three days before election day the campaign took a nasty, unforeseen twist. Ex-New South Wales Premier and federal MP Jack Lang personally attacked Ben and Lizzie Chifley. The animosity between Lang and Chifley dated back to 1935 when Chifley contested Lang's state seat and played a

---

1 Heather Henderson in discussion with author, 6 July 2021.
2 *Sydney Morning Herald* (Sydney), 9 December 1949, p. 1.
3 Crisp, pp. 370–371.
4 *Daily Telegraph* (Sydney), 9 December 1949, p. 8.
5 *Daily Telegraph* (Sydney), 8 December 1949, p. 1.

part in Lang's expulsion from the ALP. Lang formed the Australian Labor Party (Non-Communist) in 1940. There was a brief reconciliation with the ALP before Lang broke away one more time in 1943. He was elected to Federal Parliament in 1946 and was the leader of a small cluster of former Labor MPs.

Lang was a formidable presence in Parliament and known for his forceful and bitter attacks on the Government. Labor MPs called him the "de facto leader of the Opposition" since he voted against the Government 117 times during his single term in Parliament.[1] When he stood in the House of Representatives to wallop the Government, the chamber was packed and Liberal and Country MPs were delighted.[2] Yet despite his ferocity Chifley always treated Lang's attacks as political rather than personal.

Twenty-four hours before the radio blackout Lang went on radio to allege that from 1930 to 1942 Ben and Lizzie Chifley had lent money at exorbitant interest rates to working people in Bathurst. He repeated the accusations to a stunned town hall audience. Lang said Chifley had attacked the banks for high interest rates during the Depression but did the same thing himself. Lang argued Australians needed to know the real Ben Chifley.[3]

The 1949 election campaign was tough, often boisterous but attacking a man's family was seen as disgraceful. Lang might say what he pleased about the Prime Minister but people were angry he criticised Lizzie.

The Prime Minister retaliated swiftly. He chose a small amusement park in Lang's electorate and told a crowd of thousands what had really happened.[4] He explained he was well-known in Bathurst and people often sought his advice. Sometimes widows and families asked him to invest their money. Chifley loaned their funds through a solicitor to people who otherwise would struggle to get a bank loan. He did this in accordance with a New South Wales law which required a trustee to get the best possible rate of return when he managed other people's money. Lizzie became the unpaid trustee of these loans when Chifley returned to Parliament in 1940. The couple had not received a single penny from these transactions. The audience booed when Lang's name was mentioned and cheered when the Prime Minister finished. People rushed forward to shake his hand. Thus Chifley ended the efforts of the former Labor premier to drag him down in the final days of the campaign.

---

1 *Argus* (Melbourne), 8 December 1949, p. 3.
2 *Daily Telegraph* (Sydney), 18 March 1949, p. 8.
3 *Sydney Morning Herald* (Sydney), 7 December 1949, p. 6.
4 *Argus* (Melbourne), 8 December 1949, p. 3.

No Australian election had received as much international attention as the 1949 contest. The Australian poll was scheduled two months before a general election in the United Kingdom, where nationalisation and socialism were also issues. The view in Britain was that the Australian result might be a barometer for what could happen there. *The Times* offered no predictions. The *Daily Herald*, a British Labour Party newspaper, said the contest was between Liberal promises and Labor performance. The *Manchester Guardian* referred to the election as the Ben and Bob show.

A British correspondent flew to Australia to report on the campaign but was more interested in which party sang "God Save the King" the loudest and which had the most Union Jacks on stage. The BBC and the National Broadcasting Company of America (NBC) commissioned a short television documentary on the election. The Associated Press in America said the English-speaking world was watching closely and *Time Magazine* predicted the Government was facing the fight of its life. European newspapers were only interested in the fate of Victorian Liberal candidate Hubert Opperman, whose cycling triumphs were still remembered.

The odds seemed to favour the Opposition in the final days. English bookmakers listed six to four against the Government and Australian bookies had the odds at five to four.[1] One Sydney advertising executive wagered a large sum on the Liberals and there were rumours that a Labor minister had bet £4,000 on his party (over $250,000 today.) Investors sensed the mood for change. Bank shares rose on the stock exchanges and Australian shares traded higher in New Zealand.[2]

Some said it was an omen when days before the election the long-serving Labour Government of New Zealand was defeated at the polls. Canberra's small corps of diplomats speculated about a Liberal victory as staff in the offices of Labor ministers pondered an uncertain future. The latest opinion polls showed the Opposition was ahead and that Australians opposed nationalisation.

---

1 *Sydney Morning Herald* (Sydney), 9 December 1949, p. 2.
2 *Daily Telegraph* (Sydney), 8 December 1949, p. 35.

18 Bankers' Last Push

"Australia for the first time is voting on the way of life it will live – for socialism or continuance of the general way of life the nation has known up to the present."[1]

The 1949 election was grand political theatre. The major political parties were centre stage, fiercely competing to win government while a cast of diverse, mostly uncoordinated characters shouted from the wings, hoping to force the dramatic exit of the Labor Government. Some players were in plain view. Others quietly worked behind the scenes.

The private banks knew they would be the biggest losers if the ALP won the election. Constitution or not they were convinced a triumphant Labor Government would find a way to press their industry into the service of the state. A fourth-term Labor Government might bury the banking industry under mountainous red tape or bring in regulations that made it just too difficult to operate. It could aggressively buy up bank shares or direct the Commonwealth Bank to undercut the private banks on interest rates, fees and charges. It might demand the private banks pay ever greater amounts into the wartime special accounts that still continued. Some even suggested a re-elected Chifley and Evatt might stack the High Court with extra judges, similar to President Roosevelt's failed attempt in 1937 to add additional liberal justices to the US Supreme Court to resume the "task of building anew on the Constitution a system of living law".[2] Another Labor manoeuvre might be to abolish appeals to the Privy Council.

Prior to bank nationalisation the Chairmanship of the Associated Banks rotated among the general managers of the private banks. In 1949 McConnan was persuaded to stay on until after the election campaign. That made Leslie McConnan the busiest of bankers and those around him marvelled at his stamina. The head of the Union Bank was overseas for most of the year and the General Manager of the Bank of Australasia stayed largely silent. The General Manager of the ES&A, E. G. Wilson, accompanied McConnan on some visits and addressed the wives of Melbourne bank officers, warning that if the Government won,

---

1 *Maryborough Chronicle* (Maryborough), 17 October 1949, p. 1.
2 "How FDR Lost His Brief War on the Supreme Court," National Constitution Centre. February 5, 2023. https://constitutioncenter.org/blog/how-fdr-lost-his-brief-war-on-the-supreme-court-2.

bureaucrats would be in their kitchens dictating what they baked.¹

In May 1949 McConnan embarked on his own roadshow to motivate bank officers and let them know their banks wanted them involved in the election. He started in regional Victoria, then visited Central Queensland in August and travelled to Western Australia and South Australia in October. McConnan's last stop was Tasmania to meet bank staff in Hobart, Burnie and Launceston. In between he managed a holiday with his family in Surfers Paradise but still found time to visit bank officers in local branches.

McConnan knew the mathematics of unseating Labor. A National Bank memo identified that a 2.8 percent swing against the ALP would bring the Opposition a narrow victory. A 4 percent swing would give Menzies and Fadden a fifteen-seat majority. These swings depended on a relatively small number of people who supported Labor in 1946 switching their votes to non-Labor candidates. The memo recommended bank officers be persuaded to encourage four or five voters to "swing over" and each branch to target thirty-five people to abandon the Government.²

In November 1949 McConnan asked National Bank managers in Victoria to gauge local feelings and explain the importance of the poll to their customers. The Moonee Ponds manager reported he contacted 135 customers and was "pleased to report all of them are on our side including a big chain of shops who will support our cause to the hilt".

McConnan authorised a letter to National Bank customers warning them about the Government's intentions to destroy their banks despite the recent Privy Council judgment.³ Thousands of copies of the letter were printed and freighted from head office to National Bank branches, where managers personalised and signed each letter before sending them out by first-class mail. A few customers complained about the letter and bank officers were soon on their doorstep explaining the Bank's position. As the poll got closer, the National Bank cancelled leave and deployed extra staff to branches to fill in for bank officers volunteering for the campaign.

Historian Geoffrey Blainey observed that Leslie McConnan seemed to enjoy "the daily excitement, the sense of crusade, the adulation, the mingling with people".⁴ Thomas Heffer of the Bank of New South Wales was as committed as McConnan to saving the banks but shunned the

---

1 *Sun* (Melbourne), 6 October 1949, p. 8.
2 Memo for Chief Manager, Conscription of Labour, 27 September 1949, NABA/Bank Nationalisation, p. 2.
3 National Bank Circular, 21 November 1949, Arthur Calwell Papers, NLA MS 4738/Box 31.
4 Blainey, p. 370.

public spotlight.¹ Heffer preferred to stay in the background and had played a leading role in the banks' High Court challenge. In September 1949 he wrote to his customers and shareholders and sounded an alarm. Bank nationalisation was how socialists regimented an economy and the Privy Council decision had blunted not ended the threat to banking.² The President of his Board, Sir Frederick Trout, echoed his feelings.

At the Bank's annual general meeting in 1949, Trout thanked the Bank's 6,200 staff for their "loyalty in the fight to preserve the existence of the trading banks". In the press he declared the Government was "still intent on eliminating the trading banks. Its obsession with this objective is a measure of the determination of the socialists to take over the banks as the first and major step in destroying the fabric of free enterprise and individual liberty."³

Claud Victor Janes was the long-serving, enthusiastic and sometimes stormy manager of the economic department in the Bank of New South Wales. He was somewhat of a field director for Heffer and Trout in their resistance to nationalisation.

Early in 1949 the UBOA (NSW) invited Janes to address its organisers. Janes said bank officers should downplay their links with the banks since too much talk of banking would give the impression the banks were self-obsessed. Instead, they should infiltrate rather than confront their communities, presenting themselves as calm, reasonable and determined men not prone to excitement or belligerence. He advised them to act discreetly but always remember their main task was to help win the election.⁴

In February 1949 the Commercial Bank of Sydney released employees for full-time election work with the UBOA (NSW). In South Australia the ever-colourful Oscar Isaachsen of the Bank of Adelaide was more involved. His bank ran ads in South Australian papers and he even handed out non-Labor how-to-vote cards on polling day.⁵

In Victoria the Central Committee coordinated the campaign efforts of the Melbourne banks. The Committee had a full-time chief executive and a staff of officers seconded on full time duty from their banks.⁶ By September the Committee was advertising in major and provincial newspapers, sponsoring radio shows and special broadcasts and had

---

1 *Smith's Weekly* (Sydney), 22 May 1948, p. 11.
2 *Singleton Argus* (Singleton), 28 September 1949, p. 2.
3 Annual Report, Bank of New South Wales, 30 September 1949, p. 11.
4 A. H. B. Jones, Inspector Bank of New South Wales to L. J. McConnan, 1 February 1949, WGA/GM102
5 *News* (Adelaide), 12 December 1949, p. 5.
6 May, p. 18.

circulated over a million brochures, leaflets and pamphlets. It trained bank officers in public speaking, commissioned a two-minute cinema featurette and paid a *Herald* journalist to produce pro-bank material for radio stations and country newspapers.[1] There were plans for a twenty-minute documentary for screening in cinemas but these never eventuated.[2]

In October Richard Casey and Leslie McConnan lunched at the Melbourne Club. The Federal President only then became aware of what the banks were doing in the election and even then Casey felt McConnan was exaggerating.[3] It is unclear how much the private banks contributed directly to the Liberal and Country but years later Labor MP Fred Daly claimed "some members of parliament publicly admitted the banks had financed their campaigns in 1949."[4] The bank officers who stood as Liberal candidates may have received help from bank unions, but the banks themselves were guarded about how much support they gave politicians.

Throughout 1949 members of the UBOA were on a singular mission: to support any candidate who opposed socialism and oppose any who supported it. By December 400 officers were working full-time to unseat Labor and being paid by their banks. Thousands of other bank officers took unpaid leave to do union work or volunteered after hours and on weekends (sometimes with their wives.) Others campaigned during the day then worked back at night. Staff who worked behind the scenes in the banks, such as typists, cleaners, lift operators and car drivers, contributed financially to union activities.

Each state affiliate of the UBOA had a committee which developed and implemented election plans, ran ads, courted the media, sent out speakers and published literature. Some worked with political parties while others limited their operations to local communities. Individual unionists passed out literature, pasted posters, spoke with voters, addressed rallies, hosted discussion groups, verified electoral rolls and encouraged people to vote. On election day unionists stationed themselves at polling places and handed pocket-sized how-to-vote cards. Some were scrutineers who monitored the counting of votes.[5]

The private banks made staff, facilities, equipment and overdrafts available to the state-based unions. The Victorian bank officers' committee operated from the ES&A Bank in Collins Street, and the Bank of New

---

[1] Memo to Chief Manager: Opposition to Bank Nationalisation – List of Activities, 22 September 1949, NABA/Bank Nationalisation, p. 1.
[2] Memo to Chairman Associated Banks: Films, Undated, NABA/Bank Nationalisation, p. 2.
[3] Casey diary entry: 24 October 1949.
[4] Daly, p. 79.
[5] *Riverine Grazier* (Hay), 27 September 1949, p. 3.

South Wales made a garage at its Ashfield branch available for an election headquarters for the UBOA (NSW).[1] The bank unions functioned independently but loosely coordinated their activities with the banks. When the Bank of New South Wales protested about an activity, Stan Card threatened to stop the election work of his entire seven thousand-strong membership. The Bank quickly backed down.[2]

New South Wales staged the largest election campaign. The UBOA (NSW) sent full-time organisers and well-trained speakers to the state's most vulnerable electorates.[3] Between September and December 1949 the union organised 300 meetings in town halls, factories, foundries, department stores, timber yards, insurance companies and street corners. Bank officers in the country talked to shopkeepers and held discussion groups for farmers.[4] There was an enormous amount of literature including a weekly union newsletter with a circulation of half a million copies.[5]

New South Wales also pioneered disruptive tactics. Young bank officers appeared at ALP rallies to disrupt proceedings and heckle Labor candidates. This was completely unexpected behaviour from bank officers and clearly rattled some ALP candidates. Young officers clashed with Labor supporters at a meeting addressed by John Dedman. Fred Daly MP said, "The private banks were paying officers at double rates to attend and disrupt ALP election meetings."[6] There were rumours that bank cars ferried young men from rally to rally to break up ALP meetings.

These troublemaking tactics spread. Obstreperous bank officers were ejected from a South Australian meeting addressed by Arthur Calwell. He called the boisterous protesters "educated larrikins" out for rapid promotion. Menzies chuckled at Calwell's anger. "For the Minister for Immigration to describe bank officers as larrikins was a perfect example of an iron pot calling an aluminium kettle black."[7]

The employee committee in Melbourne had thirty-five bank officers on full-time duty plus liaison officers in key suburbs.[8] The Committee ran seminars on door-knocking and campaign tactics. Menzies, McEwen and McConnan spoke at some of these sessions, while at other seminars Eric Butler of the League of Rights taught finance and economics. Bank officers

---

1 Harry Jago interviewed by Peter Coleman, 22 March 1989.
2 May, p. 123.
3 Harry Jago interviewed by Peter Coleman, 22 March 1989.
4 *Sydney Morning Herald* (Sydney), 8 December 1949, p. 2.
5 May, p. 103.
6 *Sydney Morning Herald* (Sydney), 19 November 1949, p. 4.
7 *Age* (Melbourne), 3 December 1949, p. 6.
8 May, p. 108.

spoke at 250 meetings around Melbourne, including at the fashionable Georges Emporium on Collins Street. Bank unionists handed out literature, wrote to newspapers, approached church groups and talked to communities who might be especially vulnerable if the banks were abolished.[1] By mid-November bank officers had visited 35,000 homes in Victoria.

Victoria had the only women's banking group. A hundred women belonged to the Bank Employees' Wives' Committee and their mission was to tell Australian women the truth about nationalisation. They conducted radio talks and advertised although the extent of their activities was unclear.[2] There were hundreds of other organisations that were more visible so this small group might have been overlooked but for Arthur Calwell. The Labor minister claimed the banks were forcing wives to protest and support their husbands otherwise their partners' careers would be in jeopardy. Calwell immediately drew attention to the committee and was howled down for an unchivalrous slur on these women.[3]

The UBOA (QLD) had a particularly effective campaign. It had a speaking squad that took the anti-socialism fight into every corner of Queensland. The speakers were chosen for their personality, banking experience and presentation skills. Of the eight individuals, most were members of veteran, service or community organisations which provided ready connections in provincial centres and country towns. They were on extended leave from their banks and funded by a shilling-a-week fee levied on each bank unionist in Queensland.

The speakers travelled in pairs starting in Labor strongholds and marginal seats. By polling day they had crisscrossed Queensland three times. In each town they motivated fellow unionists, bank staff and local sympathisers and spoke at public meetings in the evening. Typically one speaker talked about bank nationalisation and the other broadened the talk to cover the perils of socialism and Communism.[4] They mocked Labor governments and the absurdity of their past attempts to run fish-and-chip shops and other enterprises.

A large map of Queensland in an operations centre in Brisbane tracked the progress of each speaking team. The centre also arranged the distribution of almost a million pamphlets and comic strips, and blotters, cricket fixtures and bus timetables branded with anti-nationalisation

---

1 *Westralian Worker* (Perth), 1 April 1949, p. 2.
2 May, p. 109.
3 *Herald* (Melbourne), 26 November 1949, p. 2.
4 *Townsville Daily Bulletin* (Townsville), 2 September 1949, p. 5.

messages.¹ The *Courier Mail* reported that 3,000 bank officers volunteered during the election and "many were key workers for the Country and Liberal Parties".² The Country Party was so impressed with how the bank officers organised themselves they recommended primary producers should adopt a similar model at the next state election.

Western Australian bank officers had a committee which educated the state's swinging voters through a monthly newsletter and material supplied to country newspapers.³ By December 1949 twenty-five West Australian bank officers were employed full-time as public speakers, researchers, writers and publicists.⁴ South Australian bank officers said they would "do everything in [their] power to protect the rights and liberties of the people of Australia ... and remove the socialist government from power on 10 December".⁵ Forty bank officers, mostly in Adelaide, worked full-time, publishing a monthly newsletter and supporting citizens' protest groups. Seven full-time officers worked on the election campaign in Tasmania. It would be wrong to suggest banks and bank officers were the only aggrieved groups to campaign in the 1949 election. Australia's doctors were as incensed with Labor's socialist agenda.

One worthy goal of the Chifley Government was to make healthcare available to all Australians regardless of their financial status. This included universal coverage for doctors' services, hospital stays and pharmaceuticals to be paid for by a taxpayer funded insurance scheme. The British Medical Association of Australia (BMA), the peak body for the medical profession, saw Labor's policy ambitions as socialised medicine that would turn doctors into public servants and erode patient confidentiality.

The BMA launched its own healthcare plan which GPs readily passed to their patients. Doctors vehemently criticised Labor, and in northern Tasmania GPs and specialists went on the radio from morning to night to assail the Government.⁶ The Government in turn accused BMA members of callous indifference towards the sick and Labor newspapers said they were the enemy of the people. With neither side willing to compromise, surgeries joined bank branches as centres of resistance committed to seeing the ALP did not get another term.

Australian women had grievances too. Four years after the war there were

1 May, p. 110.
2 *Courier-Mail* (Brisbane), 14 December 1949, p. 6.
3 *Kalgoorlie Miner* (Kalgoorlie), 29 March 1949, p. 2.
4 May, p. 110.
5 *Advertiser* (Adelaide), 8 November 1949, p. 3.
6 *Mercury* (Hobart), 7 December 1949, p. 29.

still rationing, shortages, big queues, high prices, black markets and coal strikes. Living costs, rents and the lack of affordable housing compounded the problems for women. One correspondent said "Mrs Australia" was fed up. The President of the Housewives Association of New South Wales said, "The housewife knows [she] has been unduly ignored and resents it. She is eagerly awaiting her opportunity to show that she knows her politics on 10 December."[1] The President of the Liberal Party in New South Wales forecast a silent rebellion among women and that many would break with tradition and vote differently from their husbands and fathers.[2]

The AWMAS was perhaps the most vocal of all women's groups. Seven thousand women belonged to eighty-eight branches including twenty-five branches in marginal seats.[3] The AWMAS held meetings, advertised, passed out anti-nationalisation literature, canvassed homeowners and took every opportunity to engage voters. Three days before the election the Movement held a final rally in the Sydney Town Hall. Women wore Union Jack flags pinned to their dresses and Preston Stanley composed a special song for the occasion. The audience clapped after a teenage girl declared, "We were born during a depression, we grew up during a war and we have entered adolescence in a period of inflation. We have little to look back upon. We are hoping that we may look forward with optimism to a happier and more contented future."[4]

Preston Stanley understood the power of celebrity. Earlier, the AWMAS engaged Englishwoman Jennie Broad for a speaking tour of provincial New South Wales. Broad was Britain's first female test pilot and had ferried Spitfires around England during the war. She migrated to Australia hoping to become a pilot, but finding Australian aviation closed to women, she became a beauty consultant. She warned country women about socialism and told them the Labor Government in the United Kingdom had turned Britain into a land of industrial turmoil and perpetual queues.

During the election campaign Preston Stanley invited Sir Winston Churchill, then out of office, to come to Australia and tell voters how socialism was ruining Britain.[5] She offered to pay his expenses and arrange a national speaking tour for the British stateman which would draw huge crowds. This was Preston Stanley's boldest move and whether

---

1 *Sydney Morning Herald* (Sydney), 8 December 1949, p. 2.
2 *Daily Examiner* (Grafton), 2 December 1949, p. 1.
3 *Sun* (Sydney), 28 July 1949, p. 18.
4 *Sun* (Sydney), 7 December 1949, p. 33.
5 *Brisbane Telegraph* (Brisbane), 4 November 1949, p. 10.

the invitation was genuine or a brassy stunt was unclear. Churchill diplomatically declined the invitation, stating he had no plans to visit Australia in the near future.

The major parties had very few female candidates but they did recognise the importance of women voters. The Liberal Party formed an alliance with the Australian Women's National League and advertised regularly in the *Australian Women's Weekly*. One campaign ad showed two dimpled toddlers with the text underneath, "This will be your last chance to save your children from a life under a socialist dictatorship, from living under conditions which are basically wrong ... conditions which will destroy family life, take away freedoms and make everyone a slave of the state."[1]

The cash-strapped ALP ran fewer ads in the *Weekly*. These focused on the Government's achievements and the failings of previous conservative governments but otherwise offered few incentives for women to turn out for the Government. For its part the *Weekly* maintained a neutral editorial policy and encouraged women to learn about the issues before they voted.[2]

Petrol rationing was as irksome and perhaps as emotive as bank nationalisation, socialised medicine and the myriad of issues that frustrated Australian women. Fuel rationing was introduced during the war but had been progressively eased since 1945. After the war demand for petrol grew by ten percent each year and the nation's supplies of oil could not keep up. The Government insisted rationing was essential because the global market was still affected by war-damaged oilfields, there was limited shipping and Australia had limited foreign currency reserves to buy more oil. Arthur Fadden and the Country Party were the most persistent critics of Labor's petrol policy because farmers needed fuel for machinery and country drivers had to cover great distances.

Halfway through 1949 the High Court struck down the Commonwealth's petrol supply regulations and the Government was forced to return the responsibility for setting petrol prices and distribution to the states. Chifley warned premiers there would be chaos unless they enacted regulations. The states failed to act and for a time there seemed to be no shortage of petrol. Motorists threw their petrol coupons in the air and crowded the forecourts of service stations. This apparent abundance was short-lived and by October there was a severe shortage of petrol.[3] Service stations closed on weekends or some only served loyal customers. Doctors

---

1 *Australian Women's Weekly* (Sydney), 19 November 1949, p. 24.
2 *Australian Women's Weekly* (Sydney), 10 December 1949, p. 18.
3 *Argus* (Melbourne), 7 June 1949, p. 5.

and nurses could not get enough petrol for home visits and country rounds. People blamed hoarders, the oil companies and the Government.

The states quickly handed their responsibilities back to Canberra and the Government reintroduced petrol rationing. Australian motorists again fretted over coupons and queued wherever they could find petrol. It was just three weeks before the election which meant the timing was appalling for the Government.[1] The Opposition seized on the occasion and promised to end petrol rationing if they won. Fadden urged motorists to, "Empty out the Government and fill the bowsers,".[2] Automobile clubs opposed continued rationing and distributed two million leaflets through service stations, garages and car yards. The Service Stations' Association told motorists to vote for any candidate who promised more petrol.[3] The Government ran ads justifying the reimposition of rationing but with little effect.

As polling day approached, voters across the country were increasingly irritable and asked where was the victory dividend for their wartime efforts?

---

1 *Sydney Morning Herald* (Sydney), 30 September 1949, p. 2.
2 *Herald* (Melbourne), 25 October 1949, p. 1.
3 *West Australian* (Perth), 24 November 1949, p. 7.

19 Shirt-Sleeve Days End

"The tumult and the shouting dies. Many people feel that Australia has been saved while others imagine she is lost."[1]

Five million Australians voted on Saturday 10 December 1949. Outside polling stations, volunteers handed them how-to-vote cards. Inside election officials checked their names against electoral rolls and gave them ballot papers for the Senate and the House of Representatives. They marked their papers in privacy and deposited them in the ballot boxes. The process was orderly, well-organised and largely unchanged since Federation.

Election day 1949 passed without incident. Polling day was alcohol-free in New South Wales, and there were fewer arrests for drunkenness than normal. Most Victorians had voted by lunchtime, although Orthodox Jews waited till sunset to cast their votes. People in Brisbane queued in sporadic rain and an election official in South Australia reported a "remarkably clean, quiet and orderly election ... with no serious incidents".[2]

There was an early turnout in Tasmania because voters apparently had made up their minds well before polling day. Perth voters took more than usual interest and an elderly woman who climbed the steps of Perth Town Hall declared, "If there were 1,000 steps I'd climb them to vote today."[3] The 1949 election was the first time selected Indigenous people could vote. Cummeragunja-born man, minister and former tent boxer Doug Nicholls cast his vote in Melbourne.[4]

Menzies visited every voting place in his electorate before casting his vote in the leafy Melbourne suburb of Deepdene. The *Daily Telegraph* reported he left Deepdene happy.[5] Fadden voted on the Gold Coast then went surfing. The Prime Minister toured his Macquarie electorate and joined Mrs Chifley in the afternoon to vote in South Bathurst where "bank boys were unusually active in handing out voting cards and canvassing for their candidate".[6] The Chifleys then returned home for dinner and to sit by the radio to listen to early election results. Later in the evening Chifley

1 *Kangaroo Island Courier* (Kingscote), 16 December 1949, p. 1
2 *Advertiser* (Adelaide), 12 December 1949, p. 3.
3 *Daily News* (Perth), 10 December 1949, p. 1.
4 *Herald* (Melbourne), 10 December 1949, p. 1.
5 *Daily Telegraph* (Sydney), 11 December 1949, p. 3.
6 *National Advocate* (Bathurst), 12 December 1949, p. 1.

drove to the office of the *National Advocate* in Bathurst where he sat in an easy chair, smoked his pipe and listened to election updates on the radio. Fadden listened to a specially rigged wireless in the Country Party office on the Gold Coast. Robert and Pattie Menzies and their daughter Heather listened to the radio at the Windsor Hotel in Melbourne.[1] Surrounded by sheets of paper, Menzies marked off electorates one by one as the results came in. Heather told her father, "You couldn't possibly fail to win." He replied, "Be quiet dear, you never know until the votes come in."[2]

Harold Cox had accompanied the Prime Minister for most of the campaign and ran into the Prime Minister at a hotel breakfast the day before the election. Cox told Chifley he was returning to Canberra as there was little point in hanging around. Chifley replied, "You're perfectly right. It would be stupid to stay around here. I'll see you in Canberra next week." Two years earlier, Cox and Alan Reid were the reporters who broke the news of the Labor Government's bank plan. At the time Cox told Chifley that bank nationalisation would cost Labor dearly. As Cox prepared to leave, Chifley said, "You know, you were perfectly right about what you said to me that day about nationalising the banks. We've lost." Cox replied, "I'm afraid you have."[3]

The counting of votes began when the polls closed and soon after returning officers from polling places wired or phoned through the first results to tally rooms in each capital city. The New South Wales tally room in the General Post Office in Martin Place was filled with reporters, photographers, radio announcers and commentators. Station 2UW had Harry Jago, the bank union organiser, as a guest commentator. Some stations broadcast progress results live from the Post Office. Labor station 2KY reported the count between its Saturday evening racing and wrestling shows.[4] The *Sunday Telegraph* had 160 printers on standby to publish a special election edition of the paper, and a fleet of planes and trucks on call to distribute it around New South Wales.[5]

Melbourne's tally room was in the Army drill hall between the City Baths and the Victoria Markets. Announcers broadcast voting figures and a team from the *Argus* newspaper analysed the results. The Queensland tally room was in the Commercial Travellers Building in Brisbane. Messenger boys carried telegrams from the GPO to the tally room. Four

---

1 *Brisbane Telegraph* (Brisbane), 10 December 1949, p. 31.
2 Heather Henderson in discussion with author, 6 July 2021.
3 Harold Cox interviewed by Mel Pratt, 6 April–June 1973, NLA ORAL TRC 121/43.
4 *Sun* (Sydney), 6 December 1949, p. 29.
5 *Daily Telegraph* (Sydney), 12 December 1949, p. 16.

Brisbane stations broadcast updates. The tally room in Western Australia was in Perth's Commonwealth Bank where "electoral office staff worked at high speed and with unflagging energy throughout the night taking the latest figures and distributing slips containing the information to waiting press and radio representatives".[1]

Before the election, the Commonwealth Electoral Commissioner told Australians they could expect the results for the House of Representatives by midnight, but counting votes for the Senate would take longer because of changes to the Upper House voting system. As the evening unfolded it was unmistakable there was a swing away from the ALP and Labor supporters listened in astonishment as seat after seat fell. Around midnight it was clear Australia would have a new government and a new Prime Minister. The Liberal and Country parties had won seventy-four of the 123 Lower House seats and 50 per cent of the popular vote. The Country Party vote remained consistent with past elections and the ALP vote was well down from 1946.[2]

The Opposition parties won thirty-three of the new seats created under Calwell's plan and every sitting Opposition MP was returned to Parliament. The ALP only won fourteen of the new electorates and lost ten sitting MPs including the seats of four Cabinet ministers. Only two Labor MPs increased their majorities. Gil Duthie was the last remaining Labor MP in Tasmania. Queensland was disastrous for the ALP. It held only three of its previous eighteen seats.[3] The Coalition picked up three extra seats in Victoria, Menzies comfortably kept Kooyong and newcomers Richard Casey and Hubert Opperman were winners.

The Opposition won South Australian and Western Australian seats and picked up an additional seat in Sydney. Though Chifley kept Macquarie, the polling places on the coalfields recorded big swings against him. Evatt beat Nancy Wake although she fought a spirited campaign, door-knocked 15,000 homes and wore out five pairs of shoes. The public mood turned against Jack Lang after his late-minute allegations against the Chifleys and he was defeated. There was not a single Labor victory between the Harbour Bridge and Sydney's northern beaches. The Communist vote dropped by half because memories of the coal strike were still fresh. Yet a closer analysis of the final figures for the House of Representatives showed the ALP lost because 119,000 voters in key electorates had supported

---

1 *West Australian* (Perth), 12 December 1949, p. 20.
2 Gerard Newman, Federal Election Results 1949–1993, Canberra, Department of the Parliamentary Library, 1993.
3 *Daily Telegraph* (Sydney), 12 December 1949, p. 14.

non-Labor candidates.

Five weeks later the Senate results were announced. The Liberal and Country Parties gained four more senators but Labor managed to hold the Upper House, largely due to its majority from the 1946 election. Over half a million Australians submitted informal votes showing the new voting system for the Senate confused many people.[1]

On election night Menzies went to bed around 3 a.m. once he was sure of victory. As he slept, his family fielded congratulatory calls and stacked cables and telegrams on the piano in the lounge room.[2] Early next morning an *Age* photographer arrived at the Menzies home in Balwyn to photograph the family. Everyone looked surprisingly fresh. Later the Prime Minister-designate appeared at a press conference in the city wearing the tartan tie of his Scottish ancestors. Menzies said the "new Government would aim to foster real feelings of national unity, real understanding and tolerance".[3] The election outcome was a remarkable comeback for Menzies, a man many thought would never again be Prime Minister.

The day after the election Chifley drove from Bathurst through the towns and hamlets back to Canberra. The mood in the prime ministerial limousine must have been sombre although Chifley showed his usual courtesy when he thanked staff who served him a meal at the Commercial Hotel in Yass. The next morning Chifley phoned Menzies to congratulate him. He said he would tender his resignation to the Governor-General at the earliest and keep his Government in caretaker mode until Menzies formed a new government.

Chifley was disappointed perhaps even shocked by the result but urged his supporters not to be discouraged. "It is the people's verdict and we accept it. I have no complaints to make."[4] Mid-morning the Prime Minister visited the long-serving Clerk of the House of Representatives, Frank Green. Chifley sat in the Clerk's office, lit his pipe and expressed his disappointment with the defeat of the Government. He conceded he had moved too fast on bank nationalisation, saying, "It is a mistake to show the rooster the axe when you are going to take his head off. You should show him a bit of corn first." He said Menzies and Fadden would be busy keeping the many election promises they had made.[5] Later Chifley and Menzies met to discuss the transition between their administrations.

---

1   *Sydney Morning Herald* (Sydney), 10 January 1950, p. 2.
2   *Age* (Melbourne), 12 December 1949, p. 6.
3   *Advertiser* (Adelaide), 17 December 1949, p. 3.
4   *Advertiser* (Adelaide), 12 December 1949, p. 1.
5   Frank Green, *Servant of the House*, Melbourne, Heinemann, 1969, p. 131.

There was no awkwardness between the two.

Evatt, Calwell and other ministers flew back to Canberra for private meetings with Chifley. On the Wednesday after the election, ministers convened for their final Cabinet meeting and last official photographs. Chifley announced he had submitted his resignation to the Governor-General but expected ministers to remain at their posts until the new government was sworn in. He thanked the Cabinet for its support over the years and spoke fondly of the four ministers who had lost their seats. One of those ministers, John Dedman, led a tribute to Chifley. Arthur Calwell had the uneasy task of providing an update on latest polling figures.

The feeling in the Cabinet room was the Liberal and Country Parties had waged a fear campaign and artfully exploited the bank nationalisation issue. Ministers felt the unity between the Opposition parties would collapse under the weight of their many election promises. The Labor men believed they would soon be back in government.[1] There were no regrets or recriminations, but a genuine pride in what their Government had achieved in the last eight years, two months and thirteen days. How could they know it would take three leadership changes and twenty-three years before the next Labor Cabinet met in that room.

Chifley left Canberra to spend Christmas in Bathurst and Arthur Calwell remained to tidy up. Calwell wrote letters congratulating victorious Labor candidates and consoling the defeated. He began to catalogue the campaign promises Menzies and Fadden made, so Labor could hold the new Government to account in the new parliament and at the next election.

News of the result quickly spread. It was front-page news in London and the British Prime Minister and Winston Churchill were informed. British conservatives welcomed Menzies back to the world stage, praised his stand against Communism and complimented Australians for rejecting socialism and nationalisation. Some New York newspapers reported the results on the front page with pictures of Menzies. An NBC commentator said "free enterprise has become the order of the day in Australia".[2] An American newspaperman nominated the Labor defeats in New Zealand and Australia as the biggest stories of the year.[3] The *Vancouver Daily Sun* declared Australians and New Zealanders had just shot Santa Claus because "voters normally do not oust big-spending governments which

---

1 *Herald* (Melbourne), 14 December 1949, p. 5.
2 *Daily Telegraph* (Sydney), 12 December 1949, p. 2.
3 *Daily Telegraph* (Sydney), 3 January 1950, p. 3.

promise full employment".¹ The new, conservative Prime Minister in New Zealand said the two countries should enjoy harmonious relationships since now they had similar governments.² Australian newspapers began to speculate on the new Government's first step. Would it to ban the Communist Party, end petrol rationing or halt bank nationalisation?

Fadden flew to Melbourne to discuss the make-up of the new Liberal-Country Party ministry with Menzies. The meeting was businesslike, and both men showed no interest in revisiting the past differences between their two parties.³ Theirs would be the first conservative ministry in nearly a decade and the two leaders had to balance the relative strengths of the two parties in Parliament, representation from the states and the merits of ambitious individuals. They opted for a ministry with a mix of experienced MPs and enthusiastic, first-time legislators.⁴ Menzies was to serve as Prime Minister with no additional responsibilities. That would leave him free to direct the new government. Fadden was to be Treasurer and Deputy Prime Minister and there would be three other Country Party men in the ministry.⁵

Menzies' selections showed he would not be handicapped by the expectations of others. He appointed Sir Earle Page, the man who in the early war years had cruelly attacked him in Parliament, as Minister for Health. This gave the experienced Page a portfolio while keeping him away from the key decision-making processes of government. Some senior Liberals believed Dame Enid Lyons deserved a ministry. Menzies appointed her as Vice-President of the Executive Council which was largely a ceremonial position. Even so this made Dame Enid the first woman in a Commonwealth ministry.

Richard Casey was tipped to become Minister of External Affairs because of his impressive diplomatic achievements during the war. Menzies made him responsible for the new Department for National Development. Casey, an engineer by training and ever the organiser, was soon developing plans for new transport, housing, hospital, water, rural and manufacturing projects.⁶ The "Bengal Tiger" was busy but cast a somewhat lonely figure in Canberra. Harold Cox noted he had little rapport with Menzies and did not mix easily.⁷ Casey disliked the political

---
1 *Advocate* (Burnie), 14 December 1949, p. 7.
2 *Daily Telegraph* (Sydney), 12 December 1949, p. 2.
3 *Inside Canberra* (Sydney), 15 December 1949, p. 1.
4 *Sun* (Sydney), 4 December 1949, p. 2.
5 John McEwen became Minister for Agriculture and Commerce, Larry Anthony was Postmaster General and Sir Earle Page was sworn in as Minister for Health.
6 *Daily Telegraph* (Sydney), 19 December 1949, p. 9.
7 Letter: Cox to Murdoch, 27 February 1950.

combat of Canberra and when he eventually became Minister for External Affairs, he travelled aboard frequently to avoid the Prime Minister and the Parliament.

Just before Christmas the Governor-General William McKell administered the oath of office to the seventeen members of the new ministry. It was considered to be one of the most experienced and talented ministries since Federation.[1] It included former ministers, ex-prime ministers (Menzies, Fadden and Page) and Harold Holt later a future Prime Minister.[2] The swearing-in ceremony took place at Yarralumla, the official residence of the Governor-General. After the formalities the new ministers returned to Parliament for their first Cabinet meeting and briefings by departmental officials. Meanwhile staff at Parliament House trundled boxes of party files between offices and opposition rooms.

The change in government brought a fresh mood into Canberra. The small diplomatic corps in the capital had regarded the Labor men as amiable but rather dull hosts, but the arrival of the Liberals promised a return to pomp and ceremony. When Menzies and his family moved into the Lodge it became once more the apex of entertainment in the capital.[3] Commonwealth car drivers noticed the change. They were issued with chauffeur caps and instructed to wear jackets and ties when driving ministers and their wives. The incoming Speaker, South Australian Archie Cameron, announced his intention to wear the traditional Speaker's attire of gown, cravat and wig. Formality had made a comeback and the shirt-sleeve days of Labor were over.

On 22 February 1950 MPs met to elect their party leaders. Menzies and Chifley received rousing receptions from their respective party rooms. The Liberal and Country Parties unanimously elected Menzies and Fadden as their respective leaders. Menzies congratulated voters for saving Australia from becoming a socialised state and told his MPs the election was a turning point for Australia. "Australia under Mr Chifley had fast been drifting towards full regimentation but the election has restored a form of democratic behaviour in which the four freedoms could flourish."[4] He urged MPs to work hard to deliver the promises they had made to voters.

The Labor Caucus met as the Opposition for the first time since 1941. It

---
1 *Daily Telegraph* (Sydney), 22 January 1950, p. 32.
2 Menzies, Fadden and Page were ex-prime ministers, Holt and McEwen were future prime ministers and Casey and Hasluck became Governors-General.
3 Elsie Curtin and Lizzie Chifley did not live in The Lodge, opting to remain in Perth and Bathurst respectively.
4 *Canberra Times* (ACT) 22 February 1950, p. 4.

was a distinctly different party room. Missing were the defeated ministers, John Dedman, Claude Barnard and Nelson Lemmon. The room now had a more industrial, urban feel because only six MPs were from rural seats. The Caucus re-elected Chifley as leader and Evatt as his deputy. A fourteen-member "policy executive" was formed to guide party decisions and was tipped to be the next cabinet when Labor returned to office.

The Governor-General officially opened the Nineteenth Commonwealth Parliament the next day, and outlined the new Government's plans in a twenty-five-minute speech. Public interest in the event was immense. MPs and Senators could each invite only one person to the opening ceremonies and some members of the public tried to bribe attendants to get into Parliament House. Accommodation in Canberra and Queanbeyan was fully booked. After the formalities eight cooks and thirty waiters served 2,500 cakes and thousands of sandwiches and savouries to the very large crowd.[1]

The new Parliament had sixty Senators and 123 MPs, nearly double the previous number of legislators.[2] Besides Lyons, Rankin and Tangney there were two new female Liberal senators. Agnes Robertson was elected from Western Australia and Ivy Wedgwood won a Senate seat from the fourth spot on the Liberal ticket in Victoria.[3] More space was needed in both chambers so seating arrangements were expanded in the House of Representatives and the Senate. Additional microphones and loudspeakers were installed and eighty-two new offices were added to the building.[4]

The new year was extraordinarily busy for the new Government. Within months the Government ended petrol rationing, abolished four departments and established new ministries for Supply, Fuel, Shipping and Transport and National Development. Among the departments to disappear was the Ministry of Information which the Liberals always regarded as propaganda machine for the Labor Government. Its responsibilities were spread among other agencies.[5]

The Coalition Government repealed the 1947 Banking Act. It never held a referendum on bank nationalisation as it had promised but introduced legislation to restore a board of directors to the Commonwealth Bank. The new Opposition saw this as an attempt to subordinate the Bank to vested commercial interests and the legislation stalled in the Senate for

---

1 *Daily Telegraph* (Sydney), 22 February 1950, p. 6.
2 *Age* (Melbourne), 22 February 1950, p. 3.
3 Doris Blackburn lost her seat in 1949.
4 *Canberra Times* (ACT), 22 February 1950, p. 4.
5 *Sydney Morning Herald* (Sydney), 9 March 1950, p. 2.

months. Menzies used Labor's obstruction to trigger a double dissolution and called an election for April 1951. It was the first double dissolution election since 1914 and only sixteen months since the last election.

Both Coalition and the Opposition MPs were nervous about the election. The last government to call a double dissolution had been trounced, and there was risk of Labor being seen as pushing the newly elected government to the polls too soon. Banking was once more a central election issue so the banks, bank unions and conservative groups like the AWMAS campaigned against the ALP. This time however they did so with less urgency and energy. The Menzies-Fadden Government won the 1951 election and though its majority in the House was reduced it gained control of the Senate.

By the mid-1950s banking had ceased to be contentious. Historian Geoffrey Blainey observed, "In office again he [Menzies] was careful not to jump to the other extreme and completely liberate the banks. His firm decision, year after year, that they should still be closely regulated was one reason for his long retention of power. It marked him as an economic moderate."[1] In 1960 the Coalition Government established the Reserve Bank of Australia (RBA) to ensure "the stability of the currency of Australia; the maintenance of full employment in Australia; and the economic prosperity and welfare of the people of Australia".[2] The RBA Charter sounded similar to the vision Chifley had outlined for the Commonwealth Bank in 1947.

Robert Menzies went from success to success after 1949. He won seven elections though some wins were more decisive than others. He became Australia's longest-serving prime minister and retired of his own choosing in 1966. Menzies died in 1978 and is considered one of great Australian prime ministers and among the most influential people in Australian history. He left politics as a revered and statesmanlike figure and set the standard against which Liberal prime ministers are still measured.[3]

Menzies had been a formidable Opposition Leader in the early post war years. He was masterful at identifying issues such as bank nationalisation that would resonate with voters and capable of mounting powerful attacks on his opponents inside and outside parliament. On the other hand, it was clear Chifley lacked the vigour for his new role of leading the Opposition.

Don Rodgers remained his press secretary and was as loyal as ever.

---

1 Geoffrey Blainey, email to author, 25 January 2017.
2 "A Brief History", Reserve Bank of Australia, www.rba.gov.au/about-rba/history.
3 Paul Strangio, Paul 't Hart and James Walter, *The Pivot of Power: Australian Prime Ministers and Political Leadership 1949–2016*, Carlton, Miegunyah Press, 2017, p. 11.

Yet he noted Chifley's time in opposition was not good for the man or the Party. He described the ex-Prime Minister as being at the "fag end of a great political career".[1]

Just when Labor needed his sharp political instincts, Chifley's political effectiveness was in decline. An instance was when Menzies introduced the Communist Party Dissolution Bill in 1950. The purpose of this legislation was to dissolve the Communist Party and associated organisations and ban Communists from public service and union appointments. Menzies had argued for years that Communists were fifth columnists and part of a global revolutionary movement set on espionage and sabotaging Australia.

The Prime Minister presented the Dissolution Bill knowing it would divide Labor MPs. Chifley and Evatt were against an outright ban on the Communist Party, arguing it could make martyrs of their leaders and drive the Communists underground where they would be much harder to fight. Instead they wanted to modify the more draconian parts of the legislation. Other Labor MPs, particularly the Victorians, were inclined to support Menzies' proposals. They thought the Communist-led coal strike in the dying months of the Chifley Government had cost Labor the 1949 election. They saw Menzies' plan as a way to remove Communists from the union movement, and argued that if the ALP was seen as defending the rights of Communists, the next election could be so much harder to win.

The debate in Caucus was harsh and disagreeable and only resolved when the ALP Federal Executive instructed Labor MPs to support the legislation. That forced Chifley into a rare and embarrassing backdown and he could only advise Caucus, "Accept your humiliation and we can go forward. Recriminate and we shall split."[2]

Around this time Chifley was grappling with poor health. Heart disease ran in the male line of the Chifley family and this genetic predisposition plus his still punishing workloads took their toll. Outwardly Chifley looked robust but with each passing week those around him began to notice signs of his declining health. He had always been an excellent listener, now he talked non-stop to everybody and about everything. He was spending more and more time lying on the couch in his office and in his bedroom at the Hotel Kurrajong.

Late in 1950 Chifley suffered a heart attack while driving to Bathurst.[3] He was hospitalised and his doctor ordered him to rest. Chifley ignored

---

1 Don Rodgers interviewed by Mel Pratt, 29 April 1971.
2 Crisp, p. 396.
3 *News* (Adelaide), 29 November 1950, p. 1.

this advice and led the ALP in the 1951 election. Chifley remained as Opposition Leader after Labor's defeat despite having lost the last two elections.

In June 1951 the Commonwealth Parliament held a gala ball with music, medals and elegant gowns to celebrate the fiftieth anniversary of the Federation of Australia. Chifley disliked such occasions and spent the evening at the Hotel Kurrajong. After dinner he headed to his bedroom to read. Mid-evening he suffered a seizure. Phyllis Donnelly, his secretary of twenty-three years, called a doctor who immediately arranged an ambulance to rush Chifley to Canberra Hospital where a Catholic priest stood by to administer last rites. News reached the ball that Chifley was in hospital and, shortly afterwards, Menzies announced Chifley had died. The celebrations quietly ended and many ball-goers left in tears. The sudden death of the sixty-six-year-old former Prime Minister shocked Australia.

Tributes poured in as the body of the former train driver lay in state in Parliament House. Thousands of mourners filed past his coffin and later an RAAF DC3 aircraft carried Chifley's body to Bathurst. Forty thousand people attended the state funeral for Ben Chifley in his hometown and newsreel cameras captured the moment he was laid to rest in the Catholic section of the Bathurst Cemetery.[1] Prime Minister Menzies visited Lizzie Chifley in her Busby Street home to convey the condolences of the nation.

The following year a large crowd gathered at the Bathurst Cemetery as a simple marble-and-stone memorial was dedicated to honour Chifley. Etched around the base were the lines from a Chifley speech: "If an idea is worth fighting for, no matter the penalty, fight for the right and truth and justice will prevail."[2] For many years Labor supporters remembered John Curtin as "our great leader" but Ben Chifley as "our beloved leader".[3] A 2020 Monash University survey of political scientists and historians ranked Chifley fourth among Australia's best prime ministers.[4]

Federal Labor MPs elected "Doc" Evatt to lead them after Chifley's death. Evatt was leader for ten years, but at times it was not clear if Evatt was acting in his own or his party's interests. Caucus meetings were often marked by dissension and angry scenes. In 1955 nine disenchanted Labor Senators and MPs plus some trade unionists and party members left the

---

1 Sue Martin, *A Sacred Trust*, Canberra, The Chifley Centre, 2020.
2 *Advocate* (Melbourne), 26 June 1952, p. 3.
3 Don Rodgers interviewed by Mel Pratt, 29 April 1971.
4 Misha Ketchell. "Who Were Australia's Best Prime Ministers? We Asked the Experts." The Conversation. 2 August 2021. https://theconversation.com/who-were-australias-best-prime-ministers-we-asked-the-experts-165302.

ALP to establish the Democratic Labor Party (DLP.) They claimed the new organisation was the real heir to the Curtin and Chifley legacies. The DLP was a third party in Australian politics well into the 1960s and a factor in Labor's defeat in three elections.

The tempestuous Evatt survived leadership challenges in 1954 and 1959, and when he finally left politics, he became Chief Justice of New South Wales. He resigned because of ill health and died in 1965. Fred Daly, whose relations with Evatt were strained, observed that Evatt's performance as Opposition Leader gave Menzies "an armchair ride through the fifties and sixties".

After the 1949 election, there was a noticeable lack of celebration among McConnan and other bank leaders. The banking industry was subdued after its hard-fought and expensive victory. Bank employees received a five percent Christmas bonus which McConnan said was standard practice. However it was most likely a well-timed reward for the part bank officers played in the battle for the banks.[1] Half of the bank officers who led the anti-nationalisation campaign in Queensland received significant promotions within a year which suggested their contributions had not gone unnoticed by their banks.[2]

McConnan stepped down from chairing the Associated Banks after the election. He rarely spoke about politics but continued to talk about economic and financial issues. In recognition of his role in saving the banks, the National Bank commissioned the acclaimed artist William Dargie to paint McConnan's portrait. Telegrams of goodwill poured into the Bank headquarters and staff from every state attended the ceremony when the portrait was presented to the General Manager. McConnan and his wife then sailed for an extended holiday in Britain, Europe and the United States and on their return McConnan was knighted for services to banking.

Fourteen hundred people attended his retirement dinner the following year. The *Age* said McConnan had always been a tireless fighter who worked to defeat the nationalisation plan, earning the respect of his opponents for his tenacity, clear thinking and unwavering will to win.[3] In retirement McConnan fished, golfed and held positions on the boards of leading companies and charities. The National Bank honoured his legacy by naming a staff scholarship for him and a decade later the Institute of Public Affairs featured him in a book on prominent Australian businessmen. For such a prominent figure in the early post-war years,

---

1 *Herald* (Melbourne), 19 December 1949, p. 6.
2 *Sunday Mail* (Brisbane), 26 November 1950, p. 1.
3 *Age* (Melbourne), 2 January 1951, p. 2.

McConnan quickly faded from public memory.

Despite the Menzies-Fadden victory the private banks were not confident they had seen the last of hostile Labor governments. Or that Australians would continue to support a competitive banking system.[1] They established a coordinating committee to promote the virtues of the banking industry and forestall criticism. Each bank boosted its public relations capability in case Menzies fulfilled his promise and called a referendum on banking or Labor won a future election.

The Bank of New South Wales developed a public relations model that other banks copied to some degree. In 1950 the Bank appointed its first full-time public relations officer whose early task was to produce a communications framework. This included a press agent to uncover newsworthy stories about the bank, goodwill ambassadors, films and an in-house magazine. Public relations positions were established in state offices and the Canberra branch was assigned to lobby senators and MPs. Branch managers were encouraged to create "a family spirit" among their staff.[2]

In 1954 the bank upgraded its public relations officer to management level and appointed Russell Prowse to the role. Prowse had worked on the Bank's anti-nationalisation campaign, and over the next twenty years became a highly visible advocate for the banking industry. He played a key role in establishing the Australian Bankers Association and took on the role of industry spokesperson. Prowse was Australia's most recognisable banker when he died in 1982.[3]

Since the 1950s banking in Australia has completely transformed. In 1951 the Union Bank and the Bank of Australasia joined to become the Australian and New Zealand Bank (ANZ) then the country's second-largest bank.[4] Then the Bank of Adelaide merged with the ANZ Bank. In 1981 the Commercial Banking Company of Sydney merged with the National Bank and a year later the Melbourne-based Commercial Bank combined with the Bank of New South Wales to form Westpac. By the 1990s four powerful institutions dominated Australian finances. Yet while the Commonwealth Bank, nab, ANZ and Westpac are the industry heavyweights, a myriad of small banks, credit unions, foreign banks, building societies, crypto traders, wire services, payday lenders and fast loan merchants offer Australians an ever-expanding array of financial services.

---

1 Assistant General Manager of the Bank of New South Wales, Sydney to Chief Inspector of the Bank of New South Wales, Melbourne, 25 January 1950, WGA/Bank Nationalisation.
2 Public Relations Officer to Inspector Bank of New South Wales, Melbourne, 16 August 1950, WGA/Bank Nationalisation.
3 *Canberra Times* (ACT), 16 June 1982, p. 3.
4 *Economist* (UK), 20 January 1951, p. 161.

20 A Sickening Loss

"The attempt to create a monopoly bank goes into history as the most serious mistake made by the Chifley regime."[1]

In 1949 Australians were wealthier, better fed and more educated than ever before. The Chifley Government had laid the groundwork for a social security and national health scheme which underpins many of the payments and services, today's Australians routinely access. The Australian economy was prosperous and stable and there was full employment. The country's manufacturing base was expanding and farmers were doing well. A migration program was underway that would transform the country culturally, economically and politically. Work had started on far-sighted national projects such as the Snowy Mountains Scheme, the Commonwealth Scientific and Industrial Organisation, the Australian National University and a modern security and intelligence service. Australia was finishing the forties as a respected global middle power. So why did voters turn their back on Chifley and his government at the 1949 election? The explanation goes beyond voters simply wanting a change from eight years of Labor Governments.

Historian Ross McMullin has written, "Shattered Labor activists knew it was an election that never should have been lost. In fact there has probably never been – neither during the half century that followed nor the preceding half century since Federation – an ALP federal election defeat more avoidable, more undeserved and therefore more sickening for party supporters."[2]

Robert Menzies agreed with the *Age* newspaper which reported two days after the election that, "The disappearance of bank nationalisation ... will give general satisfaction and reassure all who were directly affected by the threat."[3] There is no question the Labor Party seriously misread the public mood in 1947 when it presented its banking plan without warning. Australians thought they had left behind the uncertainties of the wartime years yet their government was now presenting them with unprecedented and near-revolutionary change. Chifley's vision for a fairer financial future

---
1 *Age* (Melbourne), 12 December 1949, p. 2.
2 Ross McMullin, "Joseph Benedict Chifley" in *Australian Prime Ministers*, ed. Michelle Grattan, Frenchs Forest, New Holland, 2001, p. 266.
3 *Age* (Melbourne), 12 December 1949, p. 2.

was commendable, but he and his ministers failed to persuade Australians how it would benefit them or even how it would work. It needed more than a cryptic press statement and the agonising long debate in Parliament to convince people that change was necessary. After the election Senator Nick McKenna, a key player in the nationalisation episode, said the Party moved too far ahead of public opinion.[1]

It is difficult to pinpoint the exact moment a government loses favour. Yet around midday on 16 August 1947 is one of those rare occasions in Australian history. The moment Chifley's press statement left Canberra was the moment support for his Government began to wane. In the face of growing and raucous opposition the Government did not modify its position despite three clear opportunities to do so: after the High Court ruling in 1948, after the savage loss in the Referendum that same year and following the verdict from the Privy Council.

It would have been mortifying to back down but on each occasion the Government could have privately if not publicly conceded that it was swimming against the tide of events and public opinion. It could have changed course and recalibrated with the community. Instead the Labor men pressed stubbornly on shielded by a parliamentary majority and convinced of their own righteousness. With less hubris and more humility, bank nationalisation need not have become a crisis.

From the start the Government knew the banks would oppose their plans but it seriously underestimated the ferocity in their fight and the enormous sums they would spend to save themselves. The Sydney banks probably spent £461,000 on campaign and legal fees (around $27 million today) and the Melbourne banks spent as much, possibly more.[2] And the value of support they provided to anyone who might help them is incalculable. Without bank help, political parties, bank unions, powerful third parties and citizens groups could not have resisted bank nationalisation as fiercely as they did. The banks had over a hundred years of avoiding political storms, or at least publicly. That changed in 1947 when they broke their own conventions. They allowed and supported their officers to become political agitators and turned to the media to help make their case. Editors and journalists were engaged on an industrial scale. Little wonder one ALP candidate moaned that only Superman could have saved Labor.[3]

Labor's loss also came about because the Opposition parties ran a

---
1 *News* (Adelaide), 10 April 1950, p. 2.
2 Eather and Cottle, "Sydney Banks and the IPA", p. 180.
3 *Northern Star* (Lismore), 13 December 1949, p. 4.

highly effective election campaign.¹ Their simple but effective strategy was to take every occasion to associate Labor with Communism and socialism. In doing they capitalised on the fears of Australians in the Cold War-era. They successfully used this strategy like "a bilious crimson triennial vegetable" in every election for the next sixteen years.²

The ALP knew it had been outspent in the 1949 election but would never concede it was out-generalled. Instead it blamed the press for playing a huge role in the Party's defeat. Weeks before the election Chifley told a Melbourne audience, "The press had unleashed a tremendous barrage against Labor and only four newspapers stood out for their impartiality."³ Evatt talked of "propaganda fed by vested interests".⁴ ALP Senator Gordon Brown wrote that "no Labor leader has been more bitterly assailed than Ben Chifley. Ben has been lampooned, cartooned, vilified and abused with greater intensity than any previous leader."⁵ John Dedman believed "the principal reason for our defeat was the fact the press was against us and they were not averse to telling downright lies about what would happen if the Labor Party got another term of office."⁶

Chifley carried his distrust of the media into opposition. In 1950 the *Sydney Morning Herald* told Chifley it wanted to improve its political coverage and was posting an associate editor to the Press Gallery. The paper asked Chifley to meet their new man so he could learn Chifley's views. Chifley met the reporter twice but then withdrew access. He had seen what he considered unfavourable coverage in the paper and concluded the newcomer was an unofficial publicity officer for Menzies.

In 1950 Tom Truman from the University of Queensland set out to assess whether Labor's allegations of press bias were true. Truman asked Don Rodgers for examples of media distortion. Rodgers produced two minor examples but hinted at "many local instances of unfairness, distortion, under-playing and over-playing in the treatment of political events". Rodgers promised more examples but nothing was forthcoming.⁷ Truman then compared press coverage of Labor policies with what was said in Parliament and with government press releases. He concluded that, despite occasional lapses, newspapers reported all parties fairly. Truman did similar research after the 1951 election. He found that news

---

1 Allan Martin, *Robert Menzies*, Carlton, Melbourne University Press, 1996, p. 126.
2 *Woroni* (Canberra), 23 September 1965, p. 5.
3 *Age* (Melbourne), 24 November 1949, p. 3.
4 *Daily Examiner* (Grafton), 17 December 1949, p. 2.
5 *Worker* (Brisbane), 3 October 1949, p. 7.
6 Stephens, *Australian Quarterly*, p. 90.
7 Letters Truman-Rodgers, January-February 1950, NLA MS 4738/3/31.

coverage of the ALP was accurate but commentary and cartoons favoured the Liberal and Country Parties.[1] He concluded the ALP had trouble distinguishing fact from opinion.

The ALP blamed the banks, the Opposition and the media for its loss, but showed little interest in introspection, reflection or learning from defeat. Maybe an arrogance lingered on from the second Chifley ministry whose ministers were in office for eight years. For example it puzzled people how a government could let things get so bad – petrol shortages, industrial disruption, rising living costs and the coal strike – yet go to an election promising more of the same. The Catholic *Advocate* said voters were repelled by "the growing self-assertion of certain of its [Labor's] leaders as though they were assured of remaining in office forever" and many felt "it would do them good to have a rest and think things over".[2]

Visiting US academic Louise Overacker observed in 1946 the ALP organisation suffered from "apathy, intrigue, frustration and defeatism". Party supporters did not attend meetings and two or three branch members did the work. She reported an instance where a senior official went to a branch meeting and found four people waiting outside. "Nobody could find a key to the hall so the meeting was cancelled ... this meeting was to decide office bearers for the next year."[3] Overacker also noted the Party shunned "tall poppies," those academics and intellectuals who could help explain Labor policies and reach broader audiences.[4]

---

[1] T. C. Truman, "The Press and the 1951 Election", *Australian Quarterly* 23, no. 40 (1951), pp. 33–44.
[2] *Advocate* (Melbourne), 15 December 1949, p. 6.
[3] Louise Overacker, *The Australian Labor Party*. Unknown publication details NLA Bib ID: 914230, p. 681.
[4] *Age* (Melbourne), 30 January 1950, p. 1.

21 An Erosion of Trust

"Many companies were too focused on maximising profit over doing what was right for customers."[1]

The banking sector was among the first Australian industries to use modern communications methods to mobilise community anger to resist government interference. Since then other industries have used the model the bankers pioneered. In 2009 the Australian Coal Association orchestrated a well-funded media campaign and organised resistance on the coalfields to oppose the Emissions Trading Scheme proposed by the Rudd Labor Government. BHP Billiton, Rio Tinto and other mining companies waged a $100 million newspaper, radio and television campaign to attack proposals by the same Government for a super profits tax. The gambling, licensed clubs and tobacco industries have tried to enlist community support and third parties to defeat government regulation.

Sir Leslie McConnan and his contemporaries might be pleased their resistance model is still being used but would be aghast at the dramatic changes in modern banking. These postwar bankers met their customers face-to-face in grand buildings of stone, wood, gleaming bronze and in galvanised iron outposts. There was a friendly banter between bank officer and customer and bank officers were expected to be, and were willing participants in the life of their communities. Seventy five years on those relationships have vanished and been replaced with disembodied voices in distant call centres, terse texts and conversations with digital bots. Bank branches around the country have closed and many that remain trade for restricted hours.

Cash dispensing machines, phone apps, toll-free telephones, internet portals and other technologies may be efficient but have separated Australians from their bankers. This isolation led to public frustration and anger and in 2017 a Royal Commission was appointed to investigate the banking industry.

Headed by former High Court Justice Kenneth Hayne, the Royal Commission held public hearings and received thousands of submissions, many of which pointed to poor ethics, malpractice and sometimes of

---
1 *Financial Review* (Sydney), 30 May 2023, P.2.

outright criminality by the banks.[1] Ordinary Australians, sometimes in tears, described the mendacity of their banks and the power imbalance between those who need financial services and those who provide them. Witnesses told how banks pursued profits above all other considerations.

The inquiry took two years and ended in the most damning indictment of Australian banking anyone could remember. Hayne accused the banking industry of prioritising profits over people, abandoning their duty of care to customers and said that bank boards and bank executives were responsible for numerous legal and moral transgressions.[2] The Royal Commissioner's stinging report ended with numerous recommendations to restore public trust in banking. The evidence was so conclusive and damning the bankers of Sydney and Melbourne could only pledge to do better while the Government was pressured to pass legislation to improve integrity in Australian banking.

In 1949 Australians voted to save their banks. In 2019 Australians had to be saved from their banks.

---

[1] Kenneth Hayne, *The Final Report of the Royal Commission into Misconduct in the Banking, Superannuation and Financial Services Industry*, Canberra, Commonwealth of Australia, 2019.
[2] Hayne, *The Final Report of the Royal Commission*.

Acknowledgments

I have tried to be fair to those involved in the bank nationalisation fight and to understand the texture and tone of their times. I bear responsibility for any errors, missing information or misinterpretations of their motivations. This account uses information from books, letters, diaries, and interviews of people directly involved in the battle for the banks. I have also relied on newspaper accounts and government records of the time.

I have tried to obtain permission to use the works of authors referenced in this book. Many have passed away, and despite extensive research and attempts to contact their estates or representatives, it has not always been possible to secure explicit approvals. If any copyright holder believes their rights have been inadvertently infringed, I ask them to contact me so appropriate acknowledgement can be given.

I am indebted to A. L. May, whose 1968 book *The Battle for the Banks* is the most exhaustive account of the bank nationalisation story. May interviewed key people and had good access to bank records. It is half a century since May published his book and the banking industry has dramatically changed. The private banks of the Chifley era have merged or disappeared, records have thinned and the main players have died. I am grateful therefore for Allan May's scholarship in providing material which now appears lost.

Warwick Eather and Drew Cottle published a book in 2012 on the opposition of the private banks to Labor governments from 1930 to 1949. They also wrote noteworthy journal articles on the banks which were enormously helpful. Professor Robert Crawford of RMIT University has written widely on advertising in Australia including work on the banks and their anti-nationalisation campaign. Professor Bridget Griffen-Foley of Macquarie University specialises in the history of Australian media and has published on the 1949 election and the "new discipline" of public relations, which was so important in defining the image of Robert Menzies. Both were very helpful, as was Professor Geoffrey Blainey, author of the first official history of the National Bank. Professor Blainey was always reassuring and ready to provide advice.

I am indebted to the Noel Butlin Archives Centre at the Australian

National University, particularly Kathryn Dan and Sarah Leithbridge, who guided me through union and corporate records. Helen Cadzow at the National Australia Bank Archives in Melbourne was most accommodating in facilitating my research, helping me understand post-war banking and bringing to life the character of Sir Leslie McConnan.

At the Westpac Group Archives Kim Eberhard was equally supportive in making available the records of the Bank of New South Wales and guiding me through the different approaches the Melbourne and Sydney banks brought to the nationalisation fight. Regrettably, Covid lockdowns and organisational changes meant the ANZ Archives in Melbourne were unavailable for research. This was disappointing since this depository includes the records of the Bank of Australasia, the Union Bank, the English, Scottish and Australian Bank and the Bank of Adelaide.

The Reserve Bank of Australia in Sydney holds the post war records of the Commonwealth Bank. These include over 1,000 pages that show how the Government planned to turn Australia into a one-bank town. Reserve Bank archivist Sarah Middleton-Jones was tremendously helpful in making those plans digitally available and they will be rich pickings for future researchers.

Ben Chifley died suddenly in 1951 and left no papers. However he did leave an indelible impression on those who knew him, and the National Library of Australia has captured their memories in its treasure of manuscripts, photographs and oral histories. I am grateful to the officers of the National Library for helping me access this material.

Heather Henderson, the daughter of Sir Robert Menzies, was gracious with her time and encouragement. She colourfully described some of the public meetings she attended with her father to such a degree I almost felt the excitement of those post-war audiences. My neighbours Ian Harris and Erika Harris spent years working in Parliament House. Ian was Clerk of the House of Representatives and Erica had important roles with various ministers. Our coffees and curbside chats gave me a sense of the drama that so often surrounds Australian politics. Richard Farmer, another neighbour and who spent a lifetime in the printing industry, was unfailingly helpful in describing the postwar newspaper industry.

Barrister Doug Hassall helped me understand the complexity of the decisions of the High Court of Australia and Privy Council which are so much part of the nationalisation story. He also provided lively descriptions of the legal advocates and justices involved in the case.

Professor of History Frank Bongiorno at the Australian National

University guided me through the history, culture and personalities of the Australian Labor Party. Frank was hugely generous in sharing his deep knowledge of Australian politics and I am most grateful for his encouragement, comments on my research and various drafts and answering my many questions. Former Army colleagues Chris Roberts, Colin Campbell, Peter O'Brien and David Mason Jones are all accomplished authors and each was always on hand to listen, check on my progress and offer advice.

Above all, I value the years-long support of my children, Joseph, Sally, Rusty, Charlie, and grandson Freddie. And I am eternally thankful for the guidance, patience, and forbearance of my wife Barbara, who never wavered in her belief that this book would be published.

Bibliography

Australian Dictionary of Biography

The following biographies from the *Australian Dictionary of Biography* were accessed during 2021 and 2022:

Malcolm Allbrook, "Hasluck, Sir Paul Meernaa (1905–1993)"

Grant Anderson and Daryl Dawson, "Dixon, Sir Owen (1886–1972)"

Peter Baume, "McKenna, Nicholas Edward (1895–1974)"

Margaret L. Black, "Isaachsen, Sir Oscar Lionel (1885–1951)"

T. P. Boland, "Gilroy, Sir Norman Thomas (1896–1977)"

G. C. Bolton, "Evatt, Herbert Vere (Bert) (1894–1965)"

Frank Bongiorno, "Rosevear, John Solomon (Sol) (1892–1953)"

David Clune, "McGirr, James (Jim) (1890–1957)"

Lenore Coltheart, "Rankin, Dame Annabelle Jane (1908–1986)"

Murray Goot, "Ashby, Sylvia Rose (1908–1978)"

Murray Goot, "Rubensohn, Solomon (Sim) (1904–1979)"

Bridget Griffen-Foley, "Holt, Edgar George (1904–1988)"

Bridget Griffen-Foley, "Howard, William Stewart McPhee (1903–1983)"

Bridget Griffen-Foley, "White, Eric (1915–1989)"

Stephen Holt, "Reid, Alan Douglas (1914–1987)"

Diane Langmore, "Lyons, Dame Enid Muriel (1897–1981)"

Diane Langmore, "Menzies, Dame Pattie Maie (1899–1995)"

Carmen Lawrence, "Tangney, Dame Dorothy Margaret (1907–1985)"

Valerie Lawson, "Goldberg, Frank (1889–1958)"

C. J. Lloyd, "Rodgers, Donald Kilgour (1906–1978)"

Stuart Macintyre, "Latham, Sir John Greig (1877–1964)"

A. W. Martin, "Menzies, Sir Robert Gordon (Bob) (1894–1978)"

J. D. Merralls, "Rich, Sir George Edward (1863–1956)"

J. D. Merralls, "Starke, Sir Hayden Erskine (1871–1958)"

D. T. Merrett, "McConnan, Sir Leslie James (1887–1954)"

Heather Radi, "Preston Stanley, Millicent Fanny (1883–1955)"

Jack E. Richardson, "Bailey, Sir Kenneth Hamilton (1898–1972)"

L. L. Robson, "O'Donnell, Thomas Joseph (1876–1949)"

Martha Rutledge, "Cowper, Sir Norman Lethbridge (1896–1987)"

D. B. Waterson, "Chifley, Joseph Benedict (Ben) (1885–1951)"

Author interviews and correspondence

Interview with Heather Henderson (daughter of Sir Robert Menzies), Canberra, 16 July 2021.

Interview with Ian Harris (former Clerk of the House of Representatives) and Erika Harris, Canberra, 12 September 2021.

Interview with Doug Hassall (barrister), Canberra, September 2021.

Emails with Professor Geoffrey Blainey (historian), January 2017.

Books

Ayres, Philip. *Owen Dixon*. Carlton: Miegunyah Press, 2003.

Barwick, Garfield, Sir. *A Radical Tory: Garfield Barwick's Reflections and Recollections*. Leichhardt: Federation Press, 1995.

Blackshield, Tony, Michael Coper and George Williams. *The Oxford Companion to the High Court of Australia*. South Melbourne: Oxford University Press, 2001.

Blainey, Geoffrey. *Gold and Paper: A History of the National Bank of Australasia Limited*. Melbourne: Georgian House, 1958.

Calwell, Arthur A. *The Australian Labor Party and the Press: The Twenty-Second Arthur Norman Smith Memorial Lecture in Journalism delivered at the University of Melbourne, 30 July 1959*. Carlton: University of Melbourne Press, 1959.

Chalmers, Rob, edited by Sam Vincent and John Wanna. *Inside the Canberra Press Gallery: Life in the Wedding Cake of Old Parliament House*. Acton: ANU E-Press, 2011.

Crawford, Robert. *But Wait There's More: A History of Australian Advertising 1900–2000*. Carlton: Melbourne University Publishing, 2008.

Crisp, L. F. *Ben Chifley: A Biography*. London: Longmans, 1960.

Daly, Fred. *From Curtin to Hawke*. South Melbourne: Sun Books, 1984.

Day, David. *Chifley.* Sydney: HarperCollins, 2001.

Donoghue, Jed, and Bruce Tranter. *Exploring Australian National Identity: Heroes, Memory and Politics.* Bingley: Emerald Publishing Limited, 2018.

Duthie, Gil. *I Had 50,000 Bosses: Memoirs of a Labor Backbencher 1946-1975.* Sydney: Angus & Robertson, 1984.

Eather, Warwick, and Drew Cottle. *Fighting from the Shadows: The Private Trading Banks, Political Campaigns and Bank Nationalisation 1930-1949.* Shanghai: Australian Centre for Labour and Capital Studies, 2012.

Goldberg, Frank. *My Life in Advertising.* Self-published: undated. (NLA Bib ID 971790.)Grattan, Michelle, editor. *Australian Prime Ministers.* Chatswood: New Holland Publishers, 2016.

Green, Frank. *Servant of the House.* Melbourne: Heinemann, 1969.

Griffen-Foley, Bridget. *Party Games: Australian Politicians and the Media from War to Dismissal.* Melbourne: Text Publishing, 2003.

Hancock, Ian. *National and Permanent? The Federal Organisation of The Liberal Party of Australia 1944-1965.* Carlton: Melbourne University Press, 2000.

Hasluck, Paul, Sir. *Sir Robert Menzies.* Carlton: Melbourne University Press, 1980.

Hasluck, Paul, Sir, edited and introduced by Nicholas Hasluck. *The Chance of Politics.* Melbourne: Text Publishing, 1997.

Haylen, Leslie. *Twenty Years Hard Labor.* South Melbourne: Macmillan, 1969.

Holder, Reginald. *Bank of New South Wales: A History.* Sydney: Angus and Robertson, 1970.

Holt, Edgar. *Politics is People.* Sydney: Angus and Robertson, 1969.

Hudson, William. *Casey.* Melbourne: Oxford University Press, 1986.

Kemp, C. D. *Big Businessmen: Four Biographical Essays.* Melbourne: Institute of Public Affairs, 1964.

Lloyd, C. J. *Parliament and the Press: The Federal Parliamentary Press Gallery: 1901-88.* Carlton: Melbourne University Press, 1988.

Lyons, Enid, Dame. *Among the Carrion Crows.* Adelaide: Rigby, 1972.

Manning, Geoffrey H., and Haydon R. Manning. *Worth Fighting For: Work and Industrial Relations in the Banking Industry in South Australia.*

Adelaide: Australian Bank Employees Union, South Australia and Northern Territory Branch, 1989.

McMullin, Ross. *The Light on the Hill: The Australian Labor Party: 1891-1991*. Melbourne: Oxford University Press, 1992.

Martin, Allan. *Robert Menzies*. Carlton: Melbourne University Press, 1996.

May, A. L. *Battle for the Banks*. Sydney: Sydney University Press, 1968.

Menzies, Robert. *The Measure of the Years*. North Melbourne: Cassell Australia, 1970.

Merrett, D. T. *ANZ Bank: A History of Australia and New Zealand Banking Group Limited and its Constituents*. Sydney: Allen & Unwin, 1985.

Mills, Stephen. *The New Machine Men: Polls and Persuasion in Australian Politics*. Ringwood: Penguin Books, 1986.

Newman, Gerard. *Federal Election Results 1949-1993*. Canberra: Department of the Parliamentary Library, 1993.

Overacker, Louise. *The Australian Labor Party*. Unknown publication details NLA Bib ID: 914230.

Overacker, Louise. *The Australian Party System*. New Haven: Yale University Press, 1952.

Remington, G C. *Public Relations: An Integral Part of Policy Making: Building of Public Confidence and Public Interest*. Sydney: Public Relations Institute of Australia, 1964.

Stargardt, A. W. *Things Worth Fighting For: Speeches by Joseph Benedict Chifley*. Carlton: Melbourne University Press, 1953.

Truman, Tom. *Ideological Groups in the Australian Labor Party and Their Attitudes*. St. Lucia: University of Queensland Press, 1965.

White, Bob, and Cecelia Clarke. *Cheques and Balances: Memoirs of a Banker*. Ringwood: Viking Press, 1995.

Winterton, George. "Barwick, Garfield Edward John" in *The Oxford Companion to the High Court of Australia* edited by Tony Blackshield, Michael Coper and George Williams. South Melbourne: Oxford University Press, 2001.

Commonwealth Parliamentary Debates

House of Representatives, 13 November 1941, 430 (Arthur Calwell, Minister for Information).

House of Representatives, 9 March 1945, 533 (Ben Chifley, Prime Minister).

House of Representatives, 15 October 1947, 796 (Ben Chifley, Prime Minister).

House of Representatives, 23 October 1947, 1273 (Robert Menzies, Leader of the Opposition).

House of Representatives, 28 October 1947, 1382 (Dame Enid Lyons, Member for Darwin).

House of Representatives, 5 November 1947 (Doris Blackburn, Member for Bourke).

House of Representatives, 27 November 1947, (John Lang, Member for Reid).

House of Representatives, 28 September 1949, 643 (Arthur Calwell, Minister for Information).

Senate, 10 July 1974, 28, (Lionel Murphy, Attorney-General).

Exhibitions

New South Wales Rail Museum, *Railway Trades Display*, Thirlmere, 20 July 2018.

Journal articles

Ansell, R. D. "Advertising in Relation to the Public Service." *Journal of the Australian Regional Groups of the Institute of Public Administration* 6, no. 1 (1946).

Boyer, R. J. F. "Radio in Education." *Australian Quarterly* 18, no.1 (March 1946): 94–101.

Courtney, Caryn. "John Curtin's Forgotten Media Legacy: 1941–45." *Labor History* 105, no. 4 (November 2013): 63–78.

Crawford Robert. "Supporting Banks, Liberals and The Australian Way: The Freelands and the 1949 Election." *History Australia* 2, no. 3 (2005): 84.1–84.23.

Eather, Warwick, and Drew Cottle. "Keep Government Out of Business:

Bank Nationalisation, Financial Reform and the Private Trading Banks in the 1930s." *Australian Journal of Politics and History* 59, no. 2 (June 2013): 161–77.

Eather, Warwick, and Drew Cottle. "The Mobilisation of Capital Behind the Battle for Freedom: The Sydney Banks, The Institute of Public Affairs (NSW) and Opposition to the Australian Labor Party 1944–1949." *Labour History* 103 (November 2012): 165–86.

Murray Goot. "Labor's 1943 Landslide: Political Market Research, Evatt, and the Public Opinion Polls." *Labour History*, no. 107 (2014): 149–66.

Griffen-Foley, Bridget. "A Civilised Amateur: Edgar Holt and His Life in Letters and Politics." *Australian Journal of Politics and History* 49, no. 1 (March 2003): 31–47.

Griffen-Foley, Bridget. "'Four More Points than Moses': Dr. H. V. Evatt, the Press and the 1944 Referendum." *Labour History,* no. 68 (1995): 63–79.

Howard, Stewart: "The State of Democracy." *Australian Quarterly* 18, no. 2 (June 1946): 15–22.

Maloney, James J. "The Control and Administration of Radio Services in Australia." *Public Administration* 1, no. 1 (1939): 90–104.

Morgan, Hugh. "Liberty and the Corporation", *Policy, Australian Mining Industry Council* (Winter Edition 1989): NLA Bib ID 901366.

Overacker, Louise. "The Australian Labor Party." *The American Political Science Review* 4 (August 1949): 677–703.

Ross, Lloyd. "Socialism and Australian Labour: Facts, Fiction and Future." *Australian Quarterly* 22, no. 1 (March 1950): 21–35.

Stephens, David. "Three Labor Veterans Look Back." *Australian Quarterly* 46, no. 3 (September 1974): 84–89.

Tranter, Bruce and Jed Donoghue. "National Identity and Important Australians." *Journal of Sociology* 51, no. 2 (October 2014): 236–51.

Truman, T. C. "The Press and the 1951 Election." Australian Quarterly 23, no. 4 (December 1951): 3–44.

Ward, Ian. "The Early Use of Radio for Political Communication in Australia and Canada." *Australian Journal of Politics and History* 45, no. 3 (September 1999): 311–29.

Williams, J. R. "Emergence of the Liberal Party." *Australian Quarterly* 39, no. 1 (March 1967): 7–27.

National Archives of Australia

NAA: Department of Treasury; A571; 1947/2679; Nationalisation of Trading Banks Legislation – Banking Bill 1947; 1947–1949; Item ID 134304.

NAA: Department of Treasury; A571; 1947/2680; National of Trading Banks – Acquisition of Assets and Shares; 1947–1950, Item ID 134305.

NAA: Department of Treasury; A571; 1947/3703A: Nationalisation of Banks in Australia; 1947–1948; Item ID 134389.

NAA: Australian High Commission United Kingdom [London]; A2910; 412/1/25/52; Coward Chance and Company – Bank Nationalisation Litigation 1947–1951; Item ID 30049300.

NAA: Attorney General's Department: A432; 1947/989; Protests re Proposed Nationalisation of the Banks; 1947–1948; Item no 1288453.

NAA: Department of Post-War-Reconstruction: A9790; 844; Prime Minister's Report to the Nation; 1948–1949; Item ID 257313.

National Australia Bank Archives, Melbourne

Ambler, G. Ward, *Address Given to the Constitutional Club*, Melbourne, 15 April 1940.

Bank Employee Protest Committee, *News Bulletin,* Melbourne, Editions, 27 October 1947–28 October 1949.

Central Committee, *Summary of Activities*, Melbourne, Minutes, 10 September 1947, 28 September 1947, 28 July 1949 and 25 August 1949.

Points Against Bank Nationalisation, Facts of the Last Depression, What are the Trading Banks? Bank Nationalisation in other Countries, Statements on Bank Nationalisation, Trading Bank Profits, Information Circulars, September-October 1947.

McConnan, Leslie, *The Banking System is Safe until the Next Federal Election*, Melbourne, Press Statement, 26 July 1949.

McConnan, Leslie, *Nationalisation of Banking: Privy Council Decision*, Melbourne, Radio Script, 27 July 1949.

Malvern Citizens' Nationalisation Committee, *These Are the Facts about Bank Nationalisation*, Pamphlet, 1947.

Bank Memos to Chief Manager, Melbourne, *Dr Evatt's Submission to the High Court: 26 February 1948, Films: 1948, Opposition to Bank*

Nationalisation List of Activities: 22 September 1949, Swing Needed in Federal Elections: 27 September 1949.

National Bank of Australasia, *Public Relations Activities for 1949*, Report, 15 November 1948.

National Bank of Australasia, *Monthly Summary of Australian Conditions*, Booklet, 10 June 1947.

Associated Australasian Banks (London), *Nationalisation of Trading Banks*, Memo 4 October 1948.

National Library of Australia

ABC TV, *Mr Prime Minister–J. B. Chifley Programme: May 1966, Papers of L. F. Crisp*, NLA MS 5243/5/11.

Broadcast Bulletins (1948–), *Australian Federation of Commercial Broadcasting Stations*, National Library of Australia Bib ID 1500593.

The Banker, *United Bank Officers' Association of New South Wales*, National Library of Australia, Bib ID 1306893.

Bankers' Magazine of Australasia, *Bankers' Institute of Australasia*, National Library of Australia, Bib ID 2175287.

Canberra Survey, 1948–1970, NLA Bib ID 119714.

Correspondence of C.D. Kemp 1963-1964, NLA MS 1548.

Diaries of Gil Duthie, 1943–1976 (Manuscript) NLA MS 7076.

Discussion Pamphlet no 5, 1945, *Films*, Australian Army Education Service, NLA Bib ID 397387.

Discussion Pamphlet no 22, 1945, *Radio*, Australian Army Education Service, NLA Bib ID 397387.

Inside Canberra, 1948–2012, NLA Bib ID 1948286.

Liberal Party of Australia, Circa 1945–1990 (Manuscript), Australia, NLA MS 5000.

Papers of Arthur Calwell, 1896–1973, NLA MS 4738.

Papers of the Casey Family, 1820–1978 (Manuscript) NLA MS 6150.

Papers of P. J. Clarey, 1923–1959 (Manuscript) NLA MS 2186.

Papers of Frederick Osborne, 1945–1984 (Manuscript) NLA MS 3662.

Papers of L. F. Crisp, 1878–1984 (Manuscript) NLA MS 5243.

Papers of Sir Robert Menzies, 1905–1978 (Manuscript) NLA MS 4936.

Papers of Donald Kilgour Rodgers, 1930-1949 (Manuscript) NLA MS 1536.

Papers of Dorothy Margaret Tangney, 1938-1986 (Manuscript) NLA MS 7564.

Records of the Liberal Party of Australia, NLA MS 5000.

Typescript Reports of Erle Harold Cox, 1944–1964 (Manuscript), NLA MS 4554.

National Portrait Gallery of Australia

Ben Chifley n.d. Max Dupain OBE, gelatin silver photograph on paper (sheet: 39.0 cm x 31.5 cm, image: 38.5 cm x 31.5 cm) © Max Dupain/Copyright Agency, 2021, NPG 2017.25.

National Film and Sound Archive of Australia

Prices and People, 1948, Film, Realist Film Unit, NFSA title no 233839.

In the Wake of The Storm, 1946, ALP Cinema Advertisement, NFSA title no 111849.

The Golden Age, 1946, Liberal Party Cinema Advertisement, NFSA title no 111848.

The House You Built, 1949, Liberal Party Cinema Advertisement, NFSA title no 52317.

Noel Butlin Archives Centre, Australian National University

Bank Officials' Association Federal Office and Victorian Branch Deposit, A2/2/7 Correspondence with Victorian Branch, January to December 1947.

Bank Officials' Association Federal Office and Victorian Branch Deposit, A2/8/3, Correspondence File, 1945–1950.

Bank Officials' Association Federal Office and Victorian Branch Deposit, A2/14/1/3A General Correspondence File, 1933–1951.

Syd Butlin Research Papers Deposit Z199/50, Bank of Adelaide, 1867–1972.

Syd Butlin Research Papers Deposit Z199/53, Commercial Bank of Australia, 1890–1959.

Syd Butlin Research Papers Deposit Z199/58, English, Scottish and Australian Bank (Chartered), 1854–1968.

Syd Butlin Research Papers Deposit Z199/63, National Bank of Australasia, 1931–1959.

Syd Butlin Research Papers Deposit Z199/67, Bank of New South Wales, 1931–1959.

Syd Butlin Research Papers Deposit Z199/73, Rural Bank of New South Wales, 1947–1969.

Syd Butlin Research Papers Deposit Z199/74, Rural and Industries Bank of Western Australia, 1947–1969.

Syd Butlin Research Papers Deposit Z199/92, Bank of Australasia, Colonial Superintendent to London, Confidential letters, 1947–1951.

Syd Butlin Research Papers Deposit Z199/115/U38, Union Bank of Australia, General Manager to London Private, 1928–1951.

Australian Bank Officers' Association, AU NBAC N112-262 ABOA NSW Division General Correspondence, 1947–1948.

Online

Australian Bureau of Statistics (June 1947) *Census of the Commonwealth of Australia*, ABS Website, accessed 14 April 2022.

Australian Bureau of Statistics (January 1946) *Year Book Australia*, ABS Website, accessed 14 April 2022.

Eric Butler, "Memories of the Early Years", Australian League of Rights, undated, https://alor.org/Storage/navigation/Library4.htm, accessed 3 January 2022.

Central Intelligence Agency, "Communist Influence in Australia: 11 April 1949", Australian Communist Party, undated, https://auscp.org.au/history/cia-declassified-files-on-communist-influence-in-australia/ accessed 15 September 2021.

Murray Gleeson, "The Privy Council: An Australian Perspective", High Court of Australia, 18 June 2008, https://www.hcourt.gov.au/publications/speeches/former/speeches-by-the-hon-murray-gleeson, accessed 13 April 2022.

Ian Hancock, "The Origins of the Modern Liberal Party: NLA Harold White Fellowship Lecture", 1994, https://www.nla.gov.au/ian-hancock/the-origins-of-the-modern-liberal-party, accessed 4 April 2022.

Misha Ketchell, "Who Were Australia's Best Prime Ministers? We Asked the Experts." The Conversation. 2 August 2021. https://theconversation.

com/who-were-australias-best-prime-ministers-we-asked-the-experts-165302, accessed 3 January 2022

Denis Linehan, "Chifley and the Banks 1947: Will We Ever Know What Really Happened?" 2014, www.academia.edu/8119949, accessed 12 September 2021.

Stephen Mills, "Dick Casey's Forgotten People", *Inside Story*, 25 July 2012, insidestory.org.au/dick-caseys-forgotten-people, accessed 17 September 2021.

"Petitions: Infosheet 11", Parliament of Australia, undated, aph.gov.au/About_Parliament/House_of_Representatives/Powers_practice_and_procedure/00_-_Infosheets/Infosheet_11_-_Petitions. accessed 23 September 2021.

Paula Waring, "Is It Futile to Petition the Australian Senate?" Parliament of Australia, April 2013, accessed 23 September 2021.

"Historical Statistics to End of 45th Parliament," Parliament of Australia, undated, aph.gov.au/Parliamentary_Business/Statistics/House_of_Representatives_Statistics, accessed 23 September 2021.

"Federal Election Results 1949-1993", Department of the Parliamentary Library, 22 November 1993, aph.gov.au/binaries/library/pubs/bp/1993/93bp24.pdf, accessed 23 September 2021.

National Library of Australia Oral Histories

Alexander, Joseph interviewed by Mel Pratt, 2 March 1972, NLA ORAL TRC 121/10.

Barwick, Garfield, Sir interviewed by J. D. B. Miller, 1–3 February 1977, NLA ORAL TRC 499.

Barwick, Garfield, Sir and the Hon. Clyde R. Cameron Reminisce, 30 January–1 December 1981, NLA ORAL TRC 1045.

Beale, Howard interviewed by Mel Pratt, 20–21 October 1976, NLA ORAL TRC 121/82.

Bury, Leslie interviewed by Mel Pratt, 10–14 November 1975, NLA ORAL TRC 121/70.

Chamberlain, Frank interviewed by Mel Pratt, 4 August 1972–19 January 1973, NLA ORAL TRC 121/39.

Commins, John interviewed by Mel Pratt, 22–27 March 1971, NLA ORAL TRC 121/13.

Cox, Harold interviewed by Mel Pratt, 6 April–June 1973, NLA ORAL TRC 121/43.

Craig, Hazel interviewed by Ken Begg, 25 March 1996, Museum of Democracy, OPH-OH13.

Daly, Fred interviewed by Mel Pratt, 26 August–25 November 1976, NLA ORAL TRC 121/96.

Daly, Fred interviewed by Vivienne Rae-Ellis, 2 August–19 September 1983, NLA ORAL TRC 4900/63.

Holt, Edgar interviewed by Mel Pratt, 2–3 May 1978, NLA ORAL TRC 121/93.

Fraser, Allan interviewed by Mel Pratt, 18 February–11 April 1975, NLA ORAL TRC 121/66.

Jago, Harry interviewed by Peter Coleman, 22 March 1989, NLA ORAL TRC 2606.

Lemmon, Nelson interviewed by Mel Pratt, 8 May 1978, NLA ORAL TRC 121/92.

Lyons, Enid, Dame interviewed by Mel Pratt, 13–22 March 1972, NLA ORAL TRC 121/30.

Reid, Alan interviewed by Mel Pratt, 4 October 1972–8 February 1973, NLA ORAL TRC 121/40.

Rodgers, Donald Kilgour interviewed by Mel Pratt, 29 April 1971, NLA ORAL TRC 121/14.

Reserve Bank of Australia Archives

Commonwealth Savings Bank Administration – Nationalisation of Banking – 1947–1949.

Research Department – Banking Section – Conferences with Private Banks – October 1946–November 1951.

Research Department – Central Bank – General – Board & Advisory Council Memoranda – Advisory Council Papers – File 2 – April–June 1949 and July–December 1947.

Research Department – Central Bank – General – Board & Advisory Council Memoranda – Advisory Council Papers – File 4 – November 1949.

Research Department – Central Bank – General – Commonwealth Bank

Operations – 1931–1951.

Research Department – Central Bank – General – Bankers' Administrative Staff College – File 2 – Money and Credit – 1955.

Banking Department – Exchange Control – Monetary Control Policy – Nationalisation of Banking – Compensation to Non-residents of Australia, 1949.

Research Department – Legislation – Banking Act 1947 – Memoranda and Correspondence – June–September 1947.

Research Department – Legislation – Banking Act 1947–1949 – Planning for Nationalisation – 1947–1949.

Research Department – Legislation – Banking Act 1947–1949 – Draft Plans for the Assessment of Compensation under Bank Nationalisation Registration – 1948–1949.

Research Department – Legislation – Banking Act 1947–1949 – The Bank Nationalisation Case – Plaintiff Banks' Writs, Affidavits, Etc. – Volume 1 and 2 – c.1947.

Research Department – Legislation – Banking Act 1947–1949 – Bank Nationalisation Case – Commonwealth Bank Memoranda – c.1947.

Research Department – Legislation – Banking Act 1947–1949 – Bank Nationalisation Case – Court Judgments – c.1947.

Secretary's Department – Banking Legislation – Banking Act 1947 – Section 26 – Nationalisation of Banks in Germany, Italy & Russia.

Secretary's Department – Banking Legislation – Banking Act 1947 – Section 53 – Nationalisation Plans – June 1949.

Secretary's Department – Banking Legislation – Banking Act 1947 – Section 54 – Nationalisation Plans – July 1949.

Secretary's Department – Urgent and Confidential Air Letters – From London (Indexed).

State Library of New South Wales

Scripts of "John Henry Austral Presents" and "Candid Comment", The Liberal Party of Australia, NSWSL 74Vv6djyxmll.

Ashby Research Services, MLMSS 8907.

Westpac Group Archives, Sydney

A. B. Jones to General Manager, *Banking Legislation*, 18 August 1947.

A. B. Jones to Chief Inspector New South Wales, *Nationalisation of Banking*, 21 August 1947.

A. B. Jones to Chief Inspector New South Wales, *Banking Legislation*, 30 August 1947.

A. B. Jones to R. R. McKellar, *Banking Legislation*, 16 September 1947.

A. B. Jones to Chief Security Officer, *Banking Legislation*, 12 November 1947.

A. B. Jones to Chief Inspector, *Nationalisation of Banking*, 16 December 1947.

A. B. Jones to L. J. McConnan, *Address by C V Janes*, 1 February 1949.

Bank of New South Wales Circular, *Political Control of Banking*, 5 May 1931.

Bank of New South Wales, *Public Relations Newsletter to Staff*, November 1950.

Bank of New South Wales, *Trading Banks in Australia, New Zealand, Fiji and the Pacific Islands*, 31 March 1947.

Central Committee Minute, *Public Relations: Future Activities*, 15 December 1949.

M. Dunn, *Mantle of Greatness*, Radio Script, no 64, Part 1, undated.

Memo for Chief Security Officer, *Banking Legislation*, 19 December 1947.

T. B. Heffer, *A Personal Message to the Customers and Shareholders of the Bank of New South Wales*, September 1947.

T. B. Heffer, *Nationalisation of Banking*, Sydney, Press Statement, 17 September 1947.

Tyrell to Chief Inspector Melbourne, *Public Relations*, 16 August 1950.

Tyrell to T. M. Bryce, *Bank Employee Protest Committee*, 24 October 1950.

Academic Papers

Bennetts, Ron. "Development of the Federal Parliamentary Press Gallery: 1901–1968". MA thesis, Australian National University, 1968.

Mills, Stephen. "Campaign Professionals: Party Officials and the Professionalism of Australian Political Parties." PhD dissertation, University of Sydney, 2002.

Petersen, Neville. "Policy Formulation in the ABC News Service." PhD disseration, University of Sydney, 1977.

Vickery, Edward. "Telling Australia's Story to the World: The Department of Information 1939–1950." PhD dissertation, Australian National University, 2003.

Index

Ashby, Sylvia Rose 62–3
Australian Communist Party (ACP) 37, 48–9, 143, 157, 161, 164, 168, 190, 194
Australian Labor Party (ALP) passim
  attitude to nationalisation 3
  ALP split 33, 194
Australian Public Opinion Polls 62
Bank of Adelaide 26–7, 29
Bank of New South Wales 23, 26–30, 40, 45, 54, 93, 96, 98–9, 102–4, 123–5, 131–2, 134, 136–7, 176–9, 197
Banking Act 1947 43n1, 93n1, 95n2, 96n3, 109, 117, 131, 192
Calwell, Arthur Augustus 4, 48, 59–60, 70, 72, 82, 101, 108, 140–1, 158, 161, 164, 179–80, 189
Casey, Richard Gavin Gardiner 21–3, 45–7, 53, 67, 70–1, 73–4, 99, 115, 119–20, 122, 124, 144, 146, 151, 162–6, 178, 187, 190
Caucus 15, 16, 17, 41, 52, 63, 82, 83, 84, 85, 88n2, 90, 126, 133, 160, 191, 192, 194
Chifley, Elizabeth ("Lizzie") 11–3, 16, 145, 167, 172–3, 195
Chifley, Joseph Benedict (Ben)
  1945 Banking Act 2, 5, 39, 109, 126
  1946 election 21, 62, 70, 74, 83, 84, 85, 149, 161, 187, 188
  Abercrombie Shire Council 13, 16, 144, 145, 146
  becomes Prime Minister 6, 9, 15, 16, 17
  Great Strike 12, 110
  Lizzie (wife) 12, 16, 145
  New South Wales Government Railway Service 11
  realtions with the press 1, 6, 7, 39, 48, 56, 58, 59, 78, 86, 91, 136, 139, 142, 144, 157, 164, 200
  Royal Commission Monetary Systems and Banking 14, 15, 24, 36, 44, 202, 203
  Scullin Labor Government 3, 4, 13, 22, 33–5, 39, 40, 44, 55, 75, 93, 145
  Treasurer 13, 15, 22, 23, 31
  work ethic 16
Churchill, Winston Leonard Spencer 23, 146, 182–3, 189
Commercial Bank of Australia 26
Commercial Bank of Sydney 45, 98, 102, 166, 177
Commonwealth Bank
  early years 3, 31
Cox, Harold 6–7, 39, 58, 92, 128, 143, 153, 186, 190
Dedman, John Johnstone 4, 25, 38–40, 55, 62, 108, 139, 166, 172, 179, 189, 192, 200
Depression 4, 10, 13–4, 24, 33–7, 49, 83, 86, 94, 110, 114–5, 124, 148, 173
Duthie, Gilbert Willam 48, 78, 147, 187
election, 1949 ix, 8, 56–7, 113, 118–21, 146–9, 158, 160–1, 167–8, 173–7, 181, 184–9, 191, 194, 196, 198, 200, 204

English Banks
  Bank of Australasia 26, 29, 130, 175, 197
  English, Scottish and Australian Bank 23, 26–7, 104, 131, 175, 178
  Union Bank 26–7, 29, 93, 175, 197
Evatt, Herbert Vere 2, 3, 4, 5, 41, 55, 62, 82, 83, 84, 102, 126, 127–9, 130, 133–8, 142, 143, 144, 149, 163, 164, 166, 169, 175, 187, 189, 192, 194, 195, 196, 200
  High Court case 127–8, 130, 133, 135
  Privy Council case 127, 133–7
Fadden, Athur William 20, 49, 141, 143, 153, 166–7, 170–2, 176, 183–6, 188–91, 193, 197
Gilroy, Norman Thomas 51
McConnan, Leslie James
  early career 24–5, 44–5
  Royal Commission on Monetary Policy and Banking 24
McGirr, James ('Big' Jim) 98, 106
McKell, William John 90–1, 106, 151, 191
McKenna, Nicholas 2–5, 82, 126, 132, 199
Menzies, Robert Gordon
  election victory ix, 139, 185–93
  growing up 18
  political style 19
Murdoch, Keith Arthur 6, 57–9, 62, 64–6, 92, 114
National Bank of Australasia (National Bank) ix, 24, 26–7, 29, 40, 44, 89, 130–2, 140, 162, 176, 196–7
O'Donnell, Thomas Joseph 52–3, 99, 132, 141
Packer, Douglas Frank 57–8
Reid, Alan Douglas 6–7, 15, 186

Returned Sailors, Soldiers and Airmen's Imperial League of Australia (RSL) 53, 111
Rodgers, Donald Kilgour 6–7, 64, 74, 169, 194, 200
Scullin, James Henry 3–4, 13, 33–4, 36, 66
State Banks 94
Ward, Edward John (Eddie) 4, 48, 169

www.ingramcontent.com/pod-product-compliance
Lightning Source LLC
Chambersburg PA
CBHW021353300426
44114CB00012B/1200